DREAM LANGUAGE
Self-Understanding
through Imagery and Color

by Robert J. Hoss, MS

foreword by David Feinstein, PhD

Innersource
Ashland, OR

Published by: Innersource, PO Box 213, Ashland, OR 97520
                 www.Innersource.net

Cover art and design by Bowen Imagery, www.bowenimagery.com

Library of Congress Control Number: 2005903618

Catalog Information:

Hoss, Robert J.
       Dream Language: Self-Understanding through Imagery and Color
       First Edition paperback
       Includes bibliographic references and index
       ISBN 0-9725207-1-6 (Pbk)
       1. Dreams 2. Dreams - Self-Help 3.Psychology
       4. Dreams-Therapeutic Use
       I. Title 2005
       154.6/3 - DC 21

Printed in U.S.A. by DeHART's Media Services, Inc.

QUICK REFERENCE GUIDE FOR DREAMWORK

This guide provides a simple but powerful approach for understanding a dream in relation to your waking life and inner self. Understanding the dream is the first stage in a three-stage process for using your dreams to help transform your life. Refer to chapter 11 to explore your dream further.

1) **Record the Dream** – as if you are re-experiencing it (use first person, present tense). Also note any emotionally significant situation that is going on in your life at the time.

2) **Metaphors in the Dream Story:** Look for statements in the dream story that sound like they also might describe something going on in your life at the time.

3) **Work on a Dream Image (the 6 "magic" questions):**
   a) **Pick one or more** dream images that seem important, curious or emotionally significant.

   b) **Let the Image Speak:** Go back into the dream and "become" the dream image. Speak as the dream image and record your statements. Speak in the first person present tense.

   1a) Who or **what are you** (describe yourself and how you feel): "I am _____"
   1b) Alternatively - if the dream character is someone you know, then as that person:
       a) describe your personality; b) in what ways are you like the dreamer;
       c) in what ways you are different.
   2) What is your **purpose or function** (what do you do)? "My purpose is to _____"
   3) What do you **like** about being that dream element? "I like _____"
   4) What do you **dislike** about being that dream element? "I dislike _____"
   5) What do you **fear most** as that dream element? "I fear _____"
   6) What do you **desire most** as that dream element? "What I desire most is to _____"

   c) **Relate to a Life Situation:** Do one or more of the statements sound like a way you feel or a situation in your waking life? Recall a specific situation and define your feelings at the time. Do the "I am" and "My purpose" statements sound like a role you are playing in waking life? Do the "I like" versus "I dislike" statements sound like a conflict going on? Do the "I fear" and "I desire" statements sound like waking life fears and desires, perhaps feeding the conflict? If the dream character is a person you know, do one or more of the personality statements relate to a manner in which you are approaching the waking life situation? Or alternatively, does this dream character have a personality trait that you admire or wish you had more of, in order to better handle this waking life situation?

4) **Color Work -** If there was a unique color in the dream or dream image:
   a) Pick the closest color in the **Color Questionnaire** table (also see tables 9-2 and 9-3).
   b) Read the statements for that color and select any that trigger a "connection" with feelings or a situation in your waking life (note: the emotional themes in the table are intended to trigger your own personal associations; they are NOT the "meaning" of the color).
   c) Recall the waking life situation and your feelings at the time. Relate that connection to the dream and the imagery work above. What new perspective does the color add?

Color Questionnaire

The table contains emotional themes intended to trigger your own associations. It is derived from color psychology research, the *Color Test* by Luscher, the works of Jung and research by the author.

RED	1) I feel intense, vital or animated. 2) I feel transformed. 3) I feel assertive, forceful. 4) I feel creative. 5) I want to live life to its fullest. 6) I want to win, succeed, achieve. 7) I feel sexy or have strong sexual urges. 8) I have a driving desire. 9) I need something to make me feel alive again. 10) I need to be more assertive and forceful. 11) I need to get out and enjoy myself. *12) If red appears as blood or inflammation – it may relate to an illness or injury*
ORN	1) I want to expand my interests and develop new activities. 2) I want a wider sphere of influence. 3) I feel friendly and welcoming. 4) I want more contact with others. 5) I feel enthusiastic, outgoing and adventurous. 6) I am driven by desires and hopes toward the new, undiscovered and satisfying. 7) I feel driven but need to overcome my doubts or fear of failure. 8) I must avoid spreading myself too thin.
YEL	1) I feel a sense of joy and optimism. 2) I feel alert. 3) I am seeking a solution that will open up new and better possibilities and allow my hopes to be fulfilled. 4) I feel the new direction I am taking will bring happiness in my future. 5) I am hopeful. 6) I need to find a way out of this circumstance or relationship. 7) I need a change. 8) I may be compensating for something. 9) I am acting compulsively.
GREEN	1) I need to establish myself, my self-esteem, my independence. 2) I want recognition. 3) I need to increase the certainty of my own value and status, through acknowledgment by others of my achievements or my possessions. 4) Hard work and drive will gain me recognition and self esteem. 5) My opinion must prevail. 6) I must hold on to this view in order to maintain my self-esteem. 7) I want what I am due. 8) I must maintain control of the events. 9) Things must not change. 10) Detail and logic are important here. 11) I need to increase my sense of security. 12) I need more money to feel secure. 13) I want to withdraw and retreat into my own center. 14) I need healing or better health.
BLUE	1) I feel tranquil, peaceful and content. 2) I feel a sense of harmony. 3) I feel a meditative awareness or unity. 4) I feel a sense of belonging. 5) I need rest, peace or a chance to recuperate. 6) I need a relationship free from contention in which I can trust and be trusted. 7) I need a peaceful state of harmony offering contentment and a sense of belonging.
VIO	1) I like to win others over with my charm. 2) I feel an identification, an almost "mystic" union. 3) I have a deep intuitive understanding of the situation. 4) I feel a sense of intimacy. 5) The feeling is erotic. 6) I seek a magical state where wishes are fulfilled. 7) I yearn for a "magical" relationship of romance and tenderness. 8) I seek to identify with something or someone. 9) I need intimacy. 10) I engage in fantasy in order to compensate for my feelings of insecurity.
BROWN	1) I seek a secure state where I can be physically comfortable and relax or recover. 2) I am uneasy and insecure in the existing situation. 3) I need a more affectionate environment. 4) I need a situation imposing less physical strain. 5) I want to satisfy the physical senses (food, luxury, sex). *6) If it is a Natural or wood brown: a) I am concerned about matters of family, home, or my "roots". b) I am concerned with a son or daughter. c) I am searching for my true self or natural state of being. 7) If Dirty Brown: it may relate to a physical problem or illness.*
GRAY	1) I want to shield myself from those feelings. 2) I feel emotionally distant, only an observer. 3) It is as if I am standing aside, watching myself mechanically go through the motions. 4) I want to remain uncommitted, non-involved, shielded or separated from the situation. 5) I do not want to make a decision that will require my emotional involvement. 6) I have put up with too much and wish to avoid any further emotional stimulation. 7) I am trying to escape an anxious situation. 8) I am compensating for something.
BLACK	The unconscious realm. Moving into darkness = suppression, "death of the ego" (first stage of transformation). Beautiful shiny black = a positive view of the unconscious from which a new self emerges. Try: 1) I am anxious and don't know why. 2) I am fearful of or intimidated by the situation. 3) I have been dealt an unacceptable blow. 4) Nothing is as it should be. 5) I refuse to allow it/them to influence my point of view. 6) I can't accept the situation and don't wish to be convinced otherwise. 7) I feel the need for extreme action, perhaps in revolt against or to compensate for the situation.
WHT	1) This is a new experience. 2) I'm becoming aware of new feelings. 3) I'm experiencing a new beginning, a transformation. 4) I have a new outlook, a new awareness. 5) I feel pure and innocent. 6) I feel open and accepting. 7) I feel unprepared. 8) I feel alone, isolated. 9) It feels cold or sterile. Note: White transforms the emotions associated with the colors it mixes with; adding peacefulness, newness, renewal.

TABLE OF CONTENTS

ACKNOWLEDGEMENTS

The author wishes to thank his wife Lynne Hoss for her inspiration, ongoing support, content on dual brain research, and professional input; to extend special appreciation and acknowledgement to Dr. Irwin Gadol for his mentoring in the field of Gestalt; and to Dr. David Feinstein, author of *The Mythic Path* and *Energy Psychology Interactive* for his inspiring work featured herein, the book content he contributed, and his generous support in publishing this book.

I wish to acknowledge the International Association for the Study of Dreams (IASD), a multidisciplinary organization dedicated to the investigation of dreams and dreaming, that opens its doors to dreamers everywhere. It has been valuable inspiration and resource to me, and I invite you to experience the organization for yourself (see appendix A). I want to thank the many IASD principals and members for their generous contributions to this book including: Stanley Krippner, PhD, co-author of *Dream Telepathy* and *Extraordinary Dreams and How to Work with Them*, for his assistance and content in the areas of cultural factors, anomalous dreams, personal mythology and dreamworking; Dr. David Kahn, Harvard Medical School, for his assistance and contributions in the area of neurobiology; Rita Dwyer, Founder of the Metro D.C. Dream Community for her encouragement and creative support; Curtiss Hoffman, PhD, author of *The Seven Story Tower*, for his collaboration on color research from long-term journaling studies; Art Funkhouser, PhD for content on dreams and aging; to Deirdre Barrett, PhD, author of *Trauma and Dreams* and *The Committee of Sleep,* for content in the areas of lucid dreams, dreams and trauma, creative dreams and symptom-focused psychotherapy; Ernest Hartmann, PhD, author of *Dreams and Nightmares* for content on nightmares and emotion as related to the central image; Bob Van de Castle, PhD, author of *Our Dreaming Mind* for his assistance with content related to dream research; Bob Haden M. Div., STM, Founder of The Haden Institute for content relating to guidelines for dream groups; Rev. Dr. Jeremy Taylor, author of *The Living Labyrinth*, for his content related to group work with archetypes; Marcia Emery, PhD, author of *PowerHunch* and *The Intuitive Healer*, for content relating to intuitive dreamwork; Gayle Delaney, PhD, author of *Breakthrough Dreaming* for a discussion of her Dream Interviewing approach; Justina Lasley, author of *Honoring the Dream* for her content on dream emotion and dreamwork; and Alan Siegel, PhD, co-author *Dreamcatching,* for his assistance with children's dreams. I also wish to thank G.William Domhoff, PhD, for assistance with the "dreambank.net" database. I also thank the many other contributors referenced herein and all those who so generously provided their dreams to this work, providing the much-needed examples from which we all can learn.

FOREWORD
DAVID FEINSTEIN, PHD
Author of *The Mythic Path* and *Energy Psychology Interactive*

If your life does not already seem extraordinary and mysterious, you may want to use this book to guide you into the world of your dreams. Whether or not you recall them, your psyche regularly produces internal dramas that in their own way rival great literature—with ingenious plots, exquisite symbolism, rousing intrigue, unlikely heroes, memorable villains, moral dilemmas, wise instruction, and unforeseen pathways into the realm of the spirit.

Bob Hoss is perfectly positioned to have produced this superb guidebook for the many people who are finding that it is possible to work with their dreams in ways that tangibly enhance their lives. As the Executive Officer and past President of the world's most influential organization for promoting the study of dreams and for bringing the art of dream work to the general population, he has been able to create a book that is interactive *and* comprehensive, useful for the general reader *and* for the clinician, immensely practical *and* at the cutting edge scientifically, informed by the most recent neurological findings about dreams *and* by the ancient recognition that messages from the spirit world are revealed in our dreams.

In short, the book is friendly, comprehensive, and authoritative. It will show you how to remember your dreams, and it offers dozens of time-tested techniques for exploring their language and discovering their meanings. It will teach you about special kinds of dreams, such as nightmares, paranormal dreams, lucid dreams, and children's dreams. It also introduces and provides the latest research into the highly innovative, informative, and fascinating area of the meaning of color in dreams.

Dream Language is an unusually flexible book. You can use it to learn the basics of dream work, to review the latest scientific understanding about dreams, or as a guidebook for working with your own dreams, and you can skip around according to your interests. Many dream books that are written by professionals have one of two slants. This book, however, embraces both what has come out of the clinician's office and out of the researcher's laboratory, giving it a two-pronged authority that reflects the latest in the study of dreams today.

With the re-emergence of interest in dreams in Western cultures, this book will be welcomed and will contribute to this grassroots movement where so many people are meeting for the purpose of systematically exploring their dreams with one another. One hundred years ago, it was felt that only psychoanalysts had the key to the meaning of dreams, but now we know that the dreamer is the ultimate authority on the meaning of a dream. This book is designed to give you the most up-to-date tools for assuming that authority in decoding these messages from the night.

I felt highly honored to first see that my own work was listed among the theorists who have made a contribution to the modern understanding of dreams, and then privileged to be asked to write this introduction to the book. You are in for a new adventure every night.

INTRODUCTION
TO THE COLORFUL WORLD OF DREAMS

In my dream the Angel shrugged & said, if we fail this time, it will be a failure of imagination & then she placed the world gently in the palm of my hand – Brian Andreas [67]

It is exciting to imagine that dreams have meaning for us, a message that can help us better understand and transform our lives. Although many of us have experienced the therapeutic value of dreams when we apply solid dreamwork principles, there is still controversy over whether dreams are meaningful. It would indeed be a failure of imagination if we relegate dreams to the babble of a sleeping mind, or miss the message, simply because we are unable to understand the language of the dreaming brain. We dream every night, in stages all through the night. Much our brain remains active when we dream, particularly those centers that process emotion, memories, associations and our social and spatial relationships. Dreams contain story lines that can be associated with our waking life situations. Could it be that dreams provide a window into the thought processes that influence our daily lives, if we could but understand their "language"? I think you will find that this is the case, after reading this book.

There are many approaches for dreamwork (i.e., working with dreams). No single technique can unlock all of the secrets a dream has to reveal, because the dream material comes from many levels of consciousness and pertains to so many aspects of our waking and inner life. In this book, I will introduce you to a number of proven approaches for group and individual dreamwork. I will also introduce you to a new approach that I call Image Activation dreamwork that will "let the dream speak" in its own language. It is a quick, simple, and powerful approach for personal or professional dreamwork that takes you quickly, effectively and safely into a deeper understanding of the dream and its relation to your waking and internal life. It's origin lies in an unique combination of Gestalt therapy, the works of Jung, and the work of Stanley Krippner and David Feinstein which introduced the concept of the personal myth as it applies to dreams. I have enhanced the approach with an investigation into the significance of color, as well as recent neurological research that helps to explain the nature of dream content. At its core is a role-play technique, which I call "the 6 magic questions," and a color questionnaire. Both are designed to reveal the hidden emotional content within a dream image.

Understanding the dream is only the first step however. You will be introduced to an approach for using the dream to explore your inner life and to reveal potential solutions to the waking life issues the dream is dealing with. You will find that there is more to learn from a dream than you ever realized, once you understand the language.

Dedicated to:

My wife Lynne, who dreamed that I would write this book, and

my mother Ruth, whose inspiring dreams are contained herein.

CHAPTER 1
SLEEP AND DREAMING

Sleep is by no means an inactive state for the nervous system – *Ernest Hartmann* [1]

Whathat are dreams? In the simplest terms, dreams are the recall of images, thoughts, feelings and stories from the sleep state. A dream is the state of consciousness we achieve in the sleep state. Domhoff[104] states that there are four conditions required for dreaming: 1) an intact fully mature neural network for dreaming; 2) a mechanism for activating the dream; 3) exclusion of external stimulus; and 4) loss of self control or shut down of the "cognitive system of self." To many, the resulting dreams are considered interesting and mysterious but of no consequence, since they contain imagery and a story line that seem illogical and bizarre. What I hope to show in this book is that dreams make a lot of sense once we understand the "language" of the dreaming mind. In fact, we may find that dreams can be more truthful and revealing than waking reality! We will also discover that understanding and working with dreams in a proper manner can help maintain a healthy sense of well-being.

Why do we Sleep and Dream?

Research has shown that sleep and dreaming are linked to learning and to repair of the body and mind.[1,38] Our most vivid dreaming occurs during REM sleep (for rapid eye movement) which is characterized by eye movement, as if we are indeed watching our dreams. The periods between REM sleep (devoid of rapid eye movement), called non-REM sleep or NREM, contain less dreams and less vivid dreams. If we deprive ourselves of dream or REM sleep, the body recovers by increasing dream sleep first, in fact recovering the loss of REM almost precisely, suggesting that dreaming is important. It has been observed that sleep and dream deprivation causes effects such as: waking dreams (visual and auditory hallucinations); interference with memory and learning; a loosening of associations; impaired waking ability to do tasks requiring focused attention; or difficulty maintaining a straight line of thought, creating irritability and suspiciousness. It has therefore been suggested that REM or dream sleep is associated with restoring mental well-being.

Dream sleep seems to play a key role in revitalizing new and old experiences so that they become more permanently etched in long-term memory. Alan Hobson, at the Massachusetts Mental Health Center, shows that dreaming rehearses memory patterns, either to harden them into long-term memory or to keep fading connections alive (based on brain wave activity in the hippocampus).[38] For example, one study demonstrated that the exact neuronal firing patterns present when rats explored a maze were repeated precisely when the rats were in the dream sleep.[38] In Israel, researchers at the Weizmann Institute found that consistently interrupting dream sleep in a night completely blocked learning, whereas just as frequently interrupting non-dream sleep did not.[38]

Different types of memory tasks seem to respond to different parts of the sleep cycles, with visual and perceptual tasks relating more to dream sleep. The Weisman researchers found that "procedural memory," or tasks requiring practice (as opposed to "declarative memory" or fact recall), was directly tied to quantity of dream sleep. Further research by Stickgold and Walker indicated that those learning a task in the evening, who were retested after a good nights sleep, were 15% to 20% faster and 30% to 40% more accurate than those simply tested twelve hours after learning the task at other times of the day. [cited in 70]

There is some evidence of this learning effect in the dream experience itself. On the occasions when we recall multiple dreams from the same night, it is often observed that a similar theme runs through each dream segment, but that each segment approaches that theme with a slightly different storyline or set of characters and outcome. Could it be that dreams act as our testing ground for practicing various scenarios on a situation, in order to find and reinforce the best solutions (strengthening the best neural paths)?

Some research supports the hypothesis that dreams help us adapt to stressful waking events by activating habitual defense mechanisms, and by integrating the stress situation with earlier solutions to a similar problem.[2] A critical step in the memory cycle is the step that matches representations of new experiences with the representations of closely related past experiences. This is observed to take place during dreaming.[3] It is as if the dreams are helping us adjust to new threats and experiences, by comparing them to an internal model of how we dealt with similar situations in the past, and then making those slight reprogramming or learning adjustments that are needed to better accommodate the experience. How often have you gone to sleep angry about something and awoke the next morning feeling less concerned? Thus the old saying, "better sleep on it." Sleep and dreaming appear to play critical roles in memory and learning, as well as in stress reduction and generally keeping our mental state in good repair.

Do We All Dream?

Research has shown[1] that all humans, birds and mammals, with minor exceptions,[38] exhibit REM sleep. It is known that humans dream during the REM stage because when awakened during REM sleep, laboratory subjects reported dreams or dream-like experiences an average of 82% of the time.[39] It is uncertain what animals experience during this stage, since the "network for dreaming" in the animal brain is uncertain.

Early thought was that dreaming was stimulated by REM activation. However, the dream or dreamlike state is now known to also occur at the onset of sleep, during NREM sleep and even in some waking states. Dreaming occurs to a lesser degree between REM cycles, the average rate of dream recall being only about 42%. There is also a marked difference in the dreams recalled from these two states. According to the research findings compiled by Hobson,[39] reports from REM states are typically longer, more vivid, more animated, more emotionally charged, have more dream elements in them and are less like waking life events than NREM reports. NREM reports are more thought-like, and contain more representations of actual waking life events than do REM reports. Krippner et. al.[80] report on a study by Hobson (performed on 146 dream reports by 73 subjects) using an equal number of REM and NREM dreams. Hobson applied a standardized "Bizarreness Scale" to the dreams. The results indicated that about 70% of the REM dreams were reported as bizarre, compared to 20% of the NREM dreams.

The time spent in dream sleep varies with age. Adults spend about 25% of their sleep time in REM, children about 50%, and in premature infants it has been reported to be as high as 70% to 80%.[37] In older persons, REM sleep may reduce to about 15%. Art Funkhouser[82] indicates that dreaming continues as people age, but the themes they dream about change, as do their daily concerns. It seems there are fewer nightmares, less frequent aggressive dreams, shorter average length of dreams and less frequent dream recall. While shorter dreams and lower dream recall can be partly explained by the fact that memory no longer functions as well as it used to, research into aging and dream recall has shown that there are other factors involved since the largest drop-off in dream recall occurs at a relatively young age, around 26 (especially among males).[83] As we age, the content may eventually evolve into concerns about death. Research on this subject can be found in a book by Mary-Louise von Franz.[84]

Sleep and Dream Cycles

Figure 1 illustrates the cycles of sleep in a normal human that occur every night.[1] The horizontal scale is sleep time in hours, and the vertical the stages of sleep. In simple terms, it shows that we cycle between deep NREM sleep and shallow dreaming REM sleep multiple times per evening. These cycles continue throughout the night, in approximate 90-minute periods. We typically go through four to six dream periods in an eight-hour night, which might be surprising since we are often unable to recall even one of these dreams.

Let's follow figure 1 through a night of sleep. Dream sleep or REM sleep is also known as D (for desynchronized or dreaming), stage 1 sleep, or "slow wave" sleep. Non-REM or NREM sleep is also known as S sleep (for synchronized sleep) or stage 4 sleep. Often at sleep onset we awake with a jerk, sometimes recalling some dream-like images. This is known as a period of hypnogogic sleep, or light sleep where we have entered REM sleep and re-awakened. Normally at sleep onset there is a rapid movement from stage 1 sleep to stage 4, i.e., we go right into the deep NREM sleep. Pulse, respiration rate and blood pressure are lowered and no eye, facial or body movements are noted. The brain waves are more regular and lower frequency (1 to 4 cycles per second). Muscles relax, although whole body jerks may be observed. In this deep sleep stage it becomes more difficult to arouse the person. If awakened, dream reports, if any, tend to be more thought-like and devoid of imagery.

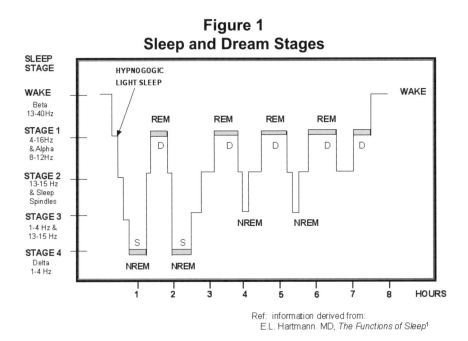

Figure 1
Sleep and Dream Stages

Ref: information derived from:
E.L. Hartmann. MD, *The Functions of Sleep*[1]

About 90 minutes later, the sleeper will begin REM sleep and vivid dreaming. As we continue through the night, we enter deep S sleep less often, and after about 6 hours remains between stages 1 and 2. The REM sleep stage is characterized by: eye movement, small movement in the muscles of the face, faster and more irregular pulse and respiration, and higher blood pressure. An EEG reading called a PGO spike often marks the onset of REM and many of these spikes appear during REM. Resting muscle potential is almost non-existent (we can't move). It is easier to arouse someone from this stage. When aroused, dream reports are full of vivid imagery and content, more so at the end of the sleep period than at the beginning.

In addition to the differences in dream reports, there are differences in brain activity observed between NREM and REM sleep. The medulla of the brain appears to regulate NREM sleep, whereas it is the pontine brain stem that regulates REM.[1] Single neurons in the brain have been seen to reduce their activity during NREM sleep and then increase during REM to a level as high or higher than in waking. During REM, a section of the forebrain is in a state similar to that of alert waking, and high levels of activity are found in the visual associative cortex and parts of the brain responsible for processing emotion. The central brain is also active, suggesting learning and memory processing.

Are Dreams Meaningful?

In the dream state, our dreams appear similar to normal waking-life adventures. Upon waking, however, that perception changes dramatically. We notice a lack of continuity between scenes, irrational cause and effect relationships, and a host of bizarre or irrational combinations of dream elements or activities. How can such dream experiences contain any logical meaning?

We are conscious in our dreams, but it is a different state of consciousness from waking. The synchronizing signals that are signs of consciousness (firing signatures of the intralaminar nuclei from various neural paths) are present, but unlike the waking state, these nuclei are not firing in response to outside stimulus.[38] Instead, the brain is activating itself purely from within; but to what purpose? Some researchers, such as Hobson and McCartney, [cited in 80] contend that dreams result from our higher brain centers attempting to make sense of the activity in the lower centers that generate the dreams. From this viewpoint, dreams could be simply be an attempt to make a rational story out of random neural activity.

When we discuss brain function in more detail in chapter 3, however, you will see that some very important processing may be taking place in the dream state. We already discovered above that dream sleep plays an important role in memory and learning. We will later learn that the parts of the brain responsible for emotional processing, social processing, novelty detection, integration of visual and auditory perceptions, associative processing, pattern and face recognition, spatial perception, imagery construction, and self-perception are active in the dream state. Could it be that these brain centers become activated in the dream state in order to perform a meaningful function?

The brain centers that are active in dream sleep are also active when we are awake, but are processing sensory experiences of the external world. These centers are responsible for our perception of the external world in relationship to our memories and expectations (our internal model of that world). They orient our physical and social perception of self to that external world, so that we can deal with it. They stimulate our emotions in order to draw our attention to what is important and to prepare us for action in the face of a threat. They contribute meaning and inflection to our speech.

In chapter 3, you will learn that these brain centers may be performing the same function in the dream state, but rather than processing real-time sensory experiences of the day, they process the unfinished business of the day, and unprocessed emotional experiences. The dream may simply be viewing this process, a process that in the waking state occurs below our threshold of awareness. The holistic and associative nature of that processing would account for its bizarreness, as well as for the fact that the part of our brain that makes rational sense out of all this internal activity (the dorsal lateral prefrontal cortex) is inactive in the dream state. The activity is not interpreted against a rational external reference as in the waking state.

Is it Necessary to Remember Your Dreams?

If dreaming does play an important role in memory and learning, and in restoring our mental well-being, then could recall and subsequent dreamwork augment the process? Since most of our dreams are not recalled, it appears that the mental processes taking place will continue whether we recall and understand them or not. There is, however, a wealth of evidence, including the experience of therapists who use dreams in their work, suggesting that properly understanding and working with our dreams can speed the wellness process. Justina Lasley, author of *Honoring the Dream*[101] states, "In my experience all dreams are significant and can be used to come to new understanding by bringing unconscious material to consciousness - I have never worked with an individual on a dream that has not carried new information and truth for the dreamer." Dream therapy has been reported[3] to bring about the creation of a new dream, called the "corrective dream," which incorporates the originally reported dream together with the new information supplied in the therapy session. *"I was dreaming I was looking everywhere for my purse. Suddenly I saw you there in the dream. You pointed out that the purse was on my shoulder. I stated, oh thank you, I guess I had it all the while."* This dream came after a therapy session where the dreamer finally realized that the self-worth they had been seeking was there all the time. It just took the dream, and the dreamwork with the therapist, to point it out.

Nightmares may be a means for the dreaming mind to involve the waking mind in dealing with an emotionally overwhelming issue. Nightmares release energy and surface anxieties associated with past trauma or recent threats to one's inner self, which might be too difficult to deal with all at once. The forced awareness of that dark inner matter, brought by nightmares, can become a part of the healing process if properly dealt with. Hartmann and Galvin[cited in 80] have attempted to teach frequent nightmare sufferers how to attain lucidity during terrifying dreams. This can be a successful approach. I found it works well with children who are very suggestible. An example is seen in a case in which a child suffered from frequent nightmares of being chased by a big black monster. I told her that the next time she dreamed it, she should turn around and hug the monster. That night she had the same dream and the next morning reported with great joy that she had hugged the monster. I asked her what happened to the monster. She said, "It turned into my mommy." The dream never returned.

Gaining rewarding results from remembering and understanding your dreams does not necessarily depend on lucidity. *"I had a frightening dream where I was being chased away by a big buffalo with a little buffalo following it."* When we worked on his dream, the dreamer's association with the big buffalo was: *"he was huge and powerful, when he wants you to go, you go,"* which he recognized as related to his boss. His association with the little buffalo was: *"a little pipsqueak that followed the big one around -- just like that little pipsqueak at work!"* Before the dream, the dreamer was unhappy on the job but was unable to focus on the reason. The dream revealed that the source of his discontent was the actions of his boss and the relationship his boss had with the co-worker whom the dreamer considered to be a "little pipsqueak" that followed the boss around. The clarity of recalling and understanding the dream now permits the dreamer to focus on the real cause of his discontent and deal with it more appropriately.

How Can I Recall My Dreams?

As we learned above, you spend about one fourth of your night dreaming, so the problem is not one of dreaming, but one of dream recall. The mechanisms involved in dream recall remain unclear, as do the reasons for differences in dream recall between individuals. There appear to be many factors involved.

Dreams do not occur as we awaken, as some early speculation suggested. Dreams occur roughly over the time period we recall them having occurred. The measured length of the REM period has been correlated with both the dream report word count and the estimated length of the dream by the dreamer.[39]

Dream recall, on the other hand, may relate to when a person awakens, whether it is during or following the REM dream experience. Recall may also relate to how a person awakens, because certain memory processes must activate to capture the remnants of the ongoing dream and store them in longer-term memory. Hobson[39] indicates that working memory is off-line in the dream state, and that the mechanisms for storing memories are diminished to non-existent. Hobson also reports that dream recall rapidly falls off, the longer one takes to wake up after the REM period.

Assuming that you wake up while the dream is ongoing or ending, the best approach for recalling dreams is to place your attention on the ongoing dream as you wake up. Try closing your eyes and reviewing the dream before opening your eyes again and moving out of position. Go over the dream completely, to store as much as possible in permanent memory. Then open your eyes and write it down or record it. Jarring yourself awake with an alarm clock might divert you from your dream too quickly to be conducive to dream recall. Wake yourself with a more gentle system (music, more gentle alarm or such).

Recall might also relate to one's sleeping habits. Webb and Agnew[51] found that people, who sleep longer than 8.5 hours, had 50% more REM sleep than people who sleep less than 6.5 hours. Later sleep tends to be less deep and closer to waking, with longer dream periods as figure 1 illustrates. Based on this information, you would expect more recall and longer dream reports as people sleep longer. There are still mixed results on this, however. Whereas Backeland and Hartmann[52] found it to be the case, Blagrove et. al.[50] did not. The total opportunity for dream recall may be greater as you sleep longer, but spontaneous dream recall still depends on other factors, including the dreamer's interest in recalling and writing down the dream.

In a literature review cited by Lynne Hoss,[45] a relationship was shown between dream recall frequency and artistic and imagery abilities. She reports that Schechter, Schmeidler and Staal (1965) tested both dream recall and creative tendencies in 100 students of art, science and engineering. There was a significantly higher proportion of dream recall among art students (assessed as more creative, and therefore using more right hemisphere process as will be described in chapter 3). Recall was lowest among engineering students (attributed to the more linear, temporal thought process of the left hemisphere). No differences between the sexes were found. Her work also cites research by Cory, Ormiston, Simmel and Dainoff (1975) that found recall to be greater in those with greater memory capability for visual images.[45]

Spanos, Stam, Radtke & Nightingale, (1980) found that in females, dream recall was greater for those who had more ability to become absorbed in imagery and measures of creativity. Cohen[48] found a highly significant difference between dream recallers and non-recallers in ability to form clear, vivid images. Blagrove[50] found that dream recall is related to the personality factor of "openness to experience." Hartmann[103] indicates that there are only a few personality factors that closely correlate with dream recall including: tolerance of ambiguity, openness to experience, absorption, creativity, fantasy-proneness and ability to be hypnotized. He states that these factors also closely relate to "thin boundaries."

In my experience (as well as that of Hartmann[103]), recall is strongly related to your interest in recalling dreams and attitude toward dreams. If a person takes an active interest in recalling a dream on a particular night, or during a period of nights, they are more likely to do so. It often happens in my dream courses that a student, who claims they don't recall dreams, suddenly begins recalling them for a period afterwards.

Interest in dreams can help, but an active interest in recall is the key. There are many tricks to aid dream recall on a particular night. One technique is known as dream "incubation." It consists of a self-suggestion ritual, performed before going to sleep, whereby you repeat to yourself that you will dream (perhaps of a certain topic) and will wake and recall the dream. Incubation is a way of placing unfinished business at the forefront of the mind when going to sleep. The request should be accompanied with a paper and pencil beside the bed, or a voice recorder, so that the dream can be recorded. I find that incubation works best with no particular subject matter in mind, just a suggestion that you will dream and wake to recall the dream. If you want to try to dream about a specific situation, it is best to pick one that is emotionally significant, associated with some anxiety or unresolved problem.

Dream recall is only the beginning of the process. Proper recording of the dream and using proper methods to understand and work with the dream are paramount. The remaining chapters of this book will be devoted to these methods. What we will learn is that it is not only important to record the story of the dream, but also the imagery, colors, actions, settings, feelings, sensations and thoughts. It is equally important to record what experiences you had the day before that were of an emotional nature or that seem to relate to the dream.

DREAM RECALL - TRY THIS

1) Put a pad of paper and pencil by your bedside, so that if you have a dream you can write it down after you wake up. This also triggers the mind that you are serious about recalling your dreams.

2) Close your eyes and repeat the phrase; "I will have a dream tonight and I will wake up and recall it." Do this 5 to10 times before falling off to sleep, and reinforce it by envisioning yourself waking from a dream and recalling it.

3) Incubate a specific dream if you wish. Envision the dream or dream topic you want, then change the incubation phrase: "I will have a dream tonight about _____ and I will wake up and recall it." It might be a specific topic, answer or solution you are looking for. But as we will learn, dreams are like parables that speak in the language of association and metaphor; so don't expect the answer to be literal.

4) Some people try ritualistic tricks such as drinking half a glass of water and placing the rest by your bed, leaving the other half to drink upon waking and recalling a dream. Many reward-like rituals work to trigger the mind, so try one that works for you.

5) Don't expect this to always work right away. It may take some time, so keep at it.

6) Don't try to fool Mother Nature. When you wake from the dream, write it down. It is this genuine interest in your dream world that will bring forth dream recall.

CHAPTER 2
WHAT ARE DREAMS ABOUT?

Trust the dreams for in them is hidden the gate to eternity – Kahlil Gibran

Some **dreams stories** have wonderfully coherent story lines, and others provide just a glimpse of an image or short disjointed events. At times when we are ill or injured, our dreams seem to become uncomfortable and bizarre. Some people report "visionary" imagery that changed their lives, or the foretelling of events in the future or at a distant place. With these endless differences, what can dreams really mean? Is there a common purpose to dreaming?

The differences we see in our dream experiences appear to be a reflection of the many sources of information and activity that the human mind deals with in the dream state. In this chapter, I will discuss dreams in terms of the source or nature of the predominant content. This will illustrate that dreams can take on many forms, as the dreaming brain seems to be open to stimulus from various levels of the human existence. Although the principal stimulus may be the processing of unresolved emotional issues, material from body and spirit can also enter or influence the dream.

The Typical Dream

Below is a set of dream characteristics, based primarily on the compilation by Hobson,[39] which researchers most consistently attributed to the experience of dreaming:

1. Dreams mainly involve visual and motion perceptions, but occasionally other senses.
2. Dream images can change rapidly (particularly numbers and words).
3. Dreams are often bizarre in nature, but also contain many images and events that are relatively commonplace. Faces are a common feature.
4. We believe that we are awake in our dreams.

5. Self-reflection is infrequent or involves illogical explanations of the events and plots.
6. Dreams lack orientation stability. Persons, times and places are fused, plastic, incongruous and discontinuous.
7. Story lines integrate all the dream elements into a single confabulatory.
8. Dreams contain increased, intensified emotion, especially fear-anxiety that can integrate bizarre dream features and shape the dream story.
9. There is a tendency toward more negative emotion in dreams.
10. There is an increased incorporation of instinctive emotions (especially fight-flight), which also may act as powerful organizers of dream cognition.
11. Dreams are concerned more with emotionally prominent content than current events. Exception: dream incubations which focus on recent emotional events can increase their occurrence in the dream.
12. Control by the will of the dreamer is greatly reduced. A dreamer rarely considers the possibility of actually controlling the flow of dream events, and on those infrequent occasions when this does occur (lucidity), the control may be only for a few seconds.
13. Self-control of thoughts, feelings and behavior is fairly common.

In 1966 Calvin Hall and Robert Van de Castle published the book *The Content Analysis of Dreams*.[57] For the first time, there was a comprehensive standardized system of classifying and scoring the content of dream reports. With this new tool, a true measure of cultural, gender and other differences in the nature of dreams and dreamers could be achieved.

It was found that women dream equally of men and women, but 67% of the characters in men's dreams are other men (Hall 1984) and the gender difference in favor of male characters appeared in almost every culture (there was one finding from a study in India where the male % was lower than the female %). For both men and women across cultures, dreams usually contain more aggression than friendliness, more misfortune than good fortune and more negative than positive emotions. Men have a higher degree of aggression in dreams than women.[40] Some cultural influences were found. For example, dreamers from small traditional societies have a greater percentage of animals than do those of larger industrial societies. Studies of dream journals reveal continuity between the emotional preoccupations of the dreamers and their waking thoughts.[40] The dreams of older dreamers do not differ much from college students with the exception of a decline in physical aggression and negative emotions, nor does dream content change much according to long-term journaling studies.

Mental Well Being

Controversy remains around the true function and purpose of dreaming, but as we will learn in chapter 3, the most typical dreams tend to be involved with the unfinished business of the day, unresolved threats to the inner self or the processing of unresolved emotional issues. Unfortunately it is difficult to see this clearly, since the events themselves rarely appear in the dream as they occurred, but are instead represented by a mixture of related memories and emotions, and contextually associated imagery. In the simplest sense, dreams appear to reflect unresolved emotional situations and experiences, by presenting the situation as a visual analogy or metaphor. The concept of the visual analogy or metaphor is illustrated in the following dream of a woman who normally considered herself totally in control of her life, and able to handle anything that came along. Suddenly she found herself dealing with the death of her husband and feeling powerless to do anything about it: *"I dreamed about being locked in a car with no steering wheel and no door handles or window controls. It was rolling backward down a steep hill, and there was no way of stopping it, or getting out of it. I woke up in a panic."*

At times, the dream can surface subliminal information that might be important to the dreamer's life, but that went unnoticed and unfinished in the day's activity. Ann Faraday recalls how she dreamed of her pet bird that *"hit her with a brown derby hat he was wearing."* When reflecting on the metaphor, she realized she had not fed her pet bird (the "brown derby" image related to a restaurant of the same name).

The more complex function of dream processing appears to be involved in finding a way to incorporate new emotionally-charged material from the day, into the internal image we hold for self or our social world. We will learn in chapters 4 and 5 that the dreaming brain will try to bring about closure by either accommodating the material in some way, or transforming the internal model a bit to better reflect external reality.

This process was illustrated in the following "jokester" dream: *" I dreamed I was bothered by a young jokester character. I tried to make him to go away, when an influential shadowy character entered from my left and argued that this jokester had been quite useful and that we should give him a chance. After some discussion I agreed, and the jokester was told he would be given a chance to prove himself. At that point he walked off to the right down a sunlit path."* In subsequent dreamwork, the dreamer recalled a situation the day before where he had been challenged by some friends, and reacted uncharacteristically by making a joke of the situation. At first he was embarrassed by his actions, worrying that he may have caused hurt feelings. But the tactic seemed to work. This new side of self that emerged in the waking situation, appeared as the jokester in the dream.

Here we saw the existing self (the dreamer in the dream) react as he did in waking life, rejecting that side of himself at first. However, a compensating character emerged to bring about a way to accommodate this jokester behavior, by accepting it on a trial basis. The result was temporary acceptance within the conscious personality. A small transformation of the inner self occurred, bringing it into closer agreement with external experience. As we will find, most of our dreams are of this type, working on unresolved emotionally-charged waking issues.

Problem Solving or Creative Dreams

Sometimes, the unfinished business that dreams work on can be unresolved problems or unrealized creations. There are many stories about the role that dreams have played in some of our greatest inventions. For example there is a story told about how Elias Howe, the inventor of the sewing machine, had been struggling with how to mechanically move a sewing needle and thread through cloth and make a stitch. In a dream, spear throwers were chasing him, and he saw the shape of the spears as that of a sewing needle. But the hole was at the sharp lower end of the needle instead of at the blunt upper end as with a hand-held needle. In this dream image he found the solution.

Deirdre Barrett, in her book *The Committee of Sleep: How Artists, Scientists, and Athletes Use Their Dreams for Creative Problem Solving—and How You Can Too*[90] opens with the quote, "It is a common experience that a problem difficult at night is resolved in the morning after the committee of sleep has worked on it." [John Steinbeck]. Deirdre offers a rich collection of examples, a few of which follow, that show how some of the world's most creative people have used the revelations of their dream life to inform their work.

In the visual arts, for example, Jasper Johns couldn't find his unique artistic vision until he dreamed it in the form of a large American flag. Salvador Dali and his colleagues built surrealism out of dreams. Today, Lucy Davis, chief architect at a major firm, dreams her extraordinary designs into life. In the film world, director Ingmar Bergman confides, "Twice I have transferred dreams to film exactly as I had dreamed them." Other filmmakers who have alluded to the use of their dreams in their work include: Federico Fellini, Orson Welles, Akira Kurosawa, Robert Altman, and John Sayles. Mary Shelley's terrible nightmare became Frankenstein. Stephen King's haunting dream as a little boy led to his first bestseller. Musicians such as Beethoven, Billy Joel and Paul McCartney have used the music from their dreams in their work. In science, Otto Loewi worked with his dreams on the medical experiment that earned him the Nobel Prize.

Nightmares

Nightmares can be distinguished from "normal" dreams by their overwhelming anxiety, apprehension and fear. We also may consider a "bad" dream as a nightmare. Ernest Hartmann, author of *The Nightmare*[60] and *Dreams and Nightmares*[86] has performed one of the most extensive studies of frequent nightmares. Hartmann states that the dream, especially the central image (CI), pictures the emotion of the dreamer and that the intensity of the central image is a measure of the strength of the emotion. This might be seen in nightmares when there is a single powerful emotion such as in a tidal wave dream following a traumatic event. Although negative content and emotion appear frequently in most dreams, we do not usually report the dream as a nightmare unless it is extremely upsetting. Van de Castle[37] reported that a study by Bixler on sleep problems, which surveyed 1,006 households, found that only 11 percent reported being troubled by nightmares.

Nightmares can fall into various classes regarding their cause, including: a) the result of trauma; b) long-term nightmare sufferers; c) medical problems requiring attention; d) heavy stress; e) severe threat to the self-image. Nightmares are different from night terrors, which may be accompanied by screaming before awakening with extended disorientation afterwards.[37] Night terrors occur (if at all) during the first two hours of sleep in deep sleep (sleep state 4) and the dream itself is generally not recalled.

Trauma Related Nightmares

Nightmares are often a direct result of a traumatic situation. The suppression of trauma, and subsequent release through replay in dreams, is common in the dreams of veterans suffering from posttraumatic stress disorders, disaster survivors, those who had life threatening encounters and such. Their nightmares are often a repetitive replay of actual experiences they had encountered. Deirdre Barrett in her book *Trauma and Dreams*[88] indicates that a pattern evolves in which the trauma is dreamed repeatedly, much as it happened, and becomes more "dreamlike" and surreal over time. These begin to change into "mastery" dreams for people who recover from the trauma. The repetitive, unchanging replays may continue, however, in those who develop severe posttraumatic stress disorder (PTSD) in their waking life. The book describes how coaching to develop "mastery" dreams can aid in the resolution of PTSD.

Deirdre Barrett and Jaffar Behbehani[89] studied post-traumatic stress disorder and recurring nightmares in Kuwait following the Iraqi invasion and occupation of 1990-91. As described in other trauma populations, many Kuwaitis had classic post-traumatic stress nightmares involving literal repetitions of the atrocities they witnessed, with only minor distortions. One dreamer, who had a brother fighting in the resistance, had the following recurring nightmare: *We are at home and the Iraqis come to the house. They break the windows and storm in, searching everywhere and demand to know where he [the brother] is. My two little children are crying. One soldiers is pointing a gun at each of our heads one by one, saying he will shoot us if we do not tell where he is hiding. We do not know. The soldier pulls the trigger and shoots my son, then my daughter. I wake up screaming.* In real life, they came into the house almost like this, and did hold a gun to everyone's head while they asked about the brother, but never shot anyone. The dreamer's brother had not come home, however, and she feared he had been shot.

Some people showed an evolution of "mastery" in their dreams. For example, one young woman had a recurring nightmare throughout the occupation in which she was riding in the elevator of a high-rise building, along with many people. The elevator cord would break, plunging the elevator several floors and then dangling by a thread with the terrified passengers not knowing how they could get off before the cord would break and plunge them to their deaths. The dreamer would wake in terror at this point. After the liberation, changes occurred with each repetition of the dream, with the most recent ending in rescuers coming to help people climb to safety through a door in the top of the elevator. As a side note, in Kuwait, people believe that dreams foretell the future rather than reflect the past, making these dreams yet more terrifying. Kuwaitis experienced considerable relief simply from learning that victims of other traumas repeat the trauma in their dreams.

Nightmare Sufferers

Nightmare sufferers are individuals who have a long history of nightmares. Unlike trauma cases, the nightmares do not repeat the same literal event, although the themes might be similar. Frequent nightmare sufferers report their typical non-nightmare dreams as vivid and detailed, filled with very bright colors and distinctive sounds, along with tactile sensations such as pain, taste and smell, which are seldom present in typical dreams.[37] In the Hartmann study, many of the long-term nightmare sufferers had stormy personal relationships, difficult adolescent years, a high suicide attempt rate and many were in therapy.[60]

Medical Related Nightmares

Sometimes nightmares can occur to warn of something wrong physically. We have all likely experienced nightmarish or disturbing dreams when very ill. Nightmares have at times warned of the onset of illness or a threatening physical condition before we are consciously aware of it. This will be discussed in more detail in the next section on dreams related to physical factors.

Stress and Threat Related Nightmares

Although research has shown that personality factors such as thin boundaries are related to nightmare frequency, Schredl found that there is a greater relationship with current daily stress factors than with personality factors.[53]

Daily stress often translates internally to a threat to one's internal image of self. Job disputes, marriage disputes, arguments with friends and associates, etc. are all stress factors that can cause nightmares. But the more significant factor is that these types of situations threaten our sense of who we are. As we will see in later chapters, this threat to self-image may be the stimulus behind a high percentage of our dreams. As the threat grows to the point where the internal model of self and reality can no longer accommodate it, a nightmare may result.

The most common theme in children's nightmares is that of being chased by monsters. Later on in life, the pursuer might become an unidentified figure or group of figures. In chapter 4 we will learn that Jung attributes many of the dark, unidentified figures, the monsters in our dreams, to material coming from the unconscious. This is the unknown "dark side" of our psyche that is still evolving. The unconscious also contains all of our suppressed, unwanted or fearful memories, our traumas, and our undesired behavior patterns. As stressful experiences add emotional energy to this suppressed material, it emerges in our dreams. This material may appear as the dark, unidentified characters or monsters that pursue or frighten us. We are essentially running from ourselves, afraid that if our darker side catches up with us, we will be destroyed. The following dream shows this in a humorous way: *"I dreamed I was unsuccessfully trying to run from a big, black, hairy monster. My legs could hardly move, and finally I found myself trapped. So I turned around to face the monster and called out in fear 'what are you going to do to me?' The monster (now appearing less frightening) said, 'I don't know lady, it's your dream'!"* According to Jung, this cycle of impending death is part of the process of integrating the unconscious self into the personality. Since integration implies that our existing self-image (the ego) must change, or symbolically die, the fear is exaggerated in the dream.

Physical or Healing Factors

On occasion, dreams can be populated with content that is stimulated by disease, fever, severe injury, or by an outside stimulus (noise or cold air for example). Patricia Garfield, in her book ***The Healing Power of Dreams,***[5] indicates that dreams often contain references to internal physical conditions before they are known to the conscious mind or felt by the senses. As a result, she indicates that we should pay attention to the related imagery and watch for warning signs, as well as signs of healing.

It is rare that an external sensory stimulus will directly affect the dream, because the input to and output from the portions of the brain that process such stimulus, are blocked in the dream state.[39] However, at times external stimulus can find its way into our dreams, particularly if it is tactile in nature or intense enough. Van de Castle[37] reports that of three external stimuli applied during REM sleep, a spray of cold water was incorporated in 42 percent of the recalled dreams, light flashes in 23 percent and an auditory tone in only 9 percent.

When there is an external stimulus, the dream generally incorporates it into the ongoing story line, but it rarely becomes the defining plot of that night's dreams. For example, a cold room might bring snow into the dream environment, and the dream may respond to a loud noise as a gunshot. These events may be unassociated with the prior dream story, but are suddenly incorporated in the ongoing dream. Conditions in the body can alter the content of the dream: *"Suddenly in the dream I had to go to the bathroom, but every time I found one, it was broken or flooded or occupied. Then I woke up and realized that I really did have to go."* This is probably one of the most commonly recalled physical stimuli that invade our ongoing dream stories. In the case of the bathroom theme, I find that the dream will often inhibit any such action while asleep by frustrating the dreamers attempt to find or use the bathroom. Perhaps there is enough conscious cognition in the dreaming process that the dream is saying, "hold on, not here!"

Dreams of illness or injury generally contain imagery depicting the poor state of the physical body (dirty water, broken pipes, broken machinery, etc.). These are often disturbing, disjointed, non-sequential dreams that seem different from other dreams, sometimes with a lot of repetitive attempts at solving a nonsense problem. Dreams of pending disease may contain such imagery as bugs crawling around, excess dirty water, ice or cold conditions, or images of a body part and, at odd times, cartoon characters. *"I dreamed there were five of us in a room, including two big fat pink cartoon-like characters, who had been at one time friendly toward us, but had turned on us. The two other men were holding down the fat pink guys and cutting their throats."* The dreamer woke with a sore throat, swollen tonsils and the flu -- all symbolized by the dream imagery.

Sometimes dreams of this nature can hint at a remedy to rebalance the system. The following series occurred to a man who had just gone on a radical diet and was still adjusting to it. *"I dreamed of a fishing boat and on the side of it was written the words 'eat more fish'."* At that, the dreamer added fish to his diet and subsequently felt an increase in energy. A couple of nights later he dreamed, *"I was being enticed by a beautiful woman. As I approached her she stated, 'bring me tea'."* At this point the dreamer was getting used to these messages of protest from his body, and added tea to his diet. Another remedy dream comes from a man who had asthma: *"I dreamed of a hand that was pouring 2 oz. of lemon juice onto 2 ice cubes."* He took this remedy for 2 weeks and claimed it solved his coughing and fainting.

Be careful with the literal interpretation of dream remedies, since dreams speak in metaphor. Only consider the apparent remedy if it is healthy and otherwise harmless. Care must also be taken in considering the messages in the dreams as accurate medical diagnoses. *"I was in a clinic and a nurse was checking me over. She felt some lumps on my groin area and exclaimed, 'she is riddled with cancer'. I was not afraid to die but asked the nurse if she could do something to keep me from going through all the pain."* In this case, the dreamer went for a checkup and, fortunately, the dream had nothing do with a medical condition. It turned out that the dreamer was a strong believer in astrology. At the time of the dream she was having a relationship with a man who was a "Cancer." She perceived that the relationship was ending and feared the emotional pain.

Nonetheless, it is good to have a checkup if a particular body part recurs in a dream or appears in a particularly disturbing or impacting dream. *"I saw a horrible looking creature, shaped like a huge black gelatinous blob which was threatening my child, oozing out from under a platform on which there was some old inoperative rusting machinery."* This dream occurred after a bout with post-menopausal bleeding. The dreamer heeded the dream and went for a checkup, which luckily showed the cause to be hormone-related, and not life threatening. In the following dream, the medical condition was symbolically represented before the symptoms were apparent. However the dreamer was less fortunate in this case: *"My father used to have a recurring nightmare where he dreamed he looked into the mirror and had no head. He woke screaming each time. He died from Alzheimer's while still fairly young."*

On a more positive note, dreams relating to pregnancy may have elements of renewal, as well as references to body change and self-image. Patricia Garfield[5] describes common images in pregnancy dreams to include small animals, baby animals and amphibians such as lizards (representing the fetus), water (perhaps representing the amniotic water in which the baby is suspended), buildings and other architectural imagery (relating to the woman's body, the fetal home).

Color can relate to the physical condition. Many dreams that accompany flu or stomach and intestinal sickness will be filled with dirty brown fluids inside of tunnels or tubes. Rust color, accompanying broken machinery, might appear as in the woman's dream above. Other sickness-related colors are vile green or muddy yellow. Injury is often accompanied with red in the dream, representing inflammation and blood. The following dream came as a result of an eye injury: *"I dreamed of a skull with red fire coming out of a section above the eye."*

Using Dreams to Heal

The great majority of this book will be focused on how to work with your dreams, or your client's dreams, to deal with unresolved emotional situations, or inappropriate beliefs that leave the dreamer stuck in unhealthy behavior patterns. Dreams may also contain information that is key to healing other disorders, particularly when there is a basis in some earlier emotional trauma or irrational decision about self and life.

Irrational beliefs can express themselves not only as symptoms of other disorders (bereavement, depression, trauma), but also as symptoms of what may appear to be physical disorders. Deirdre Barrett,[91] in her paper "The 'Royal Road' becomes a shrewd shortcut," describes how dreams can be a useful diagnostic tool in such cases, since dreams represent a powerful metaphor, which patients may be unable to articulate otherwise.

The paper illustrates how dreamwork can be utilized in symptom-focused psychotherapy. One example is that of a 36-year-old man who came for treatment of a two-month bout with insomnia. He reported a dream in which he saw a boy sleeping in a bed, with soft morning light shining in through translucent curtains. Despite the peaceful images of the scene, the dreamer felt a sense of dread. An old-fashioned alarm clock went off, ringing loudly, but the boy did not stir. A woman appeared at the door of the room and called to the boy, who still did not move. The dream ended abruptly with the patient knowing the boy was dead.

The dreamer recalled there had been a time around age six when he feared bedtime because he might die in his sleep, as he'd heard of people doing. Talking about this long-ago fear, and being able to rationally reevaluate its high improbability, led to some improvement of his insomnia.

In the next session, he reported another dream of a little boy in a room - this time not in bed, but rather sitting against a wall crying. The dreamer knew the boy was sobbing because of a terrible feeling of being alone. This dream triggered more associations to his childhood concept of death as ultimate aloneness; not so much a cessation of consciousness, but the belief that "they put you in ground and you stay there forever." Once explicitly aware of his sleep = death = aloneness equation, he discussed how several work and relationship changes had left him more lonely in the last couple months. His insomnia disappeared as he made more effort to reconnect socially.

Paranormal or Anomalous Dreams

These are dreams that contain elements that expand our perception beyond the bounds of normal reality. The dream may start out as a typical dream, but the story line may suddenly incorporate a striking paranormal element. Paranormal dreams might contain clairvoyant information, presenting us with knowledge about an event happening in another place. They may be telepathic, revealing the thoughts or experiences of another. Precognitive information is also reported in dreams, i.e., images of events yet to take place. Some report a spiritual experience in dreams, perhaps information from those who have passed on or a visionary experience seemingly from a higher source.

Some of the first pioneering scientific work in this area was performed by Ullman, Krippner and Vaughan, who in their classic book, *Dream Telepathy,*[6] discussed the results of scientifically controlled experiments in paranormal dreaming. Much of the work was performed in the dream laboratory at Maimonides Medical Center in New York. The book studies telepathic dreaming (dreaming of what someone else is thinking or experiencing) and precognitive dreaming (dreaming of an event in the future) in a sound and systematic basis. A more recent book *Extraordinary Dreams and How to Work with Them*, co-authored by Stanley Krippner,[80] provides a wealth of knowledge and research into paranormal and extraordinary dreams, as well as a discussion on how to work with the nature of each type of dream to enhance your life. An extraordinary dream of a paranormal nature might fall into one of the following classifications according to Krippner: a) Collective dreams – whereby two persons report the same or similar dreams on the same night; b) Telepathic dreams – relating to the thoughts of another; c) Clairvoyant dreams – perceiving distant events; d) Precognitive dreams – providing information about an event that has not yet occurred; e) Past life dream – which appear to detail events in a past life we have no way of knowing about; f) Spiritual dreams – whereby we are visited by spirits, deities or those from the other side. g) Out-of-Body – which involves the sensation of leaving your body. I will discuss a few of these here, but refer you to Krippner's book for a more in-depth understanding of this extraordinary class of dreams.

I have found that paranormal dreams are often marked with a degree of lucidity (a feeling that it was more real than most), a sense that it was not a normal dream, and sometimes a presence of bright light or intense colors. In my own collection of seemingly paranormal dreams, imagery symbolic of "communications" has often appeared (perhaps as a metaphor?). *"I dreamed I was searching for my lost child and was desperate to find a phone that would work. Neither of the two phones I tried had a dial tone, but I suddenly saw a phone number. I dialed the number and, on the last digit, a screen appeared above the phone revealing that my child was safe at home."* The dreamer reported that the phone number seemed so clear and significant, that she wrote it down and called it the next day. The person she contacted was quite excited, because she too had a lifelong interest in dreams, and synchronistic with the dream, belonged to an organization that works with children. Both the dreamer and the person she phoned expressed that they were searching for something the other could provide in their lives. They formed a bond of friendship as a result.

Collective Dreams

Sometimes two persons will report having dreams on the same night, with the same identical elements in them. For example, Stanley Krippner[80] cites a dream in which the two dreamers, on the same night, dreamed of being in identical locations, describing the same hotel lobby with its unique pillars. Some emotional attachment may be involved between collective dreamers. Sometimes therapists and subjects may find themselves dreaming similar dreams, with content that is important to the session that week. I have had the experience of dreaming of one of my students and she dreaming of me on the same night. In one particular case, the dreams were not similar (other than the presence of the two of us) but, when the dreams were discussed, my dream held valuable information related to understanding her dream and her situation.

Another example of a collective or connected dream experience is one that my wife and I experienced. *I dreamed of a clock face that had a jagged shape around it. In my dream I was trying to understand the meaning and suddenly a voice said "wake your wife, she will know what it means." At that moment I woke up and so did my wife. I told her of the image of the jagged clock face and she said, "Oh I was dreaming that you were going to have a rough time".*

Telepathic

Dreaming of the thoughts or perceptions of other people at a distance has been the subject of a good degree of scientific research, because it is relatively easy to administer, control and judge. Following the experimental process that Ullman, Krippner and Vaughan had pioneered,[6] my colleague John Williams and I repeated the experimentation on a number of occasions with the students from my Dream Psychology course at Richland College in Richardson, Texas. We had a person who did not know the purpose of the experiment select three pictures on 35mm slides at random and place them in black envelopes. At about midnight, we would pick one at random and project it on the ceiling of the planetarium, and view the picture with the intention that it would be telepathically sent to the sleeping students. The night before the class, the students were given instructions to go to bed and wake themselves up with an alarm clock about a half an hour after we started the projection. Upon waking, they were to draw the key dream imagery and record their dream. The dreams were then collected the following day and judged.

The experiments resulted in a small percentage of dream reports (perhaps 2 to 4 each time out of a collection of a dozen or so dreams) that were strikingly similar to the projected picture. It is difficult to say how much could be attributed to coincidence and how much to telepathic ability, but in some cases there was such a striking similarity, that the evidence for telepathy seemed very convincing. For example, one evening the picture was of Salvador Dali's *Discovery of America*. The picture contained bishops waiting on shore, each with a staff in their hand containing a rounded cross inside an oval at the top. One student turned in their drawing stating that they did not recall the dream but they did recall some images. The drawing was of a bishop with the exact same bishops hat and the exact same staff in their hands with the oval and rounded cross at the top.

Another anecdotal experience comes from the dream telepathy contests held by International Association for the Study of Dreams (IASD) at their annual conference (see resource appendix for information on IASD). Each year the association does a fun, non-scientific version of the telepathy experiment similar to the one described above. A person transmits a target picture that is selected at random from three that have been previously placed in envelopes. The target picture is transmitted late one evening to the conference attendees. The attendees are asked to incubate a dream on the picture, and then record their dream in the morning, and place it in an envelope for judging. Each year a prize is given for the closest dream representation of the target picture. At the Copenhagen conference in 2004, there was a particularly interesting "hit." The target picture was a huge tree. The person transmitting the picture, in order to try to act it out, started jumping up and down yelling, "tree – tree". One dream report came in the next day in which the dreamer said that the only thing they recalled was the image of the person who was the transmitter, jumping up and down yelling "tree – tree". They obviously won the prize!

Clairvoyant

Some of the most memorable stories of clairvoyant dreams, the perception of events at a distance, occur between family members at a time of crisis or the death of a loved one. *"I dreamed that my father and I were walking in a beautiful field. At that point he left me and walked into the sunset. I said to him 'so long Captain'."* At that moment the dreamer woke up, and a few minutes later he received a phone call regarding the unexpected death of his father (who the family lovingly called "Captain"). Sometimes the clairvoyant dream will contain better news: *"I dreamed I was unpacking a lovely wedding dress. The next day I received a call from my daughter who said she was getting married."* Clairvoyant dreams may contain metaphors or word-play related to the event: *"I was being followed by some harmless but annoying insects that I called 'urine bees.' The day after the dream, I received a note from a urologist B. B. (name), who said that they were moving to our area and wanted to get re-acquainted."*

Precognitive

The news and tabloids are filled with reports of people who saw disasters in their dreams, before the actual occurrence. A few days before the 9-11 World Trade disaster in the U.S., a person reported the following dream to me: *"I was looking across the water and all the buildings were toppled like pick-up sticks. Everything went dark and people were rushing to the radio and TV to find out what had happened."* Evidence that these paranormal phenomena can occur in the dream state also comes from a number of research studies at the dream lab at Maimonides Medical Center, reported in the book *Dream Telepathy.* [6]

The difficulty with a precognitive dream is determining whether it is foretelling the future, or if it is just a metaphor for something happening within you. Dreaming of an airplane crashing to the ground, for example, is more often than not a metaphor relating to the dreamer's goals, or new ideas and concepts, "crashing to the ground." It is always advisable to first apply solid dreamwork practices to such a dream, in order to sort out possible psychological causes. Canceling a vacation after such a dream may be an overreaction. However, if the dream seemingly warns of some event that can easily be avoided, it may be prudent to do so, particularly if the event appeared unusually real in the dream. Successfully avoiding an event may be difficult, however, since the dream rarely depicts the scene as it is in reality. Krippner et. al.[80] report on work by Louisa Rhine with 191 apparent precognitive experiences, in which 69% of the people were successful in attempting to prevent the foreseen event. I find much less success in the precognitive dreamers I have been exposed to. Most people I have worked with, who report frequent precognitive dreams that do come to pass, report feelings of fear and frustration that they are unable to prevent the events.

In a few cases that I have observed, the dream will contain a precognitive element that has little to do with the dream itself, but acted as a trigger for later recall of the dream. *I was driving along the highway recently and a unique, bright yellow custom car passed me going the other way. I suddenly realized that I had seen that same exact car in a dream the night before. At this point the entire dream, which had been previously forgotten, flooded into consciousness. It turned out to be a very important dream to work with, but the meaning of the dream had nothing to do with the yellow car.*

Sometimes, the dream and waking life events will contain a striking synchronicity with important transitions in the dreamer's life. The following "retirement party" dream, discussed further in chapter 5, contained such a precognitive and synchronistic element. This dream came at an important transition point in the dreamer's life – his retirement. He dreamed of a retirement party where he was given four gifts, with the main gift being a brilliant golden bowl. Oddly, when the dreamer awoke, he could recall all the details of the dream except the golden bowl. That afternoon, the dreamer happened upon a Tibetan "song" bowl in a store (something he had never seen before) and suddenly remembered the golden bowl as the forgotten gift in the dream. It is a notable synchronicity that the dreamer was now able to obtain the physical manifestation of this central element in this significant transformational dream.

Some people feel that precognitive dreams are responsible for many deja vu experiences. On a few occasions, as in the examples above, I have been able to track such experiences back to a dream where the element has been clear. An alternative theory of deja vu is based on evidence that a sensory event is processed by two paths in the brain. Sensory information takes a fast track to the limbic system where emotional memories are associated with the event in order to prepare us for action. The slower track goes to the cognitive centers where the event, plus those emotional memories, raises our attention level so that we become aware of it. It is reasonable that the perception of the new event, together with the older emotional memories, could produce a feeling of having been there before.

Past Life

Many people report dreams that appear to reflect a past life: *"I was Chinese and in China as one of a large band of refugees. An army, which appeared to be Anglo-Saxon, was invading. Their uniforms were brown, and instead of helmets they wore soft brown caps. I felt I was in bondage and unable to change what would happen. I was carrying my baby girl and gave her to a young Chinese girl who was my sister saying, 'I can't take my golden child. I wish I could because I love her, but I want her to grow up Chinese. Her name is Heavenly Peace.' I then called her Tien Tai, and turned away with a deep feeling of emptiness and loss. Later when I researched the name I learned that Tien is the word for Heaven."* Care should be taken since dreams will place you in very creative settings that are likely to be metaphors, related to your present life story. Some dreams, however, present a convincing case: *"I dreamed that I was in a Roman style amphitheater. My name was Pasha. The dream switched and I was looking at a tomb with the name Pasha."* The dreamer reported that four years later she took a trip to Pompeii. While there, she walked into some unmarked ruins. She told her husband "I have been here before. This used to be a covered amphitheater, and I used to sit right here." Upon speaking to the guide, he confirmed that this was the newly uncovered ruin of what was once a covered amphitheater.

Out of Body

One form of paranormal dream, which is strikingly different than any other, is the out-of-body experience (OOBE). *"I suddenly found myself above my body looking down at myself. Upon this realization I felt myself fall into my body and could feel a thud as I woke."* And another: *"I felt myself floating up above the bed. Then I drifted down toward the floor next to the bed and looked upward at an angle and across the top of the storage chest, in order to see the sky through the window. There was a crescent moon and a few stars. When I woke up, I tested this and found that I could only see the sky and new crescent moon from that part of the room by kneeling on the floor and looking over the storage chest."* Here, the dreamers find themselves consciously present outside their body, perhaps in another location, sometimes as a whole person or as just a ball of consciousness. What is interesting is that, in many of these reports, the person sees things in this state that they could not have seen from the position they were sleeping in, and could confirm later when observed from the location they were at in the OOBE state.

The OOBE experience is similar to some reports of near-death experiences, which are filled with accounts where persons saw themselves float above their body and were able to accurately report on events at a distance, which were later verified.[7] Work has been done to substantiate that the phenomenon occurs,[8] but little is known about the mechanism or whether it is a true separation of spirit or etheric body from physical body, or simply another form of the telepathic experience. Krippner[80] reports that it occurs across cultures, and that all six countries included in his 1,666 dream database, reported out-of-body dreams. La Berge [cited in 80] indicates that out-of-body dreams occur at sleep onset (when the sensory input is shutting down) and during certain lucid dreams (he reports a study in which 9% of the lucid dream reports included out-of-body experiences). Ceilia Green, in her book *Out of Body Experiences,*[81] indicates that most of these experiences occur when a person is ill, perhaps in surgery, or is resting in bed. She cites a number of experiences during surgery when the patients found themselves out-of-body watching the surgery take place. A popular theory is that when we are asleep, with our body immobilized and essentially paralyzed, and we then become partially or fully conscious with the sleep paralysis remaining, we experience the sensation of being out-of-body. However, this does not account for the many reports, similar to those cited above, in which the person in this state was able to perceive things that they had no way of perceiving from the vantage point of their physical body.

The following dream came to one individual who, at the time, had an overactive interest in the spiritual realm. It appeared to be a combination of a dream and a near death experience, with some of the same life-changing effects that a near death experience often brings. *"I dreamed I was riding in a car with a bunch of others (whom I felt were other parts of me), and they were all in disagreement about something. I got fed up and flew out of the car. I found myself flying over the ground at a fast rate, while beautiful music played all around me. Suddenly up ahead was a tunnel, with a light at the other end. I knew that if I flew through it, I would pass on to the other side, which was appealing to me due to my beliefs about the nature of the spirit. I had to make a decision, and as I entered the tunnel, I was going to go through it. But then I thought of my family and suddenly cried 'life'. At that point, I was in total darkness and cried out 'I said Life'. I then found myself above my body and floated into my body with a thump."* The interesting therapeutic aspect of this dream was that after the dream, the dreamer began to concentrate more on his daily life than on the realm of the spirit.

Spiritual

Dream content arises from many levels of consciousness, as evidenced by the examples discussed to this point. Justina Lasley[101] considers that dreams are spirit talking to the conscious. Furthermore, she indicates that the most effective form of dreamwork comes from one's own intuition and inner wisdom. This is a belief held by a great number of dreamers and dream workers. It is not simply a matter of faith, but rather an observation that there seems to be an organizing or guiding force in our dreams. In chapter 4, you will learn more about the influence of this inner wisdom or natural balancing force, from the perspective of Carl Jung.

Aside from the possibility that dreams open us up to the influence of our own higher self, there is some evidence that the spiritual connection can extend to others. There are many reports of seeing and speaking to loved ones in dreams, after they have passed away. *"I dreamed I heard my mother (who had recently passed away) call "Ruth, Ruth!" I saw her looking at me through a window and she was smiling and younger looking."* The imagery of looking through a portal or separation is commonly reported in dreams after death, but it is difficult to determine whether such a dream comes from the normal functioning of the psyche, attempting to reduce the trauma, or whether the visitation is real. One dreamer recalls having such a trauma-reducing dream, after the death of her 5th grade friend. This dream came after many days of grieving and nightmares that woke her up screaming every night: *"I saw very vividly [name of friend] standing in the field next to an airplane. He said to me 'don't worry about me, I'm just in another plane'."* She was warmed by his presence and sense of humor, the stress was released and the nightmares stopped. Could this have been a true visitation or simply an internal release?

In some cases, the person who has died reveals some information that the living person had no former knowledge of. I recall one such report of a father's death, where the Will could not be found. One of the family members subsequently dreamed of the father, wearing an old coat he had not worn in years, and pointing to the inside lining. When they investigated the coat lining, they found he had sewn the Will inside. While these cases are usually anecdotal, when such experiences occur it is difficult to discount them.

Visionary

Throughout the ages there have been many reports of spiritual dreams of a visionary nature that provide guidance, comfort or "truth" from what appears to be a divine presence. The dreamer often perceives the vision as a connection or communication with a higher level of intelligence or a higher spiritual plane. These dreams can be so striking that they change a person's life, or the course of history (holy scripture from many cultures is filled with dream accounts that changed the course of human events). Visions of biblical proportion can come to any one of us. My mother recorded the following dream, which closely resembled the description of Ezekiel's dream in the Bible. *"I saw a wheel of fire – a strange wheel endlessly turning. Fire - yet not fire - not material fire; electrical forces like the fire seen through closed eyes. The wheel was the Wheel of Time, and hovering above it were souls of all things created; animal, vegetable and man. Much like a computer, programmed to accept each one in its time, each one descended onto the earth only when an opening appeared in the wheel. The vibrations at the opening were attuned to the vibrations of that particular soul. The return from earth happened in a similar manner. Only when the proper opening appeared and the vibrations were right could the soul return from whence it came. There were some who wandered or floated beneath the wheel, unable to return through the fire until the proper opening appeared. And I saw the wheel from above, without wonder, as something I had seen before and recognized."*

The bright colors and spectacular feelings of what might be considered a vision, can be a result of a transformation dream, or a "big dream" as some call it. Nigel Hamilton[105], who has researched dreams of persons attending spiritual retreats, observes an increase in both light and color as the person goes through various stages in the process of what he terms psycho-spiritual transformation, and a dramatic appearance of light and visionary imagery in the dreams at the point of transcendence. Such dreams can occur outside of a spiritual setting, when a long-standing conflict or behavior pattern is resolved, and the internal ego-self is transformed. We often experience a symbolic "death" of the old ego-self, a journey or search for the new self, and finally an emergence and rebirth of the transformed self, which is celebrated by the dream. The final stages of such a transformation are observed in the following "ice cave" dream: *"I dreamed all night that*

I was on a long journey as a passenger in an enclosed boat going nowhere, just aimlessly moving through tunnels and underground caves. At one point in the journey, a shadow-like character urged me to take charge of the boat's direction. When I did, the boat emerged from a white ice cave onto a crystal stream in a beautiful, sunlit colorful land with trees and mountains and singing in the air. We landed by a large rock that rang like a bell when I struck it."

Since visionary imagery often reflects personal transformation, it is useful to first explore the dream for personal meaning before considering it a higher-level revelation. We will learn in chapter 4 that Jung observed that the natural compensating and balancing forces within our psyche often appear as glorious, and sometimes divine, characterizations (which he termed archetypes). This is the case in the following "Santa Claus trinity" dream: *"I dreamed that it was the end of the world and Christ was coming in the sky as the Holy Trinity. But Christ appeared as a trinity of Santa Clauses, who merged as one and began pouring gifts of love from an urn. They were invisible, but I felt the gifts hit me, so I ran. I tripped, falling down the mountain, with the gifts pouring on me the whole time."* The dreamwork revealed that the dream indeed related to the dreamer's spiritual life, but the Santa Claus Christ was not a literal visitation. It was a down-to-earth metaphor, with a storyline that was intended to compensate for the dreamers misconceptions. The dreamer had an expectation that living a good spiritual life should bring the gift of physical rewards. The clue in the dream was the representation of Christ as a Santa Claus. The dream was compensating for a misconception that, if she were a good girl, God would bring her physical gifts. The dream showed the true gifts to be invisible and intangible gifts of love. Indeed the message was a spiritual one, but the vision of Christ was only a clever metaphor.

On the other hand, some visionary dreams appear to impart a direct, almost literal, spiritual message. Prior to having the "Wheel of Time" dream mentioned above, my mother, who was involved in a spiritual search for truth about the nature of all things, recorded the following dream in her diary: *"I was being shown a huge brightly lit triangular-shaped sign with lettering in red which said, 'Make yourself a perfect channel and wait, and all things will be given to you'."*

Lucid Dreams

This is a class of dreams where you know you are dreaming. Sometimes the scene is so strikingly real that you feel you are awake, but you know it's a dream. Often there is enough consciousness that willpower is activated and the dreamer can change the dream by pure intention: *"I suddenly realized that I was dreaming, so I decided to have some fun by making people do what I wanted them to do. At first I felt guilty asking them to do my will, but then I would tell myself that this is just my dream and they aren't real."*

False awakening is a category of dreams related to lucid dreaming. In this childhood dream example, it came after a realization that the dreamer was dreaming: *I dreamed I was at home with my parents and my dad wanted me to do some work that I did not want to do. Suddenly I realized that I was dreaming so I woke myself up in order to avoid the unpleasant duties. I was happy to have been out of that dream since I was now peacefully sitting with my dad and mom in the living room. Living room! I suddenly realized that I had not woken up and was still dreaming. At that moment I actually did wake up.*

Flying dreams are more likely to be reported by subjects who also report lucid dreams, according to Deirdre Barrett[87] who examined 1,910 dreams from 191 subjects. Contrary to previous anecdotes, when flying and lucidity occurred in the same dream, lucidity preceded flight rather than being triggered by it.

The degree of lucidity can vary in a lucid dream. The lowest degree of lucidity can be simply a sense that "this is a dream," without taking action on that awareness. With a higher degree of lucidity, you might take some personal action in the dream or even wake yourself. At the highest levels of lucidity, you may take full control over your actions in the dream, impose your will on the dream characters or transform the very environment of the dream itself. Deirdre Barrett[86] examined the lucid dreams of 50 subjects for degree of lucidity based on the following corollaries: 1) awareness that people in the dream are dream characters, 2) awareness that dream objects are not real, 3) the dreamer does not need to obey waking-life physics to achieve a goal, and 4) memory of the waking world. Though many were too brief to evaluate on all corollaries, she found that only about half of the lengthier accounts were lucid for any particular corollary and less than a quarter were lucid on all four. Experienced lucid dreamers tended to be lucid about more corollaries.

Research by individuals such as Stephen LaBerge, PhD,[9] has revealed that the lucid dreamer is maintaining a high level of consciousness, as if awake, even though the sensory input from the outside is cut off. EEG tracings are similar to the waking state, even though the dreamer is asleep. Stephen LaBerge and Keith Hearne [cited in 80] independently discovered ways that lucid dreamers could communicate with researchers in the outside world, by moving their eyes or flexing their muscles in predetermined patterns. There appears to be a relationship between lucidity and the parts of the brain that are more or less active during the dream. Reports using PET scans[49] indicated a greater sense of control over the dream (lucidity) when the medial frontal cortex (involved in consciousness) was active, and a greater sense of the dream being out of control when the amygdala (involved in emotional processing) was more active.

Children's Dreams

Interestingly, even though children exhibit more REM sleep than adults, the dream recall in children is lower than in adults according to Domhoff.[40] In research studies, the average rate of dream recall is only 20% to 30% from REM awakenings until the child reaches the age of 9 to 11 years. At that age recall rate increases to the adult level of around 79%.

Dream content matures with age, up until 13 to 15 years. Early dreams (ages under 5) are primarily bland with static images and thoughts about daily events. At ages 5 to 8 dreams become more story-like with movement and interaction, but are not well developed. The dreamer only appears as an active participant at around 8 years. The structure of children's dreams do not become adult-like until the ages 9 to 11 and they are noted to have less aggression, misfortune and negative emotions than adult dreams. The length or content don't become adult-like until the pre-teens (about 11 to 13), nor does the dream content show a good correlation to their personality until about this time.

Domhoff speculates that dreaming is a cognitive achievement which, like most cognitive abilities, develops as we grow. In particular, visual imagination may develop gradually and be a necessary prerequisite for dreaming. Young children don't dream well until their visuospatial skills are developed. The part of the brain responsible for visuospatial skills and constructing the dream space (the inferior parietal lobe) is not functionally complete until about ages 5 to 7.[54]

Patricia Garfield[56] in her book *Your Child's Dreams* collected 247 dreams from schoolchildren in the US and a few in India. She found that 64% were considered "bad" dreams and the remaining "good" dreams. Of the bad dreams, almost half had a theme of being chased or attacked, and in the remaining dreams about 40% had a sense of danger or some character being injured or killed, even though there was no direct threat. Of the "good" dreams, about half of the themes fell into two categories. The most frequent category was just "having a good time," and the next was of the child receiving a gift or having some desired possessions.

Alan Siegel, another researcher in the forefront of children's dreams, speaks of the content and evolution of children's dreams in his book *Dream Wisdom*[59] and the book Dreamcatching,[58] which he co-authored with Kelly Bulkeley. He indicates that dreaming begins in the womb and that up to 80% of sleep in premature infants is devoted to REM sleep. He discusses how dream content changes as children grow and experience transitions, from first dreams, through coming of age dreams, to leaving home dreams. Siegel speaks of the appearance of two imposing figures as representing the child's image of the power of their own parents. One of the first dreams recalled by one of my daughters was of two giant hands reaching for her.

In *Dreamcatching*,[58] Siegel and Bulkeley list the most frequent types of dreams among children of all ages as: being threatened by animals or insects; being chased by monsters; flying; falling; being paralyzed or trapped; appearing naked in public; and being tested or examined. He indicates that for toddlers and preschoolers, the most common dream characters are animals. Van de Castle[37] also found this to be true, with almost 40% of young children's dreams at ages 4 to 5 containing animals, a percentage which dropped to less than 14% by the time they were teenagers. Like Garfield, he states that being chased or threatened in dreams, and nightmares with threatening creatures, appear to be the most common negative themes in children's dreams. This indicates that they symbolize a wide variety of early childhood fears and insecurities.

Monsters were a common theme I recall from my childhood dreams. In one such dream, it all came to a head: *"I dreamed I had to sleep in the basement and I knew there was a monster just around the corner that was going to get me at any moment if I made the slightest sound. I just couldn't stand the suspense, so I shouted out. At that moment, the monster exploded out of where it was hiding and I woke up."*

Another of my most frequent recurring childhood dreams was the theme of being paralyzed or trapped, trying to run but being unable to: *"I dreamed I was outdoors watching the sky darken as if a tremendous storm was coming. I tried to run but could hardly move, as if my legs were made of lead. As the dreams recurred, they would go from the point of trying to run away from the storm to the point where I began to stare at the sky as the storm began to take on beautiful patterns and colors. After awhile, my fear of the dream turned into fascination with the colorful patterns."* Interestingly, these delightful and colorful dreams were a factor in my early interest in dreams, which began in my childhood.

Perhaps there is a learning process going on in such childhood dreams. My ability to take some control over and de-fuse the situations in my recurrent dreams spilled over into my waking life, and gave me a sense of empowerment, even in the sometimes dis-empowering environment of childhood.

CHAPTER 3
THE "LANGUAGE" OF DREAMS

*After he was quiet a long time, words began to come to him in dreams and told him
their secret names and this was the way he learned the true nature of the world –
Brian Andreas* [67]

How can we make sense of our dreams? Is it possible that we simply do not understand the "language?" *"I dreamed I was talking in a derogatory way to my friend, who appeared quite naturally in the dream as an old shoe with his face on it."* The bizarre image of a shoe with a face on it was seen as perfectly normal in the dream, but upon waking was perceived as an irrational creation, akin to a cartoon character. Is there indeed a meaning behind such a cartoon-like image?

Understanding a dream is like trying to read a pictographic language such as hieroglyphics. The organization and superposition of images (birds, people, animals and such) appear irrational, particularly when related to our modern concept of a written language. But once a pictographic code is deciphered, it is determined to be a rationally created language, in which each picture is a symbol containing a meaning that is understood by that culture. Could it be that the dreams are also a picture language of meaningful images and symbols, originating from similar regions of the brain and operating on similar principles as pictographic languages? Perhaps we simply need the code!

Indeed, we will learn that the "language" of dreams is a meaningful language of imagery association and emotion, which may actually accompany the language of the written or spoken word in our waking communications. Many parts of the brain are involved in language processing. When we communicate, certain language centers (typically in the left hemisphere) are responsible for verbal speech, and for identifying all that we think and perceive with names, titles and words. These centers determine "what" we speak or write. Other language centers (typically in the right hemisphere) are responsible for the "why" and the "how." These centers process context and meaning,[10] create a visualization of our train of thought, and supply the emotional content, tone,[11] inflection and body language. For example, a simple statement such as "I want to go outside" (a left hemisphere communication), may be accompanied in the right hemisphere by a visualization of opening the door, associations with and memories of being outside, and emotions related to the anticipated experience. Does this sound a bit like a dream?

Our waking attention is usually only on "what" is being communicated, i.e., the words and their rational meaning. The other half, the non-verbal "why" and "how," contains the more complete content, but is perceived (if at all) below our threshold of awareness. These same brain centers, that process and subliminally perceive the non-verbal communications, become active when we dream. Those responsible for verbal speech remain inactive. It is, therefore, this non-verbal content within our communications that is the "language of dreams."

The "language" of dreams is essentially the language of the waking state, but without the words. It is a language of visual imagery and association in which combinations of images identify our thoughts and experiences, rather than combinations of letters and words. Each dream image is a meaningful symbol in the "dream language," just as each letter or sound is a meaningful symbol in our waking language. When we tell a dream, images are translated (by our verbal language centers) into word associations or figures of speech. If we examine the "old shoe" dream for example, it appears that the dreamer had been treating his friend like an "old shoe." The dream presented this situation as a clear, pictorial but figurative expression of the actions and attitude of the dreamer. The face of his friend was quite logically superimposed on the image of the "old shoe" to make that statement.

The Dreaming Brain

Brain Activation

Figure 2 and table 3-1 is a compilation of some recent research on the state of the brain in dreaming sleep. They show the centers of the brain that are activated during dreaming, and centers that are less active, deactivated or with input and output disconnected. The centers of the brain in the shaded areas (sites A, B, C, D) are either partially or fully inactive or their inputs or outputs blocked. The numbered centers (sites 1 through 8) are active in dream sleep. Figure 2 was derived from the updated Activation-Synthesis model presented by Hobson.[39] Table 3-1 uses excerpts from Hobson's work as well as Domhoff,[40] Ratey,[38] Calvin & Ojemann[41] and Kahn[62] to further describe the functions typically assigned to those brain centers. Based on this data, I then extrapolate how the presence or absence of those brain functions might affect the content of the dream.

Figure 2
The "Dreaming" Brain

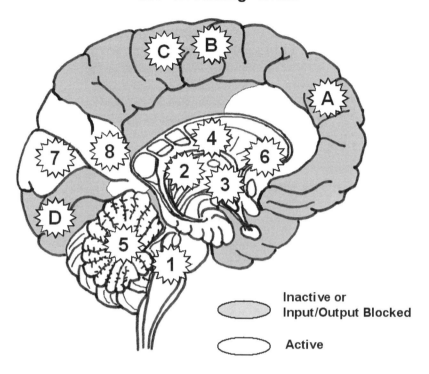

Inactive or
Input/Output Blocked

Active

1 – Pontine Stem
2 – Thalamus
3 – Rt Hypothalamus & Basal Forebrain
4 – Basal Ganglia
5 – Cerebellum
6 – Limbic and Paralimbic
7 – Visual Association Cortex
8 – Right Inferior Parietal Cortex
A – Dorsolateral Prefrontal Cortex
B – Primary Motor Cortex
C – Primary Somatosensory Cortex
D – Primary Visual Cortex

Table 3-1
Suggested Influence of Dreaming Brain States on Dream Content

ACTIVE

Brain Structure	Function	Dream Content
1 – Pontine Stem	Forebrain Arousal (PGO spikes); REM Sleep Activation	Consciousness, eye movement, movement patterns in the dream
2 – Thalamus	Control of sleep cycle; mediates arousal and attention	You are conscious in the dream.
3 – Rt. Hypothalamus & Basal Forebrain	Autonomic & Instinctual functions, motivation and reward; fight or flight; Cortical arousal	Instinctive content (fear, escape, dream emotion), motivation and reward themes
4 – Basal Ganglia	Initiation of motor activity and programmed movements	You perceive you are moving in the dream.
5 - Cerebellum	Fine tuning of movement, adds specific features such as vestibular sensations	You perceive you are moving and have bodily senses in the dream.
6 – Limbic and Paralimbic Systems (Amygdala, Hippocampus, Parahippocampal Cortex, Anterior Cingulate, Medial Prefrontal Cortex)	Emotional weighting of stimulus; perception; novelty detection; anxiety; goal-directed behavior and social processing; influences attention, memory storage, factual memory; spatial mapping of physical environment; decides what is to be processed; Motion integration; emotional processing	Selected emotional memories stimulate the dream; integration of dream emotion with actions; sense of anxiety; goal directed dream stories; focus of dream on experiences that don't fit the image of self and its relationship to others and life; integration of the resolution into memory
7 – Visual and Auditory Association Cortex	High order integration of visual and auditory perceptions; face recognition	Visual and Auditory dream content contains personal associations.
8 – **Right** Inferior Parietal Cortex	Spatial perception; spatial imagery construction; orientation and movement; image of self (physical & mental); pictographs; "speaks" in contextual or functional terms	Perception of an imaginary dream space with pictorial/symbolic imagery; emphasis on the internal image of Self (the inner model or myth)
Temporal-Occipital regions	Color, texture and shape	Color and shape stimulated by separate but associated content

RELATIVELY INACTIVE or BLOCKED INPUT/OUTPUT

Brain Structure	Function	Dream Content
A – Dorsal Lateral Prefrontal Cortex	Executive functions: Attention; Directed thought = rationalizing, logic, planning, choice, decision making, anticipation of consequences; Inhibits inappropriate behavior; Working memory.	Loss of will, reflective awareness and control of the dream (ego self is just one dream character); Irrational actions and imagery seem normal; Material enters the dream freely and "unfiltered" (you experience all parts of self)
Information flow to Precuneus	Recall and processing of visual and episodic memory.	Situations that stimulated the dream are not represented as they happened in waking life
Posterior Cingulate Cortex	Episodic and Working Memory	Sudden scene changes seem normal, no reflective awareness
B – Primary Motor Cortex	Generation of motion commands	Body is paralyzed while dreaming
C – Primary Somatosensory Cortex	Generation of sensory perceptions	Little to no external sensory input enters the dream
D – Primary Visual Cortex	Generation of visual perceptions	No external visual information enters the dream
Left Inferior Parietal Lobe and Temporal Lobe	Language association and naming; Left hemisphere "speaks" by naming things	Imagery does not represent its named identity; Dreams identify concepts via metaphor, function, association and pictographs

This state of the brain in REM sleep lead Braun et al.[cited in 39] to declare, "REM sleep may constitute a state of generalized brain activity with the specific exclusion of executive systems which normally participate in the highest order analysis and integration of neural information." In other words, we are conscious and the brain is operating, but the senses are disconnected (sites C and D). We are essentially paralyzed (site B) and much of the logic we depend on to construct the perception of a rational world is off-line (site A). All input comes from within.

The brain stem and limbic system appear to act as "activators" of the REM state of sleep we typically associate with dreaming. They arouse us into the pseudo-consciousness of REM sleep and activate the emotion-related processing that stimulates the dream. How the dream forms remains controversial. Hobson and McCarley take the position that the dream is a result of higher brain centers interpreting or try to make sense of the activity in the lower centers. Antrobus argues that higher brain centers, and some cognitive processes, are involved in the creation of dreams at the onset.[cited in 80] Citing data that similar dream characteristics occur in a percentage of both REM and NREM sleep, Solms contends that dreaming is a function of a "dream on" mechanism in the forebrain, considering REM activation independent from dream formation.[cited in 80]

The Dual Brain

The prior section discussed various centers in the brain that are active and inactive in the dream state, and how those combinations might be responsible for the content of the dream story. In this section I will discuss another view of brain processing that might contribute to the different thought processes that occur during dream sleep.

Although we may think of the brain as a single structure, it is actually divided in two halves or hemispheres. These hemispheres are linked by several bundles of nerve fibers that establish a communications path between the two halves. Perhaps one of the most surprising aspects of this is that the control of our body movements and our senses are evenly divided between these two hemispheres and this occurs cross-wise. That is, the right side of our body is controlled by the left hemisphere and the left side by the right hemisphere. Also it is the left hemisphere that is connected to the right visual field in each eye, and the right hemisphere that is connected to the left visual field in each eye.

Differences in processing have been observed between right and left hemispheres. Some of these differences were discussed in the prior section as associated with the right and left side of the frontal and parietal lobes. The left hemisphere, or "left brain," has been found to be more involved in understanding language, processing speech and reading, labeling things with words, and in linear logical thinking. It is charged with creating a model or story that makes sense. The right hemisphere, or "right brain," is more involved in processing non-verbal information (music, art, pattern recognition), forming associations and understanding what an object represents (as opposed to its name) and in visual understanding. It also detects and interprets anomalies of experience,[38] a process that is important in understanding the nature of dreams.

These distinct differences between right and left processing, however, are not pure. The more distinct differences lie with right-handed males. It is found that with left-handed individuals and with females, there is more bilateral or reversed representation of function normally attributed to one hemisphere or the other i.e., they might have speech functions in the right hemisphere rather than the left, or right hemisphere functions represented in both hemispheres. Regardless of individual variations with individual brain structure, it remains useful to understand the nature of the information processing differences, since they hold a useful relationship to differences between waking and dreaming thought.

Some of the more widely cited characteristics[10, 36, 38, 109] attributed to the two hemispheres are illustrated in table 3-2. Note the strong similarity between the right brain processing characteristics, and how you might describe the dream state. Observe how unlike the dream state the left-brain processing is. If there is a strong link between the right brain and the dream state, then perhaps viewing the dream from the standpoint of the thought processes attributed to the right brain provides a further key to understanding dreams.

Table 3-2 Functions Attributed to Brain Hemispheres

Left Brain	Right Brain
Processes peripheral details	Processes central aspects or essence
Verbal (produce speech)	Non-Verbal (comprehension only)
Temporal & Sequential	Simultaneous & Visuospatial
Language Processing (speech, words)	Emotion & Social Processing (face and body language)
Categorizing (naming, titles)	Metaphor (relation, analogy, context)
Digital (using numbers to count)	Analog (using values)
Logical (linearly linked Ideas)	Gestalt, Holistic (seeing the whole)
Analytic (step by step, part by part)	Synthetic (forming the whole)
Deductive, Convergent, Vertical thinking	Imaginative, Divergent, Lateral thinking
Thinking, Sensing (Jungian concept)	Feeling, Intuition (Jungian concept)
Rational and Realistic (reason & facts)	Intuitive (patterns, insight) and Impulsive
Ego, Persona, Conscious personality	Shadow, Id, Unconscious
"Western Thought" (Technical, Rational)	"Eastern Thought" (Intuitive, Mystic, Myth)

Research associated with hemisphere activity during dream sleep[45] resulted in a variety of theories; including Bakan's early (1977-78) theory[46] that dreaming is primarily a function of the right hemisphere. Drawing on experimental evidence from studies of EEG, brain injury, epilepsy and sleep research, Bakan contended that, "marked similarities exist between dream experience and the kind of thinking which has been ascribed to the right hemisphere, e.g., perceptual, fantasy, affective, primary process."

Much of the linking of dreaming with the right hemisphere originally came from observations of patients with damage to the right parietal region of the brain. Patients reported that they no longer had dreams and lost the ability to visualize, despite previous abilities in these areas.[11, 12, 45] In 1972, researchers[45,47] found shifts in the ratio of right and left EEG amplitude during changes from REM to NREM sleep. In a sleep laboratory study of right-handed males, they found the right hemisphere to be more active than the left during the dream state (REM). This reversed during NREM (non-dreaming) sleep.

More recent evidence with better measurement tools, as noted in table 3-1, shows that it is more than just the right brain involved in dreaming, but rather various sections of the brain activating and de-activating that make the dream state more like right brain activity and less like left brain activity. This likely occurs because some of the more influential centers that are activated in the dream state, are specific to the right hemisphere, such as the right inferior parietal cortex.[39] This is the visuospatial processing center of the brain seemingly responsible for constructing the dream space and the activity within it. Also centers that are deactivated (such as the left parietal cortex, and dorsolateral prefrontal cortex) are responsible for processing functions that are typically associated with left hemisphere. Nofzinger found an increase in activation of the right hypothalamus and the right frontal cortex during REM sleep and a decrease in the left frontal cortex.[39] Marquet found an increase in the right parietal cortex and decrease in the left during REM.[cited in 39]

Even if it is not strictly the inclusion of the right hemisphere, and exclusion of the left, involved in dreaming, the work that has gone into describing the differences in processing or "thinking" involved in the two hemispheres, is quite useful in understanding dream thought and language as opposed to waking thought and language.

The Resultant Dream

Now let's put the above findings together to better understand the nature of dreams and the "language" of the dream state. Comparing the table 3-1 with the description of the typical dream in chapter 2, it becomes more obvious why dreams have the characteristics that they do. Further, comparing the Right Brain attributes to the dream experience provides insight into how the dreaming brain "thinks" differently than the waking brain. Lets look at the characteristics of a dream and how it might relate to the dreaming brain states described above.

You Are Immobile and Isolated – Dreams Come from Within

Because the motor cortex (site B) is disconnected, there is little or no physical body motion while dreaming. This is likely an evolutionary benefit, because acting out your dreams could be harmful. But sometimes the de-activation is not perfect, as this case illustrates: *I recall one case from an early Boy Scout outing where one of the Scouts was missing from his tent in the morning. He was found walking through the woods back toward the camp, carrying his sleeping bag. He reported having had a dream that a flood was coming, so he picked up his sleeping bag and ran down the hill to get away from it.* In reality, he had acted out his dream. Obviously, the deactivation of his motor cortex in this case was not complete. An interesting side note is that he reported that when he woke up down the hill, he had no injury to his feet. All the injury came as he tried to walk back!

Since the sensory cortexes (sites C and D) are blocked, little to no external sensory information is stimulating the dream. An exception would be the minor dream-altering effects caused by strong external influences, or internal bodily needs, as discussed in chapter 2 under the topic physical factors. The intrusion of external stimuli is usually observed to modify the ongoing dream, rather than being the primary source of the dream. *"It was a long dream where myself and some others embarked on a boat trip trying to get to a party or gathering of friends. The water had become shallow and the passageway blocked with landforms, so we had to get out of the boat and walk to our destination. Suddenly the rocky terrain I was climbing over became chunks of ice and glaciers, and I could feel the cold as I touched the ice. I then awoke to a very cold room and realized my arms were outside of my bed covers and were cold."* Here is a case, typical of many cases, where the source of the dream is totally from within, until the external stimuli grows strong enough to enter the dream. The basic plot of the dream story was stimulated by a waking life search for self-identity, which in turn produces the theme in the dream of seeking, journeying and looking forward to a joyous union of the fragmented parts of the dreamer. As the physical sensation from the dreamer's cold arms became intense, it penetrated dream consciousness, and altered the physical dreamscape. The primary plot of the dream remained in place, but it gradually became diverted by the additional stimulus that the dream was attempting to accommodate.

You are Conscious in Dreams

While we generally believe that when we are asleep, we are unconscious, this is not the case. Dreams represent a sleeping state of consciousness. Because the parts of our brain that arouse consciousness (sites 1 and 2) are active, we are conscious in our dreams. Also, the same centers in the brain that process and perceive much of our waking space are active as well (sites 4, 5, 7, 8). Thus, in our dreams we perceive that we are awake. Foulkes [cited in 80] argues that dreams are little more than waking consciousness stripped of most sensory input and freed from the obligation of making coherent connections to the external world. We are not quite in the same state of consciousness as when awake, but we are consciously viewing and moving around in a dream space, which we believe to be real, since the dream space was created much the same as if it were waking life.

Dreams Appear Irrational Only to the Waking Mind

Even though we may be conscious in our dreams, the normal experience of waking consciousness eludes us because the center of our brain responsible for rational reasoning and decisions (site A) is off-line. Information that is processed in the dreaming brain is therefore not organized by this higher level of processing, nor referenced to our waking model of reality. The logical "filters" are not applied. In the dream, we perceive all of the bizarre occurrences and strange combinations of events and images as normal. Talking to our friend, who appears as an "old shoe" for example, seems perfectly normal until we reflect on it after waking. This knowledge is useful in establishing an approach to dreamwork. In a sense, the content of the dream or a dream element is more pure since it is not filtered or categorized by the rational organization of the waking state. Adopting dreamwork techniques that explore the content within dream elements in their raw or pictographic state is a key to understanding dreams.

Dream Imagery – a Language of Emotion

There is much to support the notion that emotions or emotional memories are the primary influences on dream content. Emotion is a key factor in Hobson and McCarley's hypothesis that the intensity of dreams is reflected in the dreamer's respiratory rate, heart rate and skin potential.[cited in 80] Seligman & Yeller view dream emotion as the primary shaper of the dream plot, rather than a reaction to it.[cited in 39] The right hemisphere (right prefrontal cortex), which is active in dreaming,[40] is involved in the comprehension and production of emotions.[38]

Dream imagery (and its hidden meaning) may be a result of what Berne and Savary term "Limbic Logic".[68] They state that the brain operates on at least three different types of logic:

1) Linear Logic, which principally resides in the left hemisphere of the cerebral cortex (off-line during dreaming), is our system for gaining knowledge, problem-solving, making choices, decisions and reasoning;
2) Kinesthetic Logic, which resides in the brain stem, responds to immediate physical sensations with the goal of finding pleasure and avoiding pain; and
3) Limbic Logic, which resides in the amygdala and other limbic centers (active during dreaming), has a goal of safety and survival in times of danger and thus associates an emotion to the sensory data it encounters.

This system, which is highly active during dreams, grasps images and emotions and processes them by association. The limbic system recognizes inner data such as emotions, and associates an emotion to the sensory data it encounters.[68] Whereas in the waking state the limbic system sees a world full of images and links them to emotions, in the dreaming state it is reasonable to deduce that the limbic system recovers emotional memories of our daily events and creates associated dream imagery. Figure 3 illustrates this concept.

Figure 3
Conceptual Role of "Limbic Logic" in the Creation of a Dream Image

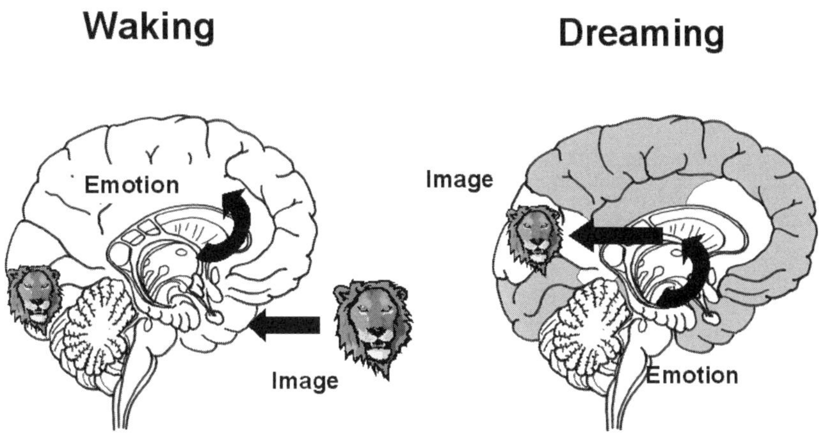

Dreams also often contain what is termed the "Central Image" or "Contextualizing" image (CI). The CI can be a striking, arresting, or compelling image, which stands out by virtue of being especially powerful, vivid, bizarre, or detailed. According to Ernest Hartmann[93] the dream, especially the Central Image, pictures the emotion of the dreamer. This is most easily seen when there is a single powerful emotion in the dream. An example of this is the frequent vivid dream of being overwhelmed by a tidal wave, in someone who has recently experienced a traumatic event. Hartmann contends that the intensity of the central image is a measure of the strength of the emotion. The more powerful the emotion, the more intense the central imagery of the dream will be. He indicates that central image intensity can be measured reliably, as supported by research, including a recent systematic study of dreams before and after 9/11/01.[93]

Hartmann indicates further that dreaming is hyper-connective, that is, the mind (brain) makes connections more broadly in dreaming than in waking (where we operate on linear, over-learned logical connections). However, the dreaming connections are not random. They are guided by the emotion of the dreamer. Dreams picture, or contextualize, the underlying emotion. For Hartmann, emotion is at the core of the language of the dream.

Dreams Are About Daily Events – but Omit the Event Itself

The emotional memories being processed in the dream state appear to be associated with recent waking life events, or long-term issues triggered by recent events. This "continuity principle" is supported by evidence that dreams contain content that is continuous with daytime events or "day residue." Day-residue is generally found in dreams from the prior day, falling off significantly after a few days. A dream-lag effect has also been observed, which shows a surprising incorporation of daytime experiences that occurred approximately one week prior to the dream.[42] Most therapeutic dreamwork approaches and results support this principle, in that they generally show the dream to be related to some recent situation, or unresolved past traumatic event, in the dreamer's waking life.

Although dreams are likely stimulated by a recent waking life event, the dream rarely represents the event that took place or even the visual memories from that event (people and places involved). The event, or waking episode, seems "hidden," which is perhaps the source of most confusion about dreams. This is because the link between the parts of the brain responsible for episodic and visual recall becomes inactive during the REM stage of sleep (the communication link between the dorsal lateral prefrontal cortex and the precuneus). Further, a number of researchers believe that the reason that we cannot recall episodes during dreaming is because of a change in the direction of information flow. In the waking state, information flows from the hippocampus to the cortical areas. Waking episodes, that are captured in short-term memories, are thereby transferred to longer-term memories. During dreaming, however, the information flow is reversed. Information flows from cortical area to the hippocampus, thus the memory of a specific episode is not accessed.[69] Emotional memories, however, may be accessed during dreaming since the center responsible for emotional processing (the limbic region) is very active. The emotional context, associations and memories of the waking event appear to be represented in the dream, but the event itself is not, all due to the unique way in which memory is processed during sleep.[61]

Dreams Focus On Self

As much as we would like our dreams to be a magical view into a greater universal reality, the typical dream appears to focus on self, perhaps the greater Self, but the self nonetheless. According to Panksepp,[43] dreams are laden with self-referential configurations and permutations of emotional problems to be solved. Revonsuo states that threat perception and harm avoidance lie at the heart of many dreams. [cited in 39] This is likely because the center of the brain that is involved in construction of imagery and our dream space (site 8) is also involved in perception of our self-image. This center of the brain plays a primary role in constructing the dream imagery and its location and movement in the dream space. It is responsible for forming a perception of one's own physical body image,[41] as well as one's abstract image of self.[44] It also plays a role in the complete perception of the spatial and social components of the world.[38] Thus in dreams, the images created in our dream space, and the dream space itself, is referenced to an internal model, an internal image of self and our social model of reality.

Dreams Deal with Material that Doesn't Fit our Social World

Dreams may not only respond to threats to self, as Revonsuo asserts, but to anomalies in our environment, things that simply do not fit our internal image of self and reality. As mentioned earlier, the right hemisphere interprets anomalies of experience, which is a processing function that seems to extend to dream sleep. This is supported by Jan Born and his colleagues at the University of Lubeck, who used a mathematical number test with a hidden trick in it, and found evidence that dream sleep more than doubled the probability of participants detecting the trick.[cited in 70]

According to Ratey,[38] the limbic system and parts of the brain stem play a major role in arousing attention, particularly novelty detection and reward. The reticular formation alerts our cognitive mind when a stimulus is novel or persistent. The hippocampus compares the present with the past, and thus relates events as either novel or ordinary. It inhibits reaction to ordinary events, and orients us to the novel, that which doesn't fit our memory store.

Perhaps this is why we observe events and characters from our past, mixed or integrated in strange ways with the present. We may be simply observing the operation of this particular brain system. Ratey also states that this process is integral to the functioning of our emotional and social brain (who we see ourselves to be in relationship to others and life's overall picture). The dream story may therefore be stimulated by daily events that are an anomaly or don't "fit" the internal perception of self and our social world.

Furthermore, certain brain centers which are active during dreaming (including the amygdala, right parietal lobe and much of the right hemisphere), are responsible for recognizing emotional body and facial expressions and are involved in processing our social interactions.[38] Dr. David Kahn[62] indicates that within a dream, the dreamer is often aware of other people's thoughts and feelings. In a study of 35 subjects (who submitted 320 dream reports containing more than 1200 dream characters), he found that in a majority of their dream reports (77%), they were aware in the dream that their dream characters had feelings about them. One explanation Kahn offers is that our awareness of the feelings and thoughts of others in our dreams prepares us for social encounters when awake.

Your Will is Absent or Diminished

This inactive logic center of our sleeping brain (site A) is also the seat of our will, plus decisions and actions based on will. In our dreams, therefore, we generally don't think to control our actions or the storyline of the dream, even though the dream is all created within our own mind. We tend to exist as just a character in the dream, which is reacting to, subject to or following the plot of the dream. The possible exception is lucid dreaming, in which control is possible, but is not always total, and generally lasts for only a short time according to LaBerge.[cited in 39] The knowledge that the dream is not subject to the will of the ego is beneficial to dreamworking. The characters in the dream, which represent, feelings, beliefs, disconnected fragments of our personality, threatening emotional memories etc., are free to express their nature in the dream outside the influence of our will.

Disconnected Scene Shifts are Typical

The executive part of our brain (A) that is off-line in the dream state is also involved in episodic and working memory. Thus dream sequences can suddenly switch on us, and we fail to even notice or reflect on what changed until we awake. This switch is perhaps a result of completing one holistic synthesis of associations, and beginning another, as a new unresolved emotional stimulus enters the dream space. When working with such a dream, therefore, it is best to treat each dream "segment" (between scene shifts) as a separate but associated dream. When each segment is analyzed separately and then compared, a more complete picture of the dream process emerges.

The loss of working memory also has implications for dream recall, and why it is hard to recall more than a few segments of a dream, usually the events closer to waking. Although there is some evidence that learning is taking place in a dream, the activation of the more permanent memory processes in the brain during waking is necessary for recall. This knowledge helps establish techniques for recall that I discussed in chapter 1.

Dream Thought is "Rational"

Look again at table 3-2 as it relates to the right hemisphere. Does the processing in the right hemisphere seem more "dreamlike" in nature, and the left more like waking thought and dialogue? Even though we may be more conscious of the left-brain processes when we're awake, both right and left-brain are active, operational, and influencing our waking actions and thoughts. The right brain processes, which dominate our dream life, are also a part of our normal rational waking functioning. As discussed at the beginning of the chapter, they also influence our waking communications. Edwards[36] describes right hemisphere information processing in the waking state as: visual imagery processing; perceptual awareness of things with minimal connection to words; no sense of linear time; not requiring a basis for reason or facts; relating to things as they are in all their perceptual complexity; seeing likeness and relationships between things; seeing metaphors and analogies; seeing how parts fit together to form a whole or gestalt; seeing the whole all at once; insight and intuition; perceiving many facets of a problem simultaneously, often leading to divergent or multiple conclusions. Does all this processing, which occurs below our threshold of awareness in waking life, sound like the landscape of a dream?

The fantasies, disconnected non-time sequential stories and non-rational imagery of the dreaming mind, bear close similarity to the characteristics of the processing performed by the right hemisphere in waking life. In dreams, association, analogy, holistic pattern and relation dominate over the linear logic and literal verbal identification. This is different from our waking life perceptions, where we name or describe our experiences with words, and where rational, deductive and time sequential reasoning is applied. Yet under all this waking rationality, our mind is actively processing all we perceive in the same dreamlike fashion that takes place in our nightly dreams. If we could learn to think in the same way our right brain perceives information, then we could understand the language of our dreams.

Putting it All Together

Putting all of this together, a picture begins to emerge regarding the focus of, and processes taking place in, a typical dream. This is a fairly simplistic view, based purely on the influence of the brain centers that are active and inactive, but it may serve a useful role in understanding the nature of dreaming. REM, which initiates the biological conditions for vivid dreaming, is activated within the brain stem. The dream is stimulated (perhaps in the forebrain, right inferior parietal region and other higher processing areas) by emotional content and memories arising from the Limbic centers. The stimulating content may be associated with unfinished business or unresolved emotional processing from the day. It might be an anxiety-provoking event requiring closure or something that presents a threat or anomaly to our internal reference of self and our social world. At night, when the flood of sensory information ceases, and our executive centers are off-line, the brain is free to process this unfinished business. A dream space is constructed in parts of the brain where the stimulating emotional material is converted to imagery associations, oriented in a visual space, and referenced to our internal model of self and our social world. The mind's natural tendency for closure then processes the content within this dream space, perhaps testing various scenarios until a fit or accommodation is found. Those scenarios are the dream stories we experience.

Learning the Dream "Language"

We can learn the "language of dreams" if we can learn to think like our dreaming brain.

Dream Images Are Rarely What They Seem

Carl Jung,[4] a pioneer of basic theories upon which some modern dreamwork is based, defined the language of imagery with the term symbol. He indicated that the various elements in a dream are symbols that represent a complex combination of emotions, precepts, and thoughts. This concept is supported by what we learned about the limbic centers of our brain, which associates images with emotion, thus providing a symbolic identity for both waking and dream imagery. In part, dream images are also creations of the visuospatial processing center of the brain, which establishes contextual relationships between the emotionally associated visual imagery and our self-image (that internal model we spoke of earlier).

So look for the dream imagery to relate to emotional events of the day, threats or unfinished business. Do not try to understand dream images in terms of the way they are commonly identified in waking life. As we learned earlier, the dreaming brain does not communicate with left-brain names and words as identifiers. It is the part of the brain that supplies the emotional associations, memories, inner meaning, and context to our communications. Therefore, a dream object rarely represents its named identity in waking life, but almost always represents a deep collage of past experiences and emotions associated with similar objects. For example, the vase in this dream was more than just a vase: *"I dreamed of picking up a beautiful vase that was laying by itself on the beach. Seeing it brought great sorrow."* During the subsequent dreamwork, the dreamer never got to the point of describing the vase before she began sobbing. Her husband had passed away and she suddenly recognized that the vase in the dream was one he had given her when they were first married. The image of the dream vase contained all of the unreleased emotions associated with that sad day. It was not a "vase," it was a personal visual representation of a complex set of emotions and memories. By defining the dream image in terms of the emotional associations within it, the true identity of the image is revealed; the true language of the dream is spoken.

Time and Linear Logic Have Little Meaning

Do not try to make sense of linear time in the dream. Working memory is off-line and the right hemisphere perceives the many facets of a problem in a simultaneous holistic fashion, often leading to divergent and multiple conclusions. Thus the dream will take off in many directions trying to resolve the same issue from all its various aspects. It will often create a series of short disconnected dream segments, each an attempt to test a potential solution that will bring closure. Possible solutions, or integrations of previously divergent content, will appear as interesting simultaneous visual combinations of dream elements or interactions between dream elements.

When working on a dream with one or more sudden scene changes, treat each scene as a separate, but related, dream. Trying to relate it as one dream, with a logical connection between scene changes, rarely works. Also working with the entire dream as a series of related dream sequences is more revealing than working with a single segment.

Don't try to use linear logic to figure out the sequence of events in a dream. It does not apply. Deductive reasoning and cause and effect do not always lead to the conclusion. Dream processing is simultaneous from moment to moment. Dreams synthesize all the emotional content and associations in a holistic manner, looking for a pattern that best accommodates it all.

Words Rarely Convey a Literal Message

With some exceptions, words in dreams, whether written or spoken, seldom convey literal meaning or "messages." The language centers in the left hemisphere (that communicate with words) are off-line in the dream state. The language processing of the right hemisphere is that of meaning, emotion, visualization, context, memory and association. It does not represent meaning with a construct of words. This perhaps explains why written words in a dream morph or change as we try to read them.

Often, words that appear in dreams are strange combinations of sounds and phrases that have no rational meaning, but that have a very direct symbolic meaning. *"In my dream there was a voice that warned, 'Beware the Nanfro bird'. I woke in a state of alarm."* Subsequent dreamwork revealed that the nonsense sentence was warning of an impending "Non Four" condition. In chapters 4 and 7 we will learn more about the appearance of "four" in a dream to symbolize a state of completion or balance. In this case the dream voice was warning of a pending state of imbalance that was being caused by his desire to "soar to new heights" (the bird).

The dreaming brain speaks by forming messages from combinations of images. It cannot form messages from combinations of words and letters as in waking life. The dreaming brain cannot say, "state of balance" because it represents this concept symbolically as "four." An imbalanced state is therefore a "non-four." The dreaming brain states, "beware the non-four bird" to represent "beware the non-balance caused by your desire to soar to new heights."

This dream also provides an example of how dreams use letters and words to form symbolic patterns. The dream morphed the written image of the word "four" into "fro." This is a three letter representation of the four letter word. As we will learn later, "three" is symbolic of a state of imbalance. Three is "four" with an element missing as needed for closure. Thus "fro" is an imbalanced "four."

Even when the dreamer has reported receiving a direct meaningful message in a dream, it is quite often an analogy for action that is to be taken, as in this "waters of the unconscious" dream: *"I dreamed it was the end of the world and water was rising all around me. Suddenly a voice said 'the water is your unconscious, jump in and you will be fine'."* The action of jumping in is not literal, but rather a metaphor for overcoming rising fears.

Dreams Speak in Metaphor
(the Natural Language of Dreams)

As we learned above, a dominant right hemisphere is generally found to be non-linguistic, although it plays a role in discriminating intonation,[11] in understanding the meaning of words, and has a great deal to do with understanding the context of speech.[10] It contributes association, analogy and context to our communications. Metaphors become apparent when we tell or write a dream; when our speech centers translate the visualizations and associations of the right brain into words.

Associations and metaphors may be formed when we perceive an event. Cook[14] proposed that when a sensory event occurs, neurons in both sides of the brain are activated, as well as the nearby neurons that illuminate closely related memories. The contextual information of the surrounding neurons is, in a sense, a stored metaphoric representation of the original event. As we learned earlier, in the dream state we do not recall the event itself because of changes in the communications path between centers in brain responsible for episodic recall. This emotionally charged contextual information, however, can be accessed by the limbic centers that remain active in the dream state.

According to Domhoff[40] there is a simple explanation for the extensive use, by the human mind, of metaphor in speech and dreams. It occurs because metaphors map our well-understood basic experiences (such as warmth) to more difficult concepts (such as friendship) - ex: "we had a warm relationship." They map physiological processes (sweetness) to more complex emotional experiences (pleasure) - for example: "what a sweet deal that was!" He states that each person learns a system of conceptual metaphors, as a result of repeated experiences in the course of childhood development.

We learn common cultural metaphors, or figures of speech, in our everyday lives and use them naturally to represent more complex concepts. They naturally find their way into our dreams, and being native to the figurative style of right hemisphere processing, are used as pictographs or wordplay to represent the more complex emotional or situational conditions that stimulated them. Dreams rely on such figurative thinking and resemblances.

Recognizing Metaphor in the Dream Imagery

Metaphors can be recognized as analogies drawn between the dream story and your waking life story. Metaphors can also be recognized in the "picture language" or picture words of dream imagery. In essence, dreams speak in visualization and pictures.

Figure 4
Metaphor

**Dream Images Picture
Common Expressions**

**A Combination of Thoughts will
Appear as a Combination of Images**

**".... then suddenly I
dropped the ball"**

Slide Rule = "Engineering"

Thermometer = "Degree"

Figure 4 illustrates two such dream metaphors. With the image on the left, the dream is trying to express the concept of failing in one's mission. It does so by combining action and imagery in a way that, when described by the dreamer, cannot help but express the common saying "I dropped the ball" (common at least in US culture). On the right is an example of how a dream might combine two images to spell out the concept it is trying to represent. This was a dream of a young engineer wondering whether his engineering degree had properly prepared him for the workplace: *"I had a troubling dream about my career and whether I made the right choice. I vividly recall the image of a slide rule with a thermometer on it."* The dream literally spelled out "engineering degree." At that time, the slide rule was an item commonly associated with an engineer, thus representing the word "engineering," and the thermometer represented the word "degree."

Recognizing the Metaphor in the Dream Narrative

Metaphors are most often recognized in the phrases used in the dream narrative. How we tell the dream, and the words we use to describe the dream and its imagery, evokes phrases that are also descriptive of a situation in your waking life. These are figurative phrases and puns, which Anne Faraday termed wordplay, that describe not only the dream, but also something going on in the dreamer's waking life. Wordplay includes accidental slips of the tongue. Even the body language exhibited when the telling the dream can provide non-verbal clues to important content in the dream story.

For example, a dream of walking along a deep ditch or depression, might be described by one dreamer as "I was in a rut" and by another dreamer as "I am in a deep depression." These statements not only describe the dream activity, but also in a figurative way say something about the dreamer's personal waking life situation. As you write and review your dream narratives, try to avoid placing emphasis on the literal meaning of the words you use. Rather consider associations you might have with the words and phrases. Look for double meanings that might apply to a way you feel, or a situation you are in, in waking life. This is the language of the dream and the key to dreamwork.

Metaphor is best revealed when the dream is told from the standpoint of being in the dream in the present tense. In the above example, stating the dream in the first person as, *"I am in a rut and can't seem to get myself out"* is much more likely to trigger associations with waking life feelings than stated it in past tense as, *"I dreamed I was walking in a rut that I couldn't get out of."* When you record your dream, record it spontaneously as the stream of words come to you. Avoid editing or thinking too much about the words you use, or you will lose the meaning altogether. In the example above, if the dreamer had applied too much rational thought when writing the dream narrative, it may have read more like *"I dreamed I was walking in a ditch in the desert."* The associations with the waking life feelings and situation would have been totally lost.

When telling a dream, it is also important to pay attention to mistakes, slips of the tongue and even unexpected body language. Never edit out a mistake or slip of the tongue, but rather underline it. The mind will often slip a metaphor into your dream description, hidden within a mistake. For example, one subject who was having some sexual problems in her marriage described a dream as follows: *"I am on the surface of a planet where it is winter time and snowing. It is a very cold climax …oops, I mean climate."* The nature of her waking life concern became immediately apparent in her "slip of the tongue" metaphor.

Furthermore the mind may produce some revealing body movement at an important point when telling the dream. For example the sudden defensive crossing of the arms at a point in the dream story could reveal something that the dreamer wants to defend himself or herself against. More on the dreamwork with metaphors will be provided in chapter 8.

Irrational Combinations are Quite Rational

Embrace the manner in which dreams combine imagery, no matter how bizarre. This is a process known as "condensation." The right hemisphere matches objects by similar appearance.[10] It also processes relationships and tries to create a whole (a Gestalt) from many parts. The right brain recognizes faces and patterns, while the left recognizes words and titles. These imagery combinations are a natural synthesis function of the right brain, which combines related emotions, perceptions and memories to form a more complete holistic representation of the situation it is dealing with. Dream images can be made up of multiple image fragments, each representing one of these different but related associations. This concept is key to both understanding the picture language of dreams, and to recognizing how modifiers such as color and shape can change the meaning of an image. This will be discussed in more detail in chapter 6.

This combined set of representations can create some interesting visual combinations such as the thermometer slide-rule combination illustrated in figure 4, or the "old shoe" dream discussed previously. In another example, actual words were combined with imagery to spell out the emotionally salient situation: *"I dreamed I saw a license plate with the words 'HIDE 45'."* The dreamer had just reached her 45th birthday and was looking for a way (a "license") to hide the fact. The dream condensed the desire to hide the dreamer's age of 45, with the desire for a legitimate way to do it, a "license." In contrast to waking life, where we combine letters and words to form meaningful sentences, dreams combine images to "spell out" meaningful associations that are quite rational once we understand the language.

Function – the Right Brain Identity of Imagery

As we discovered above, dreams are processed in a part of the brain that talks in a non-verbal language, one that deals with relationship, properties and pattern. The right hemisphere tends to identify an object by function and the left hemisphere by name.[10]

One of the early cures for certain seizure conditions was the surgical separation of the corpus callosum, the nerve paths connecting the two hemispheres. What resulted was an individual with two distinct brain halves, processing and perceiving independently.[13] A test was done where a subject's left visual field (connected to the right hemisphere) was blocked so that only his left hemisphere could see. He was shown a fork, which he correctly identified as "a fork." Then the right visual field (connected to the left hemisphere) was blocked so that only the right hemisphere could see. He could no longer identify the object as a fork, but rather called it "something I eat with." The right brain could not title the object; it could only identify its context or function.

Knowing that the right brain identifies an object by function, purpose or contextual role, is an important key to understanding the language of dream imagery. In order to identify a dream image (a right brain creation), we simply reverse the process. Ask the dreamer to describe the "function" or "purpose" of a dream image, and you will learn a little bit about what it represents to them on a personal level. Experience this by trying the imagery experiment below.

Figure 5
Dream Images can be Decoded if we Look at their Function and Emotional Content and not their Literal Identity

Left Brain

"It's a Door"

Right Brain

"It's something that keeps people out"

As you try this experiment with the image of the door, you will find that you create your own internalized door with its own personal function. Invite others to try the experiment and you will see that each will define the door a bit differently. Also note that your definition takes on a personal meaning, which usually relates to something happening in your life, or a way you are feeling at the time. If you try it again in the future, you may find that the function you attribute to the door has changed. This is a "waking dream" of sorts, in that the right brain creates its own internal image from the suggestion of a door, and that internal image is created from your own personal experiences and memories surrounding "door-ness." This is exactly what happens in a dream. Imagery is created out of associations that are contextually related to your life situation. As in this exercise, if you simply define the "function" or "purpose" of a dream image you will gain insight into it's meaning for you.

This is also a good illustration of why dream "dictionaries" can be invalid and misleading. Each image in a dream is personal, based on personal experiences and associations. A dream "dictionary" may simply contain the author's own personal associations or a collection of associations derived from other sources. Although you may connect with a few of the dream "dictionary" metaphors, there is no way that a "dictionary" can determine the true personal content within your dream image. Only the dreamer can provide that information.

Actions in Dreams Represent More Complex Concepts

In dreams, our actions and movement through the dream space may be as symbolic of something deeper, as are the characters and objects we meet in that space. For example, our ability to visualize a complex route or to find a path through a maze is a primary function of the right hemisphere. It possesses the ability to manipulate spatial patterns and relationships. Perhaps this is why so many dreams involve wandering in a maze of paths or directions, and the theme of trying to find your way. The dreaming brain presents the problem-solving and pattern-forming process as a pictorial metaphor of finding your way through a maze. We will learn more about this later when we discuss shapes and patterns of movement.

Is there a "Message" in our Dreams?

If dreams have a "language," is there a message in our dreams? The answer is: yes and no. You will learn in the next two chapters that if there is a message, it is generally a compensating message aimed at changing inappropriate beliefs that have you stuck in an unhealthy pattern of behavior. Understanding the dream message comes through solid dreamwork and not necessarily through any literal view of a "message."

Apparent dream messages usually appear in the parable of the dream story, but sometimes as spoken or written words. Remember that when the dream speaks in words, the words rarely convey a literal message. The rational language centers of the brain are inactive in the dream state, so seemingly literal verbal or written messages are presented as metaphors. To understand the metaphor, the dream must first be compared as an analogy to the waking life situation, and then the voice, words or message likewise treated as pertaining to that analogy. For example, in the "waters of the unconscious" dream, where a voice suddenly stated: *the water is your unconscious, jump in and you will be fine,*" the message was that the dreamer did not need to fear the unconscious. It was literal only within the context of the dream (embrace the unconscious). It was not about fear of water!

Dreams project internal trends; they rarely project external future events. An apparently literal story, warning or projection into the future, may merely be a reflection of your own feelings or fears about the event the dream is dealing with. As we learned in chapter 2, a plane crash in a dream is not usually a literal omen, dreaming of cancer does not necessarily predict an impending disease, and so forth. If the dream presents the "message" in a way that seems particularly "real," and it is practical to check it out, then it may be prudent to do so. However, a general fear that your dreams are always warning you of pending dangers would be unhealthy and unwarranted.

If you perceive a "message" in your dream, determine whether that "message" is appropriate before acting on it. If the "message" leads you further into an unhealthy situation, compounding the problem you are wrestling with, then you probably have read the wrong message into the dream. If, on the other hand, it is healthy and practical, and seems to reverse some unhealthy misconception, then you may have understood what your dream was telling you. Chapters 10 and 11 will provide more guidance on how to appropriately understand and work with the apparent "message" in your dreams.

Summary Exercises

a) We are Conscious in our Dreams - Recall being in a recent dream. In what ways does that state of consciousness seem or feel different than your waking experience, and in what ways does it seem the same?

b) Dreams Appear Irrational Only to the Waking Mind - Recall a bizarre situation in one of your dreams. Did it seem perfectly normal while in the dream?

c) Working Memory is Off-line - Dreams switch scenes. Recall a multi-sequence dream. Is it more understandable when you treat each scene as a separate dreamlet related to the same theme?

d) Emotions Shape our Dreams - In a recent dream, can you see a relationship between the dream story and an emotionally stimulating, or anxiety-provoking, event the day before?

e) Dreams Focus on Self and Self Image - If you were able to find a relationship between the dream and an emotionally salient event the day before, explore the event and how you felt. Did the event in any way threaten who you believe yourself to be, or the way you see the world or people around you?

f) Function is the Hidden Language in Imagery – Pick what seems like an important sentence in your dream narrative. Define the function or purpose (in general terms) of each dream element in that sentence. Insert the definition in place of the named objects in the sentence and read it back. Does that sentence now seem to refer in some way to a waking life situation?

---

g) Time and Linear Logic Have Little Meaning - Look at one of your longer more story-like dreams. Do the events follow a logical sequence from step to step, or do scenes and events shift with little relationship to cause and effect?

h) Irrational Imagery Combinations are Quite Rational - Recall a dream that combined two or more images into one. Try the function definition exercise in (f) on each image fragment in the combination. Does the new combination of definitions reveal a more complete story?

i) Metaphor is the Natural Language of Dreams – In one of your more recent story-like dreams, look for statements or phrases you used that seem like figures of speech, which also seem to apply to a way you feel, or something going on in your life at the time. Consider that waking life situation. Does the connection help explain the dream better?

j) Actions in Dreams Represent More Complex Concepts - Look at how you and other dream characters moved through a recent story-like dream. What were you attempting to do in the dream and how are these actions analogous to what you might be attempting to do in waking life?

CHAPTER 4
THE PSYCHOLOGY OF DREAMS

I think my life would be easier, he said, if I could just get my selves to agree on something – Brian Andreas [67]

We meet ourselves in our dreams. In working with our dreams, we hope to understand how our dream story relates to our waking life story and sense of self. In the last chapter, I discussed some of the biological factors that influence our dreams. In this chapter I will discuss the process in a psychological sense. I will discuss more about the concept of an "internal model" which forms both a reference for processing our perceptions, as well as a reference for our dream space. I will then compare dream theories of some of our great psychological thinkers, each of whom describes the dream process in terms of their own concept of an internal model.

Our Internal Model

In the last chapter, I introduced the concept of an inner "model" that we maintain as a reference, in order to process experiences associated with external events. Such a model is necessary since our brain has a finite capability, and we would not be able to operate from moment to moment if we had to think through and re-evaluate every bit of sensory information coming in as if it were new.

Gerald Edelman at the Scripps Institute indicates that we always perceive things, but only become conscious when we relate what we perceive to our internal experiences.[cited in 38] He also states that we judge a stimulus against references of the world stored in our long-term memories. When a match is made between the sensory information and our internal model, we become aware or conscious of that information. Our hippocampus serves the function of comparing the present with our past store of knowledge (the "model"), and monitors new sensory events as novel or ordinary based on this internal model.

There is further biological evidence for this internal model. Our brain creates neuronal "maps" to synthesize meaningful experiences from disparate pieces of information, stored by various groups of neurons. Edelman proposes a concept known as "reentrant signaling" which is the communication between these neuronal "maps" that allows the brain to further construct complex perceptions – or what we see and think.[cited in 38] Each fragment of a concept travels within the region of the brain that houses it, until various regions resonate with each other, at which point the concept becomes conscious. The many "maps" that are created are kept track of and inventoried in the core of the brain (the cerebellum, basal ganglia and hippocampus). Different experiences excite different "maps." It is the frontal cortex of the brain that then neatly organizes all of this activity into a meaningful rational story.

This handy reference, which helps us process reality, is not without problems. The brain has a finite learning ability, and cannot accurately model the totality of external reality. Thus the internal model will always be somewhat incomplete. External reality will always bring in new experiences that don't fit the internal view, stimulating the brain to reinforce old relatively unused pathways or create new ones. Our psychological or social model can be easily corrupted, because learned reactions create biases. Our internal model is heavily colored by our emotional and instinctual reactions, the "emotional tags" that our limbic system places on sensory experiences. The model is also heavily biased by the "rational" filtering of our pre-frontal cortex, which helps process our decisions and beliefs.

The "Me" and the "Not Me"

Due to the biases and perceptual flaws discussed above, our internal model presents an interesting situation regarding our self-perception versus our actual behavior or how others perceive us. We typically consider those personality states that fit this internal model to be who we are, the ego-self, the "Me." Other personality states fall outside this image of self, and become the "Not Me" or shadow self.

We will later learn the term "personal mythology" as a description of this internal model, since the many elements of the internal model make up a complex mythology from which we perceive reality and ourselves. Establishing a model of self may simplify our brain's ability to navigate through life, but has a dark downside that becomes the stuff of dreams. To illustrate this concept, and explore your own internal model a bit, try the following exercise.

Figure 6

Not Me   **Me**

Exercise - Me and Not Me

1) Place two columns on a sheet of paper and title one "Me" and the other "Not Me."
2) Under the "Me" column write down three main personality traits that you feel define who you are. You might say: *"I am a good person; I am strong; I am courteous…"* and so on.
3) Now under the "Not Me" column write down three opposite personality traits that you feel are not who you are, or that you try not to be. You might say such things as: *"I am not a bad person; I am not weak; I do not try to hurt people…"*
4) Now read through and reflect on the "Not Me" side. Was there ever a time that you acted like or exhibited any of the "Not Me" traits? Using the example above you might ask: *"Did I ever act badly; have I ever been weak; or did I ever hurt someone?"*
5) For those "Not Me" attributes that you indeed once expressed, surely that was you at the time? Are some of those "Not Me" traits therefore truly a part of you, a part of the "Me" that you would rather not admit to, that you would rather keep hidden and under control?
6) How do you feel when someone accuses you of acting like the "Not Me" traits?

If you tried the exercise you will undoubtedly realize that the mental self-image or model we create to identify who we are, the "Me," is not totally accurate. It is limited to those aspects that we want to be or that we are comfortable with exhibiting. We place the other aspects that we do not like about ourselves, or are less comfortable with, into the category of "Not Me." Other people, however, may see both sides of us, some of the "Not Me" coming out at times. When others react to your "Not Me" side or point it out, what happens? We may become shocked and defensive toward this perceived threat against self. Instinctively we may fight it (saying to ourselves or to the other person how wrong they are) or we may go into the flight mode feeling hurt and defensive. How many times have you had this happen? Have you ever been accused of acting out of one of your "Not Me" characteristics, which you later confirmed through self-examination?

The Role of the Dream

Dreams seem to explore and test various ways of accommodating anomalous experiences, that don't fit the internal model. As mentioned previously, the hippocampus plays a role in detecting the anomalies in our experience. Processing new experiences into long-term memory takes repetition and time (many hours), a process known as long-term potentiation. Dreams certainly provide both the time and the repetition for such learning. Ratey[38] supports the role of REM sleep "as a process for reliving new and old experiences so they become more permanently etched as long-term memory." At night, the emotional residue of a daily experience will surface for the dreaming brain to process. The result might be a resolution that either accommodates the experience, or alters the internal model. Even the best dreams don't transform the model all at once, because of the huge amount of past history and embedded learning that must be undone. It is generally a long slow journey with moderate successes along the way.

One possible advantage that dream-state processing might have over that of the waking state, is the absence of the rational filtering in the dream state. There may be more access in a dream sate to all available information, than the waking cognitive state will permit. In the dream state, the more disturbing emotional elements and "not me" fragments of our internal model can freely surface and be dealt with. As we saw in the "jokester" dream in chapter 2, the ego is only one of the many players in the dream, and often not the controlling one.

Dreams also appear to engage in repetitive scenarios. As we learned in chapter 2, such scenarios are necessary for creating long-term memory, and in particular "procedural memory" or tasks requiring practice.[38, 70] On the occasion when we can recall and record more than one dream from the evening, it is often observed that dreams repeat a theme, or present the same storyline from a slightly different "angle," multiple times per evening, bringing in new information each time.

The following "tornado" dream came to a person who was struggling with some new spiritual concepts she had been exposed to: *My dream had four parts: First, I dreamed there was a spirit that came up from a creek destroying trees in its path, like a tornado. Next, I was in a classroom and I knew the teacher, but could not identify her. I tried to volunteer to go out and survey the damage at the creek but I was invisible, so the teacher never recognized me. In the third part, a very old friend, who later became a missionary, was riding a tricycle down toward the creek. In the fourth part, two men, including my friend, were struggling with the spirit which was invisible and neither good nor evil."* The dream illustrates a learning progression in dealing with and accommodating the new spiritual concepts. First it shows the spirit (stirred by the new concepts) arising as a tornado-like force and destroying early beliefs that had established roots. The next sequence tackles the relationship of these new concepts to what she knows. She has an intuitive sense that she knows them (the teacher), but can't fully identify with them. She needs to see for herself. Finally, past memories are tapped in order to find a connection that might work. A childhood friend on a tricycle is brought forth, whom she relates to her childhood religious upbringing. The fourth segment shows the struggle between those childhood beliefs and the new concepts (the spirit that has been released) that appear to blur the traditional boundaries of good and evil.

As suggested by this case, dreams appear to introduce and test various scenarios in order to find the best means to accommodate the event that stimulated the dream. In the process, the brain may indeed be strengthening old memory paths and restructuring new ones, thus re-learning and reprogramming itself to find the best fit between our internal model and new external perceptions. In the above dream, the final resolution was not obviously achieved, but the core of the problem was clearly brought to the surface. Various memories (memory paths) were strengthened, and some seemingly modified as seen by the fact that each of the figures in her dream appeared in a slightly altered form or role than factual memory would suggest.

Sometimes dreams will recur through periods of our lives, trying to find a way to accommodate situations into our internal model. One teen reported: *" I have a recurring dream of being chased by two pandas. Pandas are supposed to be warm and fuzzy, but these would maul me if they caught me."* The dream related to his broken home and conflicts with his parents who were "supposed to treat him warmly." But in this case, he feared potential abuse.

Psychological Theory of Dreams

Ever since the time of Sigmund Freud, many theories on dreams have been proposed, leading to a wealth of dreamworking practices. Some of them can to be relatively ineffective, or even misleading, but many have remained useful for both therapeutic work and as building blocks for further exploration.

Freud

Sigmund Freud is probably best known for introducing the validity of dreams into the field of psychology, as well as into the awareness of the general population. Freud also introduced the concept of the unconscious as a foundation of his psychoanalytic theory. He was born in 1856 and began as a neurologist. He established a link between neurotic symptoms and dreams early on, but he considered both as arising out of sexual conflicts, many originating in early childhood. It was this extreme emphasis on the sexual source of symptoms that alienated him from his contemporaries at the time and which, to this day, creates contention as to the value of specific areas of his work.

The broader value of Freud's contribution, whether the ideas originated with him or not, was in bringing awareness of certain principles to the field of psychology such as: the validity of dreams in working with symptoms; emphasis on what he called the latent content of dreams (the wishes and fantasies within them); emphasis on the pictographic, symbolic nature of dream imagery; and the significance of metaphor in the telling of the dream. He almost always ascribed the latent content of dreams to sexual, instinctual material that had never been conscious, as well as to material that has been banished to the unconscious because it was unacceptable. He promoted the idea of "condensation," the fusion of several different elements, in which the content of a dream element is always far more extensive than what is apparent. He also promoted the idea of "displacement," or reverting one's focus from the important to unimportant elements of an event, in order that they pass our mental "censorship." He promoted the concept of "secondary revision" which is a natural tendency of the mind to organize disconnected elements into a unified whole.

He published one of the first extensive books on dreams, *The Interpretation of Dreams* around 1900. In later revisions, he discussed the topic of symbolism as disguised pictorial representations of latent thoughts. He saw symbols as a factor in the distortion of dreams and took the position that most symbols had a sexual reference. For example, he related elongated objects to the male organ, hollow objects with openings to the female organ, and various motions in the dreams such as climbing stairs to the sexual act.

His method of dreamwork was to decode, translate and "interpret" the dream, using free association, which he considered the fundamental rule of psychoanalysis. According to Freud, the motivation behind dreams was wish fulfillment and the function of dreams was the guardian of sleep - to continue sleep by censoring and disguising the disturbing latent dream thoughts so that the superego will not be offended and wake the dreamer.

Other Great Thinkers

There were many other early thinkers who established some of the lasting theories and techniques of dreamwork that we enjoy today. One of the best sources on the background of these great thinkers is Robert Van de Castle's book *Our Dreaming Mind*[37] as well as the book *Extraordinary Dreams and How to Work with Them*[80] co-authored by Stanley Krippner.

Alfred Adler believed that dreams originate in unfinished and unsolved social problems, and that they are oriented toward the future. He contended that dream images were a type of language that represented the individual's current life situation, and that individual concerns were openly revealed in dreams.[80] In the 1940's, Samuel Lowy proposed that dreams were biologically necessary and were stimulated both by psychological and physical stimulus. Erik Erikson developed an extensive dream analysis approach, which included the concepts of ego identity and socialization.[cited in 37] Menard Boss evolved the phenomenological approach to dreams, where he promoted the idea that dreams and waking life were related.[cited in 37] Calvin Hall proposed his cognitive theory of dreams, which promoted translating dream elements into the ideas to which they refer. He and Robert Van de Castle developed a systematic process for content analysis.[57] Hall proposed that a content analysis of a person's dream series makes it possible to determine the "conceptual systems" of that dreamer. He placed dream content in the following categories: conceptions of self, of others, of the world, of problems and conflicts, and of impulses, prohibitions and penalties. Montague Ullman[72] developed a non-threatening approach to working with dreams in a group setting. He taught dreamwork in a way that "respects the privacy of the dreamer and his authority over the dream." His group approach is discussed further in chapter 10.

I will review three additional theorists in the next few sections who I personally have found to provide highly effective theories and techniques for dreams and dreamwork. Carl Jung (who established a relationship between dreams and the collective consciousness and mythology of humankind) and Fritz Perls (originator of Gestalt therapy) are two whom I believe contributed much that has lasted in modern day dreamwork. David Feinstein is the third. He is a contemporary psychologist who, in conjunction with Stanley Krippner, introduced the concept of the personal myth as it applies to dreams. Table 4-1 offers a summary of these three theorists. In dreamwork, I have found it most effective to use a combination of the common themes and approaches of each.

Table 4-1
Theories Related to Dreams and Dreamwork

Source	Jung	Perls	Feinstein
Purpose of Dreaming	- Individuation - Self Realization - Evolution of the Inner Self	- Self Actualization - Wholeness - Maturation	Reconciliation of the day's events with your personal myth; glimpse into transcendent realm
Stimulus for the Dream	Unfinished business, including thoughts & feelings not experienced during the day	Imbalance creates an immediate need to correct	Waking Experience that does not fit the personal myth; latent potentials blocked by that myth
Source of the Dream Elements and Imagery	- Personal Unconscious = analogies - Collective Uncon. = archetypes, collective myth of mankind	All imagery is a part of self, "fragments" of the personality	A "complex" of associations (images) organized around a core theme
Conscious Contents in the Dream	The part of the psyche accepted by the ego	Personality "fragments" that are more readily accepted	Your internal view of self and reality, i.e., your personal myth
Unconscious Contents in the Dream	- Personal = repressed, once-conscious material; ego complexes - Collective = natural evolution of the Self - Material not integrated into the personality	Alienated or disassociated "fragments" of the personality	Opposing or alternate views of self and reality, i.e., "counter-myths"
The Mental Process Taking Place	Reconciliation between the conscious and unconscious through a process of compensation	Natural drive to unify the alienated "fragments" of the personality. 3 types of Gestalts: unfinished business; conflicts; non-actualized potential.	Accommodating the experience through: - Sustaining the old myth - Strengthening the counter-myth - Integrating the "myths"
Barrier to Resolution	Fear of the unconscious (or of accepting the unconscious and thus death of the ego)	An Impasse or experience counter to one's self-image, without a support mechanism to resolve it	Clinging to outmoded old myth, premature embrace of counter-myth, irreconcilable conflicting myths
Eventual Transform-ation	Acceptance of Self	-Maturation -Moving from environmental support to self support	A higher order synthesis of the myth/counter-myth is created
Dreamwork Approach	Recognition of motifs and archetypes and relating them to the process of individuation	Gestalt Therapy - uses role-play of the imagery to force interaction between the "fragments" and move them through the impasse	Revealing the "myth" and "counter-myth"; evoking transcendent forces in the psyche for engaging the conflict.

Jungian Psychology

Carl Jung, who lived between 1875 and 1961, was an eminent Swiss psychologist and one of the founders of analytical psychology. He became friends with Freud for a few years, but broke with Freudian psychology about the time he wrote *Symbols of Transformation*, which dealt with the symbolism of the psyche, and it's mythological orientation. He regarded Freudian psychology, and its focus on sexuality as the primary psychological force, as narrow and controlling. Jung claimed that the aim of the psyche is not to suppress or repress, but to come to know one's other side, to control the whole range of one's capacities. He believed that dream images frequently represented emerging forces in a persons life, rather than sexual wishes and troublesome past experiences.[80]

Jung had a healthy theory regarding the dream process that, unlike Freud, related dreaming more to the present state of the individual rather than traumas of early childhood. He related dreams to the "unfinished business" of waking life, observing that "thoughts that were not thought, and feelings that were not felt by day, afterwards appeared in dreams."[16] To Jung, dreams presented the current state of our mental evolution, bringing forth content related to both our unrealized potential and our less desirable weak side. He saw the dream as a method for bringing unconscious material into consciousness, whether it came from the outside (something we never became fully aware of) or whether it came totally from the unconscious.

Jung used the word "psyche" to describe our mental or psychological makeup. He roughly divided it into the conscious and the unconscious. The conscious mind is the only part of the mind that we know directly. It grows through the application of what Jung called the four functions: thinking, feeling, sensing, intuition. The ego is the name Jung uses for the organization of the conscious mind.[23] The ego has a lot of control over our perceptions since it must acknowledge something in order to bring it into awareness. We develop a personality through a process he called individuation, which is highly driven by what the ego allows to become conscious. Jung identified an alter-ego element that he called the shadow, which contains our basic animal nature and instincts as well as our insights, and parts of self that make us uncomfortable. This division of ego-self is much like the concept of the "me" and "not me" division of the internal model presented at the beginning of the chapter.

Jung divided the unconscious into the personal and the collective. The personal unconscious contains material that was once conscious but is now repressed or disregarded, perhaps because it was upsetting, unresolved or irrelevant. Within the personal unconscious lie "complexes" which act like separate little personalities that are triggered and drive our behavior at times. The contents of the collective unconscious, in contrast, have never been conscious, are linked to our evolutionary past, and are evidenced by primordial imagery ("collective" imagery) that Jung called archetypes. Two important collective archetypes are termed the Animus and Anima, or the masculine side of the female psyche and the feminine side of the male psyche. Most importantly, the collective unconscious contains the organizing principle of the personality that Jung called the "Self" (capital S). The Self drives the individuation process.

Jung indicated that one focus of dreams was to become a whole person by reconciling our conscious and the unconscious parts. The barrier to integration of the two sides appeared to be largely fear of the unconscious. This can be simply fear of the unknown, or fear of parts of yourself you repressed because you see them as evil or undesirable. Jung talked about death in dreams as symbolic of the "death of the ego" or the beginning of a cycle of "death and rebirth" which is necessary to becoming a whole and fully integrated self. In order for you to grow into your full potential, the old view of self (the existing ego) must change, or symbolically "die," so that the new self can be born. This cycle appears in dreams as death imagery or descending into darkness, followed by a period of loss or search, and an eventual discovery, acceptance and celebration of the new self. The cycle appears when you face frightening imagery in a dream. It almost always weakens or transforms into an ally, allowing the ego to accept that side of self in a different light, and to grow as a result.

Jung also indicated that dreams act on a natural tendency towards balance or wholeness. They generally employ compensation as a means to balance the misconceived beliefs of the ego. Jung called this process of self-realization and becoming a whole being "individuation." He claimed that the driving force within the collective unconscious has no deliberate plan outside of an urge towards self-realization.[17] Jung observed that this process does not complete itself in a lifetime, but is cyclical, achieving stages of "completion" little by little, sometimes in large breakthroughs, but constantly striving toward the potential whole being, the "Self."

Jung observed a strong similarity between dream narrative and imagery, the descriptions in Alchemical texts, and the common mythology of mankind. He observed how the processes, cycles, elements and geometric symbolism of the Alchemists appeared similar to the motifs, geometric patterns and cycles in our dreams. He saw similarities between the Alchemical work that described the purification and coloring of metals,[107] and the cycles of human transformation which often appear in dreams in the symbolic death and rebirth (descent and re-emergence) cycle described above. He noted that circular and center-oriented patterns and movement (for example dancing in a circle, or walking or moving around a center) depict a process that constantly and cyclically produces a "new center" for the personality.[18] The object in the center of a circular pattern might be a potential center, not identical with the ego, around which the ego revolves.[29] Spiral patterns (such as a spiral staircase) or movements (such as a tornado) might depict the dreaming personality being drawn inward toward the center, or material from the center (perhaps life-giving material) being brought forth. The tornado image, in the four-part "tornado" dream discussed previously, is an example of new material being brought forth from the unconscious center, where new concepts are destroying and replacing old ones.

Jung[4] also discussed the motif of four, or element of "four-ness," as relating to the process of individuation. He described the "four" motif as a state of completeness, the four stages of evolution, a balance of the four forces of consciousness (thought, feeling, intuition and sensation), and a pattern of order, stability, completeness or closure. He also related the balanced appearance of the "psychological primaries" (the color grouping of red, yellow, blue and green) to this same four-ness pattern of stability and closure. More on the Jungian observations on these patterns in dreams will be discussed in chapters 5, 7 and 9.

Jung also found a strong relationship between the role played by characters in our dreams and the mythology of humankind. Mythology depicts reality as mystical patterns, and life as directed by unknown forces greater than ourselves, which must be appeased by ritualistic behavior. Heroes only found their rewards after tests and long journeys, fighting beasts from the underworld, searching the unknown, proving their value along the way and collecting pieces of what or whom they encountered along the way. He observed this process to be similar to the journeys of the dreamer, in their series of dream stories. By understanding and observing archetypal imagery and patterns, Jung could relate the dream to where the dreamer was in their own mythic "journey." One of the great contributions made by Jung was the identification and naming of common "archetypes." He considered them to be instinctual in nature, and related their role within the dream and our human psyche to their collective role in the common mythology of humans across cultures. In a sense, he gave an identity to collective dream imagery, which he could relate to the psychological processes being played out in the dream. Some of the more frequently recognized archetypes are discussed in more depth in chapter 7 and will become a part of the dreamworking process in this book.

Perls - Gestalt Therapy

Fritz Perls was the originator of Gestalt Therapy. His psychoanalytic training took place at the Psychoanalytic Institutes of Berlin, Vienna and Frankfurt. He developed Gestalt Therapy while in the United States from 1946 until 1970.

Perls, like Jung, saw the process going on within the mind as a constant natural tendency toward obtaining wholeness or completion within the individual, thus the term "Gestalt" which means whole or completeness. Perls also considered the dream as part of the normal function of the mind, calling it "the most spontaneous expression of the existence of the human being."[15] Like Jung's theory of individuation, he referred to a similar singular inborn process for the individual, calling it the process of "self-actualization."

He claimed that, in essence, we are whole unified individuals, but that we "fragment" ourselves. We dissociate or alienate our conscious personality from the parts (fragments) that we don't like or can't deal with. He developed a process called Gestalt Therapy for re-owning these fragments, and for re-unification. Through this process, we accommodate alienated parts of self and restructure the internal model.

Perls claimed that each of the characters and images we see in dreams is a part of our own personality, the dissociated "fragments" so to speak. He could see a relation between how we relate to these fragments in the dream, and how we relate to others and events in waking life. These personality fragments are not only projected as images in our dreams, but are projected on other people in our waking life. If there is a part of ourselves we do not like, then we often find ourselves disliking someone who reminds us of that part.

Perls also claimed that dreams are an opportunity to get in touch with, interact with, and re-own these alienated fragments to bring about the unified, self-actualized being. He claimed that a primary biological process of "gestalt formation" drives this activity, whereby any imbalance in the personality creates an immediate need to correct this imbalance. He discussed at least three basic types of Gestalts that dreams deal with: unfinished business; conflicts within yourself or with others; and non-actualized potentials. This is similar to Jung, who also indicated that dreams work on unfinished business and are driven by evolving forces within the unconscious, forces that contain representations of the fully actualized Self.

Perls indicated that there is a regulating law, whereby the more urgent situation becomes the controller and takes over. Our dreams on any particular night, therefore, may be related to the most urgent piece of unfinished business left with us before we fell asleep. This perhaps explains why we are able, with proper self-training, to incubate and stimulate a dream on a certain problem. By concentrating on the problem as we fall asleep, we are sometimes able to place the request as the most urgent piece of unfinished business in our sleeping mind.

With Jung, the barrier to becoming individuated or self-realized, appeared to be a fear of accepting the unknown, unconscious side. Perls called the barrier to self-actualization, the "impasse."[15] The "impasse" is the point at which neither external nor internal support is forthcoming, nor has authentic self-support been achieved. It is a state of limbo and anxiety in which the person has nowhere to turn until a new support mechanism is found.

The individual will often search in a panic for something that will help them re-identify themselves in relation to the reality they are experiencing, or help them justify the rejection of that reality. In extreme cases, this is a time when an individual might join a cult, participate in protests, exhibit irrational behavior, or collapse into depression.

By becoming aware of Self, and permitting the process of "organic self-regulation" to take place, Perls indicated that the individual abandons the tendency towards self-manipulation and manipulation of one's environment. They no longer become fragmented because they experience a "fit" between the external experience and the internal view of who they are. This self-regulating principle that Perls described is similar to the natural centering force discussed by Jung.

According to Perls, as the personality becomes unified, it no longer requires support from the environment but becomes more capable of self-support. The transformation from environmental support to self-support, Perls called "maturation."

Feinstein - The Personal Myth

Whereas Jung related dreams to the mythology of humankind, dreams can relate to a more personal mythology, according to David Feinstein, PhD. In Stanley Krippner's book *Dreamtime and Dreamwork*,[19] Feinstein considers dreams as a place where we meet and reconcile the day's events. We do this within the context of how we perceive and make sense of ourselves, this context taking on the characteristics of a deep "personal mythology." He and Stanley develop this further in their book *Personal Mythology*.[71] This is, in a sense, the nature of the internal model to which I have been referring.

Our internal model is naturally structured by organizing a complex set of images, emotions and concepts around a core theme. Feinstein claims that this core theme has all the aspects of a myth. We often associate the word myth with the lack of reality. However, in its true definition, a myth relates to the way the mind interprets reality. According to J. Campbell,[20] the characteristics of a myth include: the urge to comprehend the world in a meaningful way; the search for a marked pathway through life; the need to establish secure and fulfilling relationships, and the longing to understand one's part in the mystery of the cosmos. These characteristics, according to Feinstein, are similar to the way the mind organizes its internal model or view of self and reality. Thus he terms this internal model the personal myth. This personal mythic structure is similar in some ways to the Jungian "field of consciousness" that contains the ego, the shadow and the complexes to which the ego attaches itself at times.

Since one's personal myth is the mind's interpretation of reality, rather than absolute reality, it does have an aspect of fantasy. As we mature, the myth is modified to better fit our experience, but the core theme remains an interpretation, with all of its limits and internal biases. By recognizing that events in a dream are taking their story line from the viewpoint of a personal myth, it will permit us to better understand the dream in relation to our view of self. The personal myth concept relates well to Jung's description of dreams as associated with the collective mythology of man. The approach presents a way of understanding dreams from a personal aspect, as well as explaining how some imagery and core themes are common across the human cultures. Feinstein indicates that personal myths are the product of four interacting sources:

1) Biology - capacities for symbolism and narrative found within the brain structure, along with the impact of one's physical characteristics on one's unique mythology;

2) Culture - the ubiquitous influence of the society on one's evolving personal myths;

3) Personal history - any emotionally significant experience that impacts one's evolving mythology;

4) Transcendent experiences - special episodes of profound insight and vision that expand, inspire and enlighten.

This is not unlike the teachings of Jung who saw the unfolding myth in dreams as a function of: 1) biological evolution including the evolution of the mind or psyche; 2) cultural influence; 3) personal experience and 4) the personal state of individuation and transcendence (union of conscious and unconscious).[21] Feinstein states that dreams incorporate not only the myth and counter-myth, but (like Jung) deeper archetypal mythic structures as well. Taking the Jungian approach one step further, he proposes that external experiences (a waking experience that does not fit the myth) trigger the conflict between the conscious and unconscious. He also expands the concept of the internal mythical structure to include the collective myth (the Jungian archetypes).

By looking at our dreams, we can see the structure of our personal myth. Dreams reveal how our internal view of reality may be accommodating, or failing to accommodate, our waking experiences. Feinstein[19] states that the dream process is mediation between the older myth and the emerging counter-myth. The dream works on a new experience by relating it to a reconstruction of the past; relating it to recent events; or considering possible future alternatives. The outcome can be one of three events:

1) the older myth is sustained (your mind justifies things as they are);

2) a counter-myth (an alternative view) is enhanced or created by the new experiences that don't fit the existing myth;

3) the two conflicting myths become integrated or evolve into a new mythical structure (your mind finds a new way of perceiving the situation).

The results of all of this interaction are three different types of dreams:

1) Dreams which may not come to resolution, but rehearse interactions between the myth and counter-myth;

2) Dreams which present a new mythical structure, a higher order synthesis of the most viable elements of the old myth and counter-myth (I observe these to often be the most colorful, explosive and fun dreams);

3) Dreams, which relate how one might bring that new synthesis into daily life (dreams that give us an indirect message by example or dream experience, a metaphor, or even a direct message in words, the "compensating" function Jung referred to).

This is similar to the way Jung described the stages in a sequence of dreams: 1) the unconscious first attempts to compensate for the views of the conscious mind (mediation between myth and counter-myth), and 2) the process eventually results in a "transcendence" where a union is formed between the conscious and the unconscious.[21] There is also commonality with the Perls approach whereby: 1) we first encounter the alienated parts of our personality; and 2) we interact with these parts in an attempt to create an eventual balance or Gestalt; 3) resulting in a self-actualized being. Chapter 5 will integrate these three theories into a suggested psychological model for dreaming.

Exercise – Personal Myth

Often we find ourselves in difficult situations or stuck in dysfunctional behavioral patterns, because we are acting from the viewpoint of an inappropriate personal myth; a myth that originated with a decision made in the past at a moment of crisis.

1) If you have a disturbing dream that you can relate to a recent upsetting waking life situation, reflect on the waking life situation. Go to the most emotional point and bring to mind specifically how you felt. Name and describe those feelings.

2) Now try to go back in time to one specific emotional event earlier in your life when you felt the same way.

3) Visualize what occurred, who was involved, and specifically how you felt about what happened.

4) What decision did you make about yourself, about life or about the others involved at the time?

5) This may have been the creation point of a myth which is contributing to your behavior in the present situation. Has that decision been a driving force in certain similar situations throughout you life? Did it influence the situation the dream appeared to be dealing with? Is it an appropriate decision in the present situation, or does it leave you stuck, inhibiting your progress?

CHAPTER 5
DREAM CYCLES

There was a whole world here once, she said, but some of the smaller parts left on personal business & it's not that easy to find replacements – Brian Andreas [67]

What is happening in a dream? Jung and Perls both observed that dreams might not have any ultimate plan in mind, other than the natural tendency towards establishing stability and closure. The goal may be simple but the process can be quite involved, including the integration of a fragmented personality and restoring the self when it is under attack. Jung described the process as cyclical and evolutionary. Some cycles can last throughout a night of dreams, some throughout years or a lifetime.

As you read through the works of Jung, Perls and Feinstein summarized in the last chapter, you may recognize some common themes. The primary objective of the dream appears to be closure on unprocessed/unfinished business of the day or the re-balancing of any imbalance created from without or within. There also appears to be a synergy between the dream process and the process of human transformation. The dream both reflects the stages of this transformation, and helps to bring it about.

Transformation Cycles

As we saw in the last chapter, Jung stressed that our individuation and ego-self evolves in cycles from within the collective unconscious, under the influence of an organizing force he called the Self. He related human transformation to a symbolic death and rebirth, which can be represented as a four-stage process:

1) **Death of the Ego:** A stage of turning within, in which the ego abandons the old view of self that no longer works.

2) **Search for Self:** A search for a new self, a new decision about who we are in relation to life that will work.

3) Rebirth: As the ego accepts a new view of self or newly integrated parts of self, the old self is transcended and the new ego-self emerges.

4) Self Actualization: The new self emerges into waking life and, assuming that it is put into action and experienced, becomes actualized.

There is evidence that these stages of human transformation are reflected in our dreams. Hamilton[105] performed a recent study of fifteen hundred dreams of nineteen people who underwent silent spiritual retreats, plus an additional single case study of over a thousand dreams of a non-retreat subject who experienced a profound psycho-spiritual transformation over a period of two years. He observed that the dreams of these individuals not only reflect progressive stages of transformation similar to those listed above, but also reflect altered states of consciousness that are often encountered in such a transformation. He used Jung's nomenclature that compared human transformation to the alchemical[107] purification stages Negredo, Albedo, Citrinitas and Rubedo. He indicated that the patterns seemed unaffected by differences in age, gender, culture and the degree of exposure to spiritual ideas, texts and teachings. I will describe the observations of Hamilton and Jung and as they relate to this larger transformation cycle in more detail in chapter 7. In this chapter, I will note the imagery that Hamilton[105] and Jung[4, 16-18, 21, 28] observed in relation to transformation role of the individual dream.

Dream Cycles

The cycles within an individual dream or dream series appear to have the immediate objective of closure or balance. According to Feinstein, the dream achieves this through various means of accommodation, which may or may not include transformation. The transformation cycle, however, appears to depend on the dream to progress through each stage. Both are dependent on the waking state for actualizing the newly transformed ego. The model of a dream cycle is therefore presented as a waking/dream cycle.

1) **Balance**: This is a hypothetical waking state characterized by an ego that is in a temporary state of harmony with internal and external perceptions. The waking state is outwardly focused, but there is a feeling of inner peace. It is a state that might occur in a small way after a resolution dream, or in a bigger way after a personal transformation. As Perls indicated, however, we have various personality fragments or parts, and "parts fight." As a result, this state of temporary balance can be easily disrupted.

2) **Disruption of the Balance**: Our internal balance can be disturbed by any number of external and internal events that threaten us, activate a personal myth or counter-myth,

or don't fit our internal model. It can be something disturbing or threatening or just as easily a result of personal introspection, self-search, self-evolution or discovery. The event, and your reaction to it, creates a need for emotional closure.

3) **Encounter**: The dream begins to evolve in stages over the night, bringing forth and processing the material associated with the situation that stimulated the dream. You might encounter: emotionally associated experiences from the past, repressed memories and feelings, elements of your personal myth, and various personality fragments that have some association with that event. You may also encounter organizing and individuating forces emerging from the collective unconscious. As the dreams progress (in one evening or in a longer series) the encounters may involve progressive degrees of Self-emergence and self-awareness. Successive cycles of separation, encounter and integration (the death/rebirth cycle) will become apparent. All of these internal dynamics appear as the characters, objects and actions in your dream. You, as the dreamer, tend to play an ego role, actively negotiating the dream dance with the other fragments of self. But at times you may find yourself as a detached observer, watching all the parts of self deal with the situation. The emotional stimulus of the dream, together with the mind's natural tendency towards integration and closure, weave the dream story.

4) **Resolution/Transformation**: Some dreams seem to be a pure encounter, simply presenting the elements of the situation without an obvious attempt at closure. More often, however, dreams contemplate and test various solutions in an attempt to establish closure or restore a sense of self that is acceptable to the ego. The natural balancing forces within the psyche establish unifying patterns, compensating events, or guidance in various forms, in an attempt to bring order to the fragmented personality or to reverse misconceptions that are barriers to closure. As we learned in the last chapter, dreams attempt to bring closure by: a) reaffirming the existing view of self; b) strengthening the shadow self; or if neither of these works then c) altering and transforming the old self in a way that works. This new ego-state is only realized when brought into waking life and acted upon in the waking state (stage 1).

The net result of a successful resolution phase is some form of closure or stability in the psyche. The state of renewed inner harmony may be fleeting however, since there are always so many stimuli to be processed, personal myths to be dealt with and alienated fragments of self awaiting integration. As Jung indicates, the process of "individuation" is one of cyclic evolution and is never totally completed. It is hoped that each cycle will bring about a greater maturity, a heightened awareness of self, and a more mature mythic structure that more closely matches waking experience.

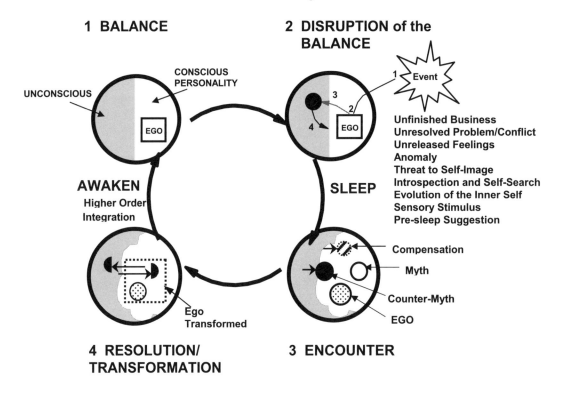

Figure 7
The Dream Cycle

1 BALANCE

CONSCIOUS PERSONALITY

UNCONSCIOUS

EGO

2 DISRUPTION of the BALANCE

1 Event

EGO

Unfinished Business
Unresolved Problem/Conflict
Unreleased Feelings
Anomaly
Threat to Self-Image
Introspection and Self-Search
Evolution of the Inner Self
Sensory Stimulus
Pre-sleep Suggestion

AWAKEN
Higher Order Integration

SLEEP

Compensation

Myth

Counter-Myth

EGO

Ego Transformed

4 RESOLUTION/ TRANSFORMATION

3 ENCOUNTER

Balance

This initial state is described as the waking state where a sense of balance has been achieved. Although a previous resolution or transformation may have taken place, the psyche remains a dual structure of conscious and unconscious parts, thus setting the stage for imbalance and conflict as soon as the environment changes.

As we learned in the last chapter, Jung termed the core of our unconscious being, that from which we evolve as individuals, as the "Self" with a capital S. As we become conscious of ourselves as individuals, our individual ego is formed (the self with a small s), by identifying ourselves with certain characteristics we are comfortable with. We further differentiate ourselves from others by suppressing certain traits we don't like. This differentiation creates conflicting parts (or personality fragments) that reside within the conscious and unconscious. On one side is the ego in all its various states and expressions, plus our personal myths. On the other is the shadow-self along with various alienated fragments, repressed feelings and memories and our counter-myths. Within the deep collective unconscious is the Self that drives both the individuation process (that differentiates the ego) as well as the integration process that brings fragmented parts back together.

Disruption of the Balance

The next phase can occur in the waking state, or can be the result of a waking event that carries over into the dream. Sleep and dreams naturally perform the beneficial role of turning within, shifting the mind's focus from external to internal matters. The particular event that stimulates the dream is likely determined by its emotional importance to us, the degree to which it threatens our inner model, as well as how much energy it contributes to an existing instability, counter-myth or unresolved trauma. Jung indicated that the most pressing unfinished business surfaces first. Even in dream life, the squeaky wheel may be the one that gets the grease. On the other hand, dreams may work on events that are barely noticed or never reach consciousness. Subliminal perceptions (body language for example) follow a different pathway in the brain, never reaching consciousness, yet are stored for later incorporation into a dream. Events that disturb the balance or demand closure can come from many sources:

- **Threat to the internal self** - An unresolved situation that does not immediately fit one's view of reality or self. Or alternatively an event that adds strength to a counter-myth that threatens the existing view of self. It could be an event devastating to the ego, such as being fired from a job, or a lesser event such as a hurtful argument with a friend that stimulates bad memories and self-doubt.
- **Unfinished business** - Jung states that dreams work on unfinished business. Events of the day that you either don't have time to deal with, or that are too emotionally hurtful to deal with, will remain in the subconscious as unfinished business, to be later worked on by the dreaming mind. Unfinished business could be an unresolved emotional problem or conflict within yourself or with another person, or something as simple as a work or school related problem, or some unfinished creative endeavor you are in the middle of.
- **Anomalies** - Experiences that don't quite fit our internal model. Perls indicated that the mind deals with information that doesn't fit by breaking it off into fragments that are at first alienated (cast into the unconscious) and later dealt with.
- **Emotional triggers** – Events that trigger suppressed emotions, emotional memories, instinctive reactions or traumas that are difficult to deal with.

- **Introspection or self-search** - The inner disruption may also be the result of introspection, an inner search, a self-discovery or the emergence of some untapped inner capability that is counter to, or expands, the existing inner view of self.
- **Internal evolution of the Self** - Jung suggests that the unconscious Self is constantly evolving and will make itself known even when no external cause for change exists. I have observed this to occur during periods of relaxation and retreat. Perhaps removal of external pressures provides an opportunity for the inner Self to evolve.
- **External physical or internal organic stimulus** - When you are ill, or some intense sensory stimulus (cold, loud noise) occurs as you sleep, that event often finds its way into your dreams, in some symbolic manner, mixed with the ongoing story line.
- **Pre-sleep suggestion or incubation** - Incubation places a strong suggestion in the mind just prior to sleep, to dream about a subject and to wake up and write down the dream. Perhaps this technique operates on the principle of unfinished business, by increasing the priority of the question just prior to sleep.

Encounter

Emotional associations triggered by the above events enter the dream. Here, we confront our shadow self, and deal with conflict between the inner and outer world. We become aware of the inner self at many levels, and encounter and surrender to the natural organizing forces of the greater Self. You encounter the "alienated" fragments of yourself according to Perls. You encounter material from your collective unconscious (your unrealized potential) and personal unconscious (your experiences and memories) according to Jung and your personal mythic structures according to Feinstein.

Encounter occurs when the event activates latent unconscious or repressed material. The amount of energy it takes to bring this material to the surface can depend on the emotional impact of the event relative to the strength of our existing views, often referred to as "ego boundaries." If our ego boundaries are "thin," then any number of daily events may have the emotional impact to stimulate a dream, and the dream may be filled with material that is always challenging and altering our internal view of self. If our view of self is strong and fairly consistent with our experiences, we may be able to more easily diffuse and accommodate the event and our dreams may be less exciting. If, on the other hand, our view of self is strong but inconsistent with external experiences, then a lot of energy may be held within the unconscious, feeding an existing counter-myth. And, at some point, our dreams may evidence dramatic and explosive releases.

Due to the inherent desire to preserve the existing ego-self, or sustain the existing myth, the dream may represent non-integrated fragments from the unconscious as frightening, dark and threatening images. The fragments that are closer to our accepted model of self, are perhaps the useful objects or more friendly players in the dream. The following "Taco Bell" dream is an example: *"I was trying to get back to a place marked by a bell in order to retrieve a wallet that I had lost, but I could not move due to a black whip, with tentacles attached to it, that was around my neck. The words 'raw ambition' flashed in my mind, as the identity of the whip."* During the dreamwork, the dreamer recognized the bell as the one in the Taco Bell (a fast-food restaurant) commercial, and recalled their jingle "south of the border" as being meaningful. With further work, the dreamer realized that he was allowing his "raw ambition" and the power of his position (the whip), to keep him from experiencing his true value and identity (the wallet), which lay somewhere "south of the border" within the unconscious. The instinctive raw ambition of his shadow side was seen as a black whip that was preventing progress. The sense of inner worth appeared as an object (a wallet). The unconscious, where the dream indicated that true value resided (in essence, the Self), was represented as something unreachable and south of the border (underneath, blocked and foreign). Here the dreamer encountered all elements of the conflict, the ego-self, the shadow self, the conscious myth and the unconscious.

Sometimes we encounter memories associated with similar experiences in the past. As a result, we may experience strange mixtures of scenes from past and present. *"I dreamed I was back in my childhood home, but in the dream I was still living there. My mother was there but she did not look like herself."* The dream may take us back to a point of trauma, and change the event slightly in an effort to transform the decisions and myths created at the time, to better fit the present situation. This was the case in the "mastery" dreams associated with trauma-related nightmares, discussed in chapter 2. It is also common to dream of a parent or loved one who has died, as alive again, perhaps in order to deal with repressed grief or unresolved issues.

What we encounter in a dream, or series of dreams, depends on our state of self-awareness and the state of the ego-self in relationship to the whole self. For example, an ego-self that is comfortable with the shadow-self will see it more as a guiding entity than a dark frightening one, as in the "jokester" dream in chapter 2: *"... an influential shadowy character entered from my left and argued that this jokester had been quite useful and that we should give him a chance."* The unconscious will be seen as something accessible rather than a dark, guarded border, and the Self perhaps as a guiding entity rather than a threatening force, as in the following "book of truth" dream, which I will discuss further in a later chapter: *"I was... looking for the book of truth. Suddenly I saw a wise old man sitting on the left, who pointed down a descending wooden spiral staircase. He said that truth lies down there."*

At some point, the ego-self may accept and integrate with aspects of the shadow: *"As I went down the stairs, I saw on my left a large stone archway and a room beyond. On the left side of this room was a young woman. As the sunlight streamed in she came forward, and I saw that she was me. She walked toward me and we blended into one person."* As more parts of self are accepted into the realm of the conscious ego, more light will enter the dream as conscious awareness "illuminates" and accepts these previously dark unconscious fragments of self. In the above dream the integration took place as the "sunlight streamed in." In the "jokester" dream, as that part of self was accepted, it went into the light: *"... After some discussion I agreed, and the jokester was told he would be given a chance to prove himself. At that point he walked off to the right down a sunlit path."* As emotions are stimulated, color will enter the dream. As emotions are transformed, the color may brighten, appear crystalline or become mixed with white (more on this will be discussed in chapter 9).

The encounter stage is similar in many ways to Hamilton's[105] discussion of the "Albedo" stage of transformation. He observed that dream encounters during this stage reflect where you are in the overall cycle of transformation and state of consciousness. In the earliest stages of transformation, he observed themes of darkness, fear, worldly concerns, animals and elements of our instinctual nature. As the individual transformation proceeded, the dream imagery showed an increase in light, color, beauty, natural landscapes and mythological imagery (archetypes?).

Resolution/Transformation

Once the dreamer has encountered the material associated with the situation that stimulated the dream, a natural tendency toward closure, balance and preservation of the inner self takes place. Jung indicated that there is a natural centering force evidenced in dreams, drawing the ego within to focus on the wholeness of the greater Self, and that dreams attempt to bring about such balance through compensation.[23] Feinstein[19] states that dreams show how your "mythic structure" is failing to account for your waking experience, and that they generate alternative "mythic structures" (counter-myths) to account for these experiences. Perls termed this tendency toward completion "gestalt" and considered it a primary biological phenomenon that any imbalance in the psyche is experienced as a need to correct this imbalance.[15]

Because of the simultaneous holistic nature of a dream, it is often difficult to differentiate between encounter and resolution since both actions often occur in the same dream. Many dreams, such as the "Taco Bell" dream above, will stage an encounter with the involved parts of self, but at the same time present a pattern for completion, often inserting a compensating "message" into the dream story to point the way toward resolution. In that dream it was a subtle message that "one's true identity lies within." A true resolution occurs when the dreaming ego accepts the message and abandons an old myth, or integrates with a previously alienated part of self, as in the "jokester" dream. As

Feinstein stated, dreams re-stabilize the personality in one of three ways: 1) Sustaining the existing myth; 2) Strengthening of the counter-myth; and 3) Integration of the two conflicting myths into a new myth.

1) Sustaining the Existing Myth

Sustaining and preserving the inner model or existing myth, involves assimilating the new, and possibly threatening waking event, into the existing mythic structure. The event may be compared with similar past events to find a fit, or projected into the future in order to dissolve the fears. I have observed that dreams sometimes accommodate the event by modifying or fragmenting it, repressing certain elements and accepting others – much as we do in waking life at times. Evidence of this fragmentation was seen in the following "office party" dream: *"I found myself in charge of an office party that was going on in three of four houses (the fourth was shadowy and incomplete). My job was to bring each of the groups through the woods into a lighted area on the right to join in a circle dance. After bringing the first group to the circle, I got so caught up in the self-importance of my role as leader, that I dallied and by the time I got back to the other three houses, most of the people had left and gone home. They exited into the darkness on the left.* Note that in this dream example some fragments (characters at the party) were incorporated into the conscious personality (the lighted circle dance), but this only seemed to feed the existing myth or complex around which the ego revolved (the role of the ego self as leader). Other fragments of self remained separated, and eventually fell back into the unconscious (party-goers who had returned into the darkness to the left). The dream shows how the ego plays a role in accepting the new parts of self into the conscious personality, and how it can also stand in the way of full integration as it holds too tightly onto the existing myth. The ego must play a role in integration, but also must diminish itself a bit in the process, letting go of the old myth, if new potential is to be integrated and sustained.

2) Strengthening the "counter-myth

Sometimes, when an event threatens our view of self, we suppress it or relegate it to the unconscious. Unfortunately such events do not disappear, they join a complex of similar memories, perhaps strengthening a counter-myth. At some point, a counter-myth may grow strong enough to make itself known, as illustrated in the following "entity" dream: *"I dreamed that a person I consider evil was alive again and realized that an "entity" was at work. I went through a ritual of exorcism, but the more I tried, the darker the sky became. Suddenly a voice said, 'stop - you are only making it worse'."* When we worked on the dream, it was revealed that the "evil" person in the dream was actually a part of herself that she considered evil – a part that threatened her existing self-image or myth. In waking life, this "evil" side of self revealed itself by bursting forth in a somewhat uncontrolled manner, as if some entity was at work. The dream was revealing how her efforts to suppress this perceived "evil" side of self poured more energy into making it evil. The voice in the dream was compensating for the unhealthy behavior by telling the dreamer that her actions were making matters worse.

A counter-myth can appear as an opposing force as above, or as part of the compensating, alternative solution in the dream. The counter-myth can be wonderfully positive, relating to unrealized potential that doesn't fit one's existing self-image. For example, some who see themselves as unable to achieve in life, may discount their greatest achievements and capabilities in order to maintain the comfort of their existing myth. In this case, the counter-myth may evidence itself as something neglected (perhaps a child - the inner child) or as a compensating message in the dream. The following dream illustrates the dreamer's inner value that has been stubbornly hidden away behind the doors of their mythical construct: *"I dreamed I was wandering through my house and I was discovering all sorts of new doors and rooms, many of them filled with a lot of treasures I did not realize I had."*

As you will find later in chapter 8, the conflict of myth and counter-myth can also appear hidden within a dream image or other dream element. Perls stated that the fragments of the personality that we have most alienated, and are least in touch with, appear as the most distant and inhuman imagery in our dreams, the insignificant inanimate objects. In the example given in chapter 8 the counter myth was hidden within the most insignificant image in the dream, a sweet potato.

3) Compensation and Integration of Conflicting Myths into a Higher Order Synthesis

At some point, when daily experiences oppose one's personal myth, or when a counter-myth gains such support and energy that it cannot be accommodated, then the mythic structure must be altered to achieve balance. As Jung and Perls pointed out, this may trigger a natural inner realization that the only way the self can be preserved is through transformation. The conflicting elements will be partly modified and integrated to create a slightly renewed ego-self and a transformed personal myth.

Resolution and transformation might be experienced in dreams as finding the way, finding the key, being shown a previously unseen path, or solving a puzzle as in the following "maze" dream: *"At the end of a long dream, I had to find my way through a liquid, crystal, rectangular game of four squares. The squares were made up of three colors (red, yellow and green) that were constantly changing at a hectic pace. Finally, it appeared that I solved it, as things seemingly fell into place by themselves. The colors now covered the entire surface of the rectangular game, and the colored shapes now changed at a calmer pace. I now felt relaxed, and that there was no longer a need to control the solution. It ended with a complete yellow screen for a moment, then a beautiful snow crystal pattern in light blue and pink tones.*" At the time, the dreamer was fighting to control a threatening situation in his work life. The dream represented his mixed, rapidly changing emotions, as mixed, rapidly changing colors. A partial solution seemed to occur as the shapes changed at a more relaxed pace, and the colors settled on yellow, converging on a crystal ice pattern of blue and pink. The day following the dream, the dreamer felt relaxed and had decided to cooperate and accept the new work assignment. He suddenly began to focus on the positive and potentially enjoyable aspects. When we worked on the dream, using the color work in chapter 9, the dreamer connected with the yellow emotional theme, "I am seeking a solution that will open new possibilities" and with the theme for mixed blue and red, "harmony and cooperation for the benefit of the organization." The dream reflected this change in perception. Note that white often mixes with color to represent a transformation related to the emotions the color represents. Hamilton[105] also observed the appearance of light colors, snow and crystal structures in dreams in the later stages of a transformation cycle.

Jung stated that transformation is achieved through compensation, that the dream "serves the purpose of compensation." It can appear in the form of guiding entities or voices as in the following dream of a middle aged man who was worried about whether he had time in his life to accomplish all he had imagined he would: "*I opened my Journal and was disturbed to see that I only had a few pages left. Suddenly a voice said 'No there is more'. It was then that I realized that I had opened it too far back and indeed there was half a Journal left.*" Compensation can be seen in the parable of the dream story as in this "flowers in my footsteps" dream, where the dreamer was avoiding (running away from) expressing her own creative inner potential: "*I was running through a field trying to get away from something frightening. I looked back, and from within each footstep I took, I could see flowers spring up.*" Compensation can be seen in the bizarre little twists in the dream imagery or imagery combinations as in the "old shoe" dream from chapter 3 where the imagery of his friend as an old shoe became the revealing message.

Often the dream will take the dreamer to the point of transformation, to the verge of the transforming decision, showing the way: "*Some foreigners have invaded and taken over the government. The invaders are gathering us up and the leader, in order to identify and separate the group, announces: "everyone that lives beyond four, tense up." A large group is tensing up and the remainder moved away to the right toward the windows. I am confused, not knowing what the command means or what I should do, since I don't know whether I am within or outside of four. I tense my fists. Someone behind me says, "No, you're OK." I relax and know that I can now move to the right, feeling I am one of the lucky ones allowed to stay. I ask the leader what will happen to the others, and he states that they will be led out (to the left) and dealt with in some (undetermined) fashion."* This "foreign invader" dream will be discussed as a detailed example in chapter 12, where you will learn that the dreamer's self-image and sense of worth (myth) was suddenly threatened by a change in management at work, and pending cutbacks. The myth was a sense of worth tied to external factors; management approval and a successful management career. Unable to determine from his management whether he was "OK," he was frozen with tension. When told by the compensating voice behind him, "no you are OK," the dreamer gained an inner sense of worth without the confirmation of his management. This new sense of self-worth became the new myth that opened the dreamer to consider elements of counter-myth (a more relaxed non-career focus). At that point, certain fragments aligned with the counter-myth, moving to the right into acceptance. The remaining fragments (likely those associated with the old myth) moved to the left to be suppressed into the unconscious. As the dream ended, the dreamer had not moved, but the direction was clear.

When a degree of transformation is achieved, the dream appears to compensate by reinforcing the new decision or direction, often with celebration of light, color and natural beauty as in the "ice cave" dream, discussed in chapter 2. The dreamer was on an endless boat journey in an underground ice cave, and only emerged when he accepted the guidance to take charge of the direction of the boat. *"When I did, the boat emerged from a white ice cave onto a crystal stream in a beautiful, sunlit, colorful land with trees and mountains and singing in the air."*

Often when the dream ends in a degree of resolution, the dreamer will awaken with a feeling of closure. This was the case in the "retirement party" dream I briefly discussed in chapter 2: *"I dreamed that my friends at the office gave me a retirement party. They bring me four presents that are intended to be symbolic of my retirement. The first was popcorn, my favorite snack. The next was a set of wooden skis, representative of my favorite sport. The third is an electric guitar, representing my musical talent. The final gift impressed me in the dream as the greatest of all – but upon waking I could not recall what it was. There were a couple of amazing things about this dream. In waking life, I never had a retirement party and had really wanted one. The dream seemed so real that when I awoke, I felt a sense of closure and satisfaction as if I really had a retirement party. The other amazing thing is that I did not recall the fourth gift until I saw it in a store the next day. It was a golden Tibetan "song" bowl used for meditation.*

It is interesting to note the transformation imagery. For one, the dream seemed to celebrate a transformative event, the completion of one stage of life and entry to another. The four-ness motif (which Jung related to a state of completion) was apparent in the four gifts. The skis and guitar related to elements of the myth that drove the dreamer's prior career life. The popcorn represented a snack (a prior hobby) that would now provide a nourishing new life in retirement. The golden bowl was a golden sphere or symbol of the

Self, which appeared to integrate the gifts into the whole. When the dreamer attempted to role-play the golden bowl, no personal association resulted. As might be expected with an archetype, he instead sensed a powerful energy, a sense of being at the center, bringing all parts together.

This higher order synthesis is in some ways similar to what Hamilton[105] referred to as the Cintrinitas or Rubedo transcendence stages. He stated that it is often difficult to differentiate the boundaries between the two stages (the transcendence and the incorporations of the new awareness into waking life). He indicated that the dreams during this cycle evidenced a dramatic increase in color and light, and the appearance of what he called "clear light." The color combinations tended to be opposites (colors at opposite ends of the spectrum), gold and silver and combinations with white. He observed dream elements aligning more along the vertical (north/south, above and below) and commented that while the "Albedo" (encounter) stage was more a resolution of opposites, this "Cintrinitas" stage indicated a general balancing of the psyche in the form of a cross.

Does this Process Relate to All Dreams?

Dreams rarely obey a set of rules. However, the various classifications of dreams we talked about in chapter 2 appear to, in some way, include parts of the self-preservation/self-transformation process discussed here. In healing dreams we find ourselves trying to deal with threats to self, although in this case the threat is physical harm or illness to our physical self. Regarding paranormal dreams, Ann Faraday[24] once stated that the reasons dreams often contain extrasensory phenomenon is that the ego is using all resources available to it, even paranormal ones, to remain in the "top dog" position. This is her term for preserving the superiority of the ego-self. In lucid dreams, the will of the dreamer may come into play to change the dream, but even this conscious control is not complete. Lucid dream characters don't always cooperate, and images morph in directions the dreamer does not desire, suggesting that a deeper process still goes on. I don't mean to rule out what appears to be valid cases of paranormal or extrasensory events in dreams, but do want to represent the function of a dream in it's proper perspective, even when it contains those events. Even though dreams may contain elements stimulated by physical, chemical or paranormal events, many of the basic processes described in this chapter seem to continue in the background.

CHAPTER 6
WORKING WITH DREAM IMAGERY

The Unconscious aspect of any event is revealed to us in dreams, where it appears not as a rational thought but as a symbolic image – C.G. Jung[4]

What we experience in dreams is both visual and non-visual. Up until this point, I have mostly referred to dream content in terms of imagery, i.e., the visual content. When working with a dream, it is wise to consider all of the content, or dream "elements," some of which are not visual. The following is a categorization of the dream elements to be considered when reviewing and working with a dream. It is derived from a listing in *The Mythic Path* by Feinstein and Krippner[77] and based on the Hall, Van de Castle content analysis categorizations (with voice and words split out as a separate category). The first group, including characters, setting, objects, nature, certain activity and descriptors (color and shape for example) are primarily visual, and therefore might fall under what I have been referring to as imagery. Sensations, dream emotion and certain other descriptors (fast, heavy, warm, for example) are primarily non-visual elements of a dream that are just as important to consider as the visual imagery. Spoken or written words are both visual and non-visual and are very important elements in the dream that can often relate to compensation.

- Character – a person or people, or some animated object or creature that you interact with as a person
- Setting – the place or environment of the dream
- Object – something inanimate including buildings, vehicles, tools, clothing, gadgets, weapons, communications equipment etc.
- Nature – plants or animals or the natural elements, including earth, fire, air, water
- Activity – interactions between dream elements, including you or other characters
- Descriptors – Adjectives and adverbs, shapes, color, size
- Words and Voices – spoken or written messages
- Sensations – such as touch, sounds, smell and other sensory perceptions
- Emotions – feelings in the dream

Composition of a Dream Image

In chapters 3 and 4, I introduced the concept of condensation, whereby multiple elements combine within a dream image. Descriptors are obvious examples of combined dream elements. For example, dreaming of a *"red car"* is an obvious combination of red and car, or a dream of a *"male child"* is a combination of male and child. Also, a bizarre dream image like the one in figure 4 is an obvious combination of two associations - one related to the thermometer and another to the slide rule. A particular dream element might contain personal memories, emotions, perceptions, and contextual associations with the experiences that created the dream. That dream element might also be influenced by collective content, including unconscious, instinctual and biological patterns and forces. For example, a dream of a *"square black poker table"* might be a combination of the dreamer's personal associations with "poker table," but might also be influenced by the collective imagery of shape (square) and color (black). It is important to realize that any dream element can be a combination or condensation of multiple elements symbolically representing both: 1) personal content and 2) collective content.

Figure 8
The Composition of a Dream Image

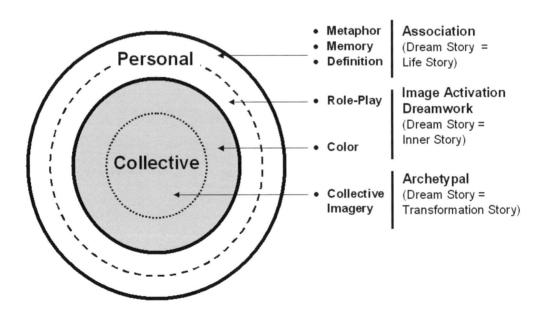

Figure 8 illustrates this concept. The circle represents the combination of personal and collective content within a dream image or element. Personal content includes symbolic representations of the dreamer's personal memories, thoughts and emotional experiences that stimulated the dream image. When the dream is told, the personal content is translated into figurative speech and metaphors descriptive of the dreamer's waking life situation. At a deeper level, personal content also includes fragments of self and elements of the dreamer's personal mythology that are activated by the situation the dream is dealing with.

Collective content includes those elements referred to by Jung as instinctive in nature, emerging from the unconscious, outside of your personal experiences. This includes the archetypal imagery discussed in the previous chapter. I also consider the appearance of dream color to be largely collective, due to the instinctual nature of our emotional response to color. Although color can have cultural and personal associations, it is the instinctual or autonomic response to which I refer here. The nature of personal and collective elements, including color, will be discussed later in this chapter, and in more detail in chapters 7 through 9.

The principle of condensation is best illustrated through an example. An obvious condensation of elements is seen in the following "change purse" dream: *In my dream I was having a long dialogue with an associate about an upcoming battle. When I awoke, I realized that I had been talking to a leather change purse! My associate in the dream was a slightly rounded, but rectangular shaped, zippered change purse, red on the top side and a green-brown color on the underside. I kept flip-flopping it over in my hands, trying to decide which side and color I liked best.* The dream came at a time of a pending "battle" that involved an organizational change, and the dreamer's perceived value in contributing to this change. The metaphors of the "pending battle" and the "change purse" were recognizable figures of speech that related the dream story to the waking life situation. The key dream image appears to be the change purse. Aside from the "change" metaphor, there were two additional combinations of elements in the change purse image. First the change purse was a bizarre combination of an inanimate object and a human character, making this object appear as a human companion to the dreamer. The second was the combination of the change purse image with color (in this case two colors). The dreamer was in conflict ("flip-flopping") over whether to pursue the situation with an assertive, win-oriented, "red" style, or to apply a bit more self-control and not take on so much responsibility, as the color green-brown might imply. You will learn more about these specific emotional associations with color later, but it is important to note that the condensation of color with the image played a key role in establishing the full identity of the dream image.

Peeling the "Dream Onion"
Working with the Layers

Figure 8 illustrates that a dream image can contains many layers or levels of meaningful content. It also hints that there are different approaches for dealing with each layer, including Associative, Image Activation and Archetypal. The objective is to discover the personal associations and mental processes that originally created the dream image. Each approach deals a bit differently with the dream and the dream imagery, and can be applied based on the nature and depth of dreamwork desired. In chapters 10 through 12, you will learn in more detail how to work with dreams using these approaches.

The first layer of dream exploration is personal association. The associative approach is mainly cognitive and consists of such techniques as recognizing metaphors or picture language in the dream and dream imagery. It also involves deeper associations, such as recalling memories of which the dream image reminds you, or defining the dream image in order to bring personal associations to the surface. Although underlying emotions can surface at this level of dreamwork, this approach typically relates the dream story to waking life events.

A deeper approach that I developed explores the underlying emotional issues, motivations and personal myths playing out within the dream story. I call it Image Activation dreamwork. The term "activation" relates to the ability of the technique to activate the emotional content within a dream element. At the core of this approach is a role-play technique derived from Gestalt therapy, but greatly condensed into a six-question script that is targeted at revealing underlying feelings, conflicts and personal myths. At this level of dreamwork, the dream story is related to the dreamer's inner story.

Exploring the instinctual emotional content contained within dream color requires yet another technique. Integral to Image Activation dreamwork is a technique for working with color, which relies on suggesting emotional themes in order to trigger the dreamer's own associations with the emotions represented by the color in the dream.

Finally, working at the archetypal level, we explore the unconscious forces at work. Recognizing and working with collective imagery: a) provides clues that help orient you to the dream and select dream elements to work on and b) at a deeper level brings about an intuitive feel for the forces at work in the dream. This archetypal level of dreamwork therefore relates the dream story to the integration and transformational story underlying the dream.

Personal Content

As noted above, personal content relates to personal and cultural associations, personal memories and recalled emotional experiences that are contained symbolically within a dream element. These associations differ from the instinctive, physiological or unconscious influences that are not direct reflections of the dreamer's personal experiences and memories. It is important to realize that a dream element can contain multiple levels of personal content. The dream element can contain something as simple as the expression of a thought in a picture form, a figure of speech that relates to the waking life events, or an emotional memory from some past experience that relates to the present experience. At a deeper level, personal content can represent an expression of emotion, non-integrated fragments of your personality, and elements of your personal mythology that are associated with the event that stimulated the dream.

You will generally find personal content within such dream elements as the characters and objects in the dream; the visual dream imagery. The setting of the dream, or certain actions and feelings, may bring forth personal memories as well. Personal content may not be immediately obvious in a dream element. The content is typically revealed when the dream element is described or re-enacted in a way that creates figurative phrases that are descriptive of both the dream and the dreamer's waking life experience. It is the figurative phrases and metaphors that emerge when telling the dream, or working on a dream element, that generally reveal the personal content. The diagram in figure 8 implies four basic dreamworking approaches for revealing personal content in a dream element: metaphor, memories, definition and role-play. The procedures for working with each approach will be presented in chapters 8 and 10.

Collective Content

The term "collective imagery" was introduced by Jung to represent dream content emerging from the collective unconscious of the human psyche, elements that are not individual and cannot be derived from the dreamer's own personal experiences. Jung linked these motifs to the evolution of consciousness, the unconscious development of mind and biological evolution in archaic humans, an evolution that, to some degree, is still taking place.

Collective images are what Jung called "archetypes" or "primordial images." They are manifestations of our collective unconscious and instinctual nature. Whereas instincts are usually perceived as an emotional reaction or experience, they also manifest as fantasies and reveal themselves as symbolic imagery.[4] According to Jung, these emotional manifestations, to which the various thought patterns of our dream imagery belong, are recognizably the same all over the world, particularly as we study human mythology that is common across cultures. The universal hero myth is an example that flows through every culture over recorded history, and is the theme of many of the most popular stories and movies in the American culture. It is the theme of the lone, powerful, super man or god-like being, which vanquishes evil in its various forms (serpents, monsters, demons, or in our contemporary society super-criminals, corporate corruption, environmental crime and such). Also, the theme of transcendence often accompanies periods of transition in a person's life. Transcendence reveals itself as release from any confining pattern of existence, another popular theme that motivated the spirit of revolution against constraint throughout history, and which we also find as a popular theme in our contemporary stories and movies.

An archetypal theme may manifest itself as a visual image in a dream. What Jung termed the Anima and Animus may appear as a representation of a male dreamer's feminine side or a female dreamer's masculine side respectively. The wise old man or goddess may appear as a representation of the guiding, organizing and compensating forces of the inner Self. The instinctive, lesser known "not me" side of our ego-self, may manifest itself as the "shadow," often in the form of a dark shadowy unknown character of the same sex that may either frighten, challenge or guide us depending on our relationship with this side of self.

These archetypal forces may also manifest themselves as patterns of psychic growth and organizing patterns relating to closure, balance and transcendence. Geometric patterns, numbers, color, illumination and darkness, or patterns of movement and directional orientation, might be representative of integration processes taking place. Activities, such as circular or spiral motion or moving around a square, even the spiral motion of a tornado, may be collective patterns representing a natural unconscious sense of order. The balanced shapes and mandala patterns, or center-oriented spirals and circular motions that we see in dreams, may be natural organizing patterns representing a desired state of balance or focal point for the ego. Jung states that the mandala is a symbol of the transcendent self, which serves both to restore a previously existing order, as well as to give expression and form to something new and unique that does not yet exist.[4, 23, 28] These collective patterns will be discussed in more detail in the next chapter.

Collective elements in the dream may be found within the descriptors, such as the shape or color of an object, or its direction of movement. Nature imagery (trees, rocks, earth imagery, fire, air, water, etc.) may represent the collective origins of the psyche and animals our collective instinctual nature.[4] Also, dream emotions and sensations may be collective representations in that they arise from our physiological and instinctual nature. An important collective element is the appearance of words or the spoken word in a dream. This often represents a compensating element or counter-myth, as discussed in the last chapter.

Recognizing collective imagery can be very useful in orienting yourself to the dream and organizing your dreamwork. Working with collective imagery, in a way that permits you to experience its essence directly, can also provide valuable insight into the forces at work in the dream and within your inner self. Both of these concepts will be discussed further in chapter 7.

Dream Color

It is curious that there has been little work done with color in dreams. This motivated my own investigation of the subject. I am often asked whether dreams are in color or black and white, even though the research on this question was completed over a decade ago. Indeed, research in the sleep lab determined that the majority of our dreams are in color.[37] Bob Van de Castle reports that when dreamers were awakened during a dream, distinct color was reported in 70% of the cases and vague color in another 13%. Why then do most people perceive dreams as colorless? It appears to be related to recall. Spontaneous non-laboratory dream reports (normal daily dream recall) indicate that only about 25% to 29% of dreamers recall color, based on studies by Van De Castle and Hall respectively. This increased to 50% for art students in one study cited by Van De Castle.

So why don't we recall the color in our dreams? Recalling color is likely subject to the same mechanisms as recalling any image in a dream, or remembering the dream at all! As discussed in chapter 2, dream recall when we are awakened during the dream is around 80%, similar to that of color recall. Although we typically spend a quarter of our night in four or more dream cycles, how many dreams and how much of the content do you remember in the morning, if any?

Perhaps our state of consciousness just prior to waking has something to do with color recall. Hartmann[1] reports that people awakened from REM sleep report more story-like and colorful dreams, whereas reports from the deeper NREM state of sleep are more thought-like with little story line or color. The nature or degree of consciousness may also affect color recall. LaBerge[9] has indicated that the EEG state during lucid dreaming (where you are conscious that you are dreaming), is in many ways similar to the conscious waking state, and lucid dreams are frequently reported in full color. As discussed in the last chapter, Hamilton[105] observed that color and light increased with increases self-awareness and progress toward personal transformation.

Whatever the mechanism for color recall, I consider the lack of ability to recall all of the colors somewhat of a blessing when working with color in dreams. It is possible that we tend to recall dream imagery, and thus color, that contains the more significant emotional content. This is supported in principle by Hartmann's contention that emotional content increases the intensity of a dream image.[86] If this is the case, then the colors that remain dominant in your dream report might be those that are the most revealing when working on the dream.

So what about the situation in which you recall a dream, or most of your dreams, in full color? When the whole dream is in color, I recommend that you work on the color associated with an important dream image that you intend to work on. In that way, you can gain two perspectives on the dream image.

Also, choose unique colors or a dream image where the color can be optional. For example, if you dream of green grass and blue sky, the color may reveal little of importance since those are the colors commonly associated with those images in waking life. Instead pick something like a red car (that could just as easily been blue), or an object that has unique colors as in the previous "change purse" dream example (where the object was red on one side and green-brown on the other).

In chapter 9, I will discuss the results of an investigation on the significance of color. I will also present a methodology for working with color in dreams. As I mentioned briefly above, the investigation led me to conclude that color in dreams contains emotional and instinctual associations, similar in nature to what Jung attributed to collective imagery. Early laboratory results with color revealed that the human nervous system responds to color at an unconscious, autonomic level.[25,33] Our physiology and brain respond very differently, and in a somewhat predictable fashion, to being illuminated by certain colors. Red, as one might suspect, stimulates our autonomic nervous system, increasing heart rate and breathing. Blue, on the other hand, calms the nervous system, reducing heart rate and breathing. This all happens at an unconscious level and is similar, in many ways, to the effect certain emotions have on our autonomic nervous system.

A primary mechanism, in generating the human response to color, may be the role the limbic system plays in associating emotion with sensory input. Associating emotion with sensory input is part of our attention system, necessary for self-preservation. If the limbic system assigns emotion to the images that we sense, then it is logical that it would also assign emotion to the colors we sense. When we consider the limbic system and the autonomic nervous system working together, it seems likely that there is a meaningful association between human emotional response and color.

Since all of the color research was based on color response in the waking state, I could only speculate that color in dreams is similar to waking emotional responses to color. I proceeded on this basis with my investigation, discussed in chapter 9. What I observed was that, indeed, specific dream colors appeared to contain specific emotional associations similar to associations in the waking state. I based the color dreamwork on the emotional themes associated with color, as derived from studies in the field of color psychology. I will discuss how to use that knowledge for dreamwork in the later chapters.

The way the brain processes color and imagery might provide a further clue as to how and why color combines with a dream image. Visual processing is distributed so that color is processed in a separate brain center than shape and other aspects of the visual image.[38] The information from the different centers of the brain are then integrated in some way to form the visual image that we "see." If color and imagery are likewise processed in separate centers when dreaming, and knowing that the dreaming brain stimulates itself from within, it is quite possible that color and imagery are stimulated by separate but associated emotional stimuli. If this is the case, then both the color and the shape of the dream image could contain valuable content. Working on the dream image, and not the color, would leave out a great deal of important information.

My investigation leads me to believe that the combination of image and color provides the true and total meaning of a dream image. Furthermore, as you will see in chapter 9, I have observed that some dream imagery evokes emotional associations that seem counter to the dreamers waking state of mind, until the color modifier is considered and understood.

Condensation of Personal
and Collective Content

Collective Influence

The influence of collective content on a dream image is best illustrated through an exercise. In chapter 3 we did an exercise with the image of a door that was illustrated in figure 5. In that exercise we defined the function of the door image in order to reveal its personal associations. If you did that exercise, then go back and review what you stated at the time. We are going to try the exercise again, but with a twist this time as described in the box below.

Figure 9
Exercise in Collective Influence

 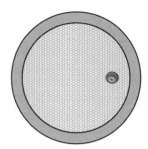

TRY THIS

1) Review the "function" you associated with the brown door in figure 5 or, if you did not do that exercise, look at the door on the left in figure 9. Close your eyes and imagine it in your mind's eye as a wooden door.
2) Define the purpose or function of this wooden door.
3) Now look at the door on the left in figure 9 again. Close your eyes and imagine it in your mind's eye as a rectangular <u>BLUE</u> door.
4) Define the purpose or function of this new BLUE door.
5) Now look at only the round door on the right in figure 9. Close your eyes and imagine the round door in any color you wish.
6) Define the purpose or function of this door.
7) Did your associations with the door change, with different colors and shapes, from that of the original rectangular brown door in figure 5?

If you had the same experience as most people with this exercise, you will have noticed that the purpose or function you attributed to the blue door and the round door changed from the original rectangular brown door. If a door is a door, then why are the associations different? Changing the shape and color of the door image changed its personal associations for you. Your responses may have changed based on a common waking life association (the round door might have reminded you of a ship's porthole for example) or your associations may have been surprisingly more esoteric than that, perhaps changed by something of a less conscious nature (finding something mystical behind the round door for example). Responses to this exercise always differ among individuals, but often the rectangular brown door relates to a control or safety function, permitting people in or out. When the door is imagined as blue, the responses change to a calmer less guarded association, more open or opportunity related. More on color association will be discussed in chapter 9.

Blending Cultural and Personal with Collective

Although I have presented a distinct contrast between collective and personal imagery here, the contrast may not be all that distinct in reality. Cultural and personal associations may condense with, or even dominate, what appears to be a collective element in a dream. It is always advisable to investigate personal associations before trying to form an understanding of the dream story from collective clues alone. I will mention a few cases here, which commonly cause confusion in dreams.

Numbers

Jung stated that numbers are not concepts for calculation consciously invented by man. He considered them as spontaneous and autonomous products of the unconscious, and thus archetypes.[4] The collective significance of numbers will be described in more detail in chapter 7, and is summarized in figure 10. Numbers with collective significance can appear in dreams as individual numbers (for example 4 as a motif for completeness) or multiple digits related to some other stage in the integration process (for example 75 representing the wholeness motif of 100 or the circle, but with a missing quarter). Sometimes, number sequences can represent various states of integration, conflict and patterns of completions. Number patterns, such as 11, 22 or longer strings such as 10201, might be representative of conflicting forces of "equal value" at play.

It is just as likely, however, that numbers or number sequences can have a personal association. Numbers in dreams can relate to the year of an event, or the age of the dreamer now, or at some time in the past or future, associated with the event the dream is focused on. *"I dreamed of a long-standing conflict that I have had between the direction that my career is taking me versus my own personal goals in life. Both conditions are equally attractive to me but take me in different directions. The number 4 appeared in pairs in various ways in the dream."* In this dream, there seemed to be a collective significance of the pair of fours, i.e. conflict between two conditions that are both satisfying (complete) in and of themselves. When we explored the personal associations however, it turned out that 44 also related to the dreamer's age at the time she entered this career, as well as to a personal item significant to the situation. Both the collective and personal significance seem valid. The "hide 45" dream from chapter 2 is another example of numbers relating to age, in this case as a birth date that the dreamer wanted a "license" to hide: *"I dreamed I saw a license plate with the words 'HIDE 45'."*

Numbers can have Personal Associations:
- Date (yr), Age
- Recalled Association such as an address
- Beliefs (Numerology for example)

Numbers can have Cultural Associations:
- 7 is considered spiritually significant and related to levels of consciousness in many cultures

Numbers can appear as "Collective" Patterns:
- Patterns relate to unification of the self (Jung)
- Numbers related to Geometric Patterns (for example 4 as related to the square, both symbolic of a state of completion)

In anomalous dreams, although rare, numbers might even be literal. You might recall the example in chapter 2 where the phone number in the dream was an actual working number which the dreamer called the next day, leading to a much needed bond of friendship that the dream story had related to. *"I dreamed I was searching for my lost child and was desperate to find a phone that would work. I suddenly saw a phone number."* The appearance of numbers in dreams can also be related to cultural or personal beliefs, as in the study of numerology. It is best to check these personal associations first when working with numbers in dreams, and then look for the collective significance.

Dream Characters - Known and Unknown

When working with dream characters, you will likely get a different result if the character is someone you know in waking life versus an unknown or ill-defined characterization. As indicated above, the unknown, ill-defined or shadowy characters are generally unconscious in origin and collective in nature, thus relatively inaccessible. For example, a male character or female character may appear in order to represent masculine or feminine forces. This is not the case, however, when the character is a person you know, or who represents a distinct role you might relate to (such as a chef, a nurse, a fireman or such). In this case, your personal associations with a specific person or their role may dominate the content within the dream image.

Sometimes the known person in your dream will represent themselves, but this usually only occurs when the dream is dealing with a situation that directly involves that person. If your dream character is a person you know in your waking life, I frequently find that your dream has "borrowed" that person to represent a personality trait or characteristic that you associate with them. The dream usually relates their personality to some aspect of your own personality. It may be a characteristic that you have been exhibiting either too much of, or too little of, in the situation the dream is relating to. Alternatively, the dream character may represent compensation, a person that has a personality characteristic you could use to better handle the situation. Perhaps they have a similar personality to yours, but more refined in that they seem to be able to deal with a similar situation more easily than you.

Natural versus Man-Made Imagery

In chapter 4, I briefly discussed the Jungian concept of archetypal imagery that includes nature motifs. Jung related these largely collective organic and inorganic nature motifs to symbols of the Self, symbols of transcendence and rebirth. These might include natural beauty and earth symbols such as the stone and the great tree: *"I had climbed into an enormous tree. My child was with me and was fascinated with the view. We sat for a long time among the leaves, feeling the gentle spring air, and looking out over the most beautiful valley I have ever seen with distant mountains and lush meadows and woods. On the branches was a thick layer of freshly fallen white snow, and the child was playing with it."* Nature motifs also include mythically-significant creatures such as the snake, fish and bird; fire or earth-fire combinations such as a volcano; air symbols such as the sun, moon, stars and the air itself; and water symbols including ice and snow.

Being of a collective origin, nature imagery may be difficult to personally associate with. On the other hand, organic and inorganic images that have a distinguishing personality, characteristic, feature or function, may contain meaningful personal associations. The image of a crystal stream, for example, may be collectively symbolic of "the source of life," but may also contain a sense of feeling "refreshed" that may be important to the dreamer's waking life experience. It is always useful to test collective imagery for personal associations, even if experienced more as feelings than words.

Whereas natural imagery is typically dominated by collective content of an instinctual nature, man-made objects or imagery in a dream tends to relate more to personal associations, conscious mental creations or concepts. The airplane in the "Latin priest" dream, for example, related to new religious concepts being studied by the dreamer. Depending on the role, machines might be metaphorically related to the "mechanical" nature of a behavior pattern, or a "mechanism" for progressing or achieving some goal, as has been observed in certain vehicle dreams. I have observed, as has Patricia Garfield,[5] that man-made objects, such as machinery, plumbing, buildings and cars, can sometimes relate to parts of the physical body (our vehicle), with broken machinery often relating to disease or sickness. In any case, it is a dreamer's personal associations with the mechanical object in the dream that is important to understanding that image in the dream.

Exercise
Recognizing Collective and Personal Combinations

This exercise is intended to help you recognize the various types of dream elements or imagery in your dream.

1) Look through one of your more interesting dreams, and using the listing at the beginning of this chapter, underline the dream elements that fit each category (character, object, setting, nature, activity, words or voices, sensations, emotions and descriptors).

2) Circle dream imagery that appears as a combination, i.e., a descriptor and the image it describes, such as a soft kitten, a dark hallway, a square room, or color descriptors such as a black car or green door. Write down your associations with the image apart from the descriptor – perhaps define the image and its function. Now write down your feelings associated with that descriptor (such as soft, dark, square, etc.). Place the two associations together to create a phrase or sentence. Can you sense how the combination of the collective and the personal association brings a different or fuller meaning to the image?

3) Next look at the imagery that has a clear geometric shape such as a square or circle or spiral, for example a tornado, which combines clouds and spiral motion. Look for objects or characters that are oriented around a geometric pattern such as four people sitting around a square table, or for activities that have a geometric pattern such as moving around in a circle.

4) Identify the known dream characters that are familiar from waking life. These you can form direct personal associations with. Identify those that are unknown and perhaps shadow-like.

CHAPTER 7
WORKING WITH COLLECTIVE IMAGERY
ARCHETYPES OF THE DREAM PROCESS

Just as the human body represents a whole museum of organs, each with a long evolutionary history, so we should expect to find that the mind is organized in a similar way – C.G. Jung[4]

Jung spoke of archetypes as a manifestation of the collective unconscious. He found a relationship between what he termed primordial or archetypal imagery in dreams and similar images and patterns found in alchemy and human mythology.[4, 17] Furthermore, he attributed psychological importance to the collective patterns that appear in both our dreams and our waking life drawings, paintings and mandala creations.

Working with Collective Imagery

The collective motifs and patterns that appear in your dreams are representations of unconscious forces. As with any dream imagery, imagery of an unconscious origin must be understood within the context of the dream and the dreamer's own associations. Therefore, avoid using the discussion herein as a "symbol dictionary" to interpret the meaning of a dream. As you recognize collective imagery in your dreams, remember that the qualities attributed to that imagery in this chapter are only suggestions to be explored.

Dream Orientation

Recognizing collective patterns can provide clues that allow you to find a better fit between the dream story and the waking life story. For example, in the following dream, recognition of collective patterns helped identify the role of the imagery in the integration process. *"I dreamed that I was watching two men boxing for sport, one was wearing red trunks and the other brown. Over to the left, I saw a shadowy figure of a dead body."* The first collective clue I noted was that the boxers were a pair of similar images (two males). As you will learn further on in this chapter, the appearance of a pair of similar elements can relate to conflict. Perhaps the different colored shorts related to the two sides of the conflict. We therefore worked on the two boxers using both role-play and color association techniques that will be discussed further in the later chapters. Although the boxers were identical (except for the shorts), the role-play and color work revealed that each boxer represented a different side of the conflict in the dreamer's life. The dreamer was also very curious about the dead body. This was the second collective clue. The figure was shadow-like, unknown, and oriented to the left, and therefore was likely an archetypal image with unconscious origins. We decided to pursue a role-play approach, even though it was unlikely that such an image would contain associations with a waking life event. While playing the role of the dead body, the dreamer stated: "I fear death" and then "I desire release." As suspected, neither statement related to waking life events or feelings. The statements did, however, relate to the very nature of the archetypal image, and provided further clues as to the nature of the forces within it. The statements appeared to relate to the collective cycle of "death and rebirth," that we discussed in chapters 4 and 5. Furthermore, there appeared to be a compensating message of sorts in the statement. The dreamer related this to needing to let some old attachments "die" (something she feared) in order to "release" herself (something she desired). This resistance to letting go was at the core of the conflict associated with the boxers.

Collective Insight

As illustrated in the "boxer" dream, using personal association techniques with an archetypal dream image rarely relates the image to a real-life personal event. Attempting to form waking life associations with a geometric shape, or an unknown shadowy male or female character in your dream, for example, may be difficult since these images originate from deep within the unconscious, a part of self we have little access to. On the other hand, as that same example illustrated, you may gain valuable insights into the deeper forces at work in the dream. An attempt at personal work with an archetype, which leads to an awareness or an experiencing of the forces within it, can be quite beneficial. In the boxer dream, the role-play statements revealed the very essence of the forces at play in the dream, as well as the compensating message. Even working with something as basic as the image of a "sphere" might lead to statements such as *"I feel complete and whole"* or insights such as *"I had a sense of completeness, a feeling of power and of drawing all the other parts into myself."* Expect insight, not direct association, when using personal imagery techniques on collective imagery.

Jeremy Taylor[96-98] indicates that all dreams reveal recurring archetypal patterns of symbolic form and meaning, which can be named and raised to greater conscious self-awareness. Jeremy uses group projective dreamwork (which will be further discussed in chapter 10) as the foundation of this work. He combines personal, associative perspectives with larger amplifications and explorations at the collective and transpersonal levels. Jeremy contributed the following personal thoughts on exploring archetypes: "When these explorations are successful in 'unpacking' a dream, or series of dreams, it most often engenders an increased awareness of deep shared common humanity, even among previously hostile parties. Encouraging people to focus attention on these archetypal patterns in their dreams, as well as in their waking lives, not only has demonstrable therapeutic effects, it is also a surprisingly effective strategy for promoting reconciliation and facilitating non-violent social and cultural change."

The Realm of the Conscious and Unconscious

The Unconscious

Theoretically, the unconscious realm can contain: threatening and suppressed material; fearful or uncomfortable fragments of self; counter-myths unacceptable to the ego-self; your shadow self and instinctual forces. For this reason unconscious material may naturally appear dark, shadowy and frightening. Undesirable fragments of our personality that threaten the existence of our image of self, might be seen as something evil or threatening, the monsters in our dreams. When representations of the greater Self arise from the unconscious, they may appear as the unknown characters in our dreams. Unconscious instinctual forces can appear metaphorically as the animals or primitive human forms. Suppressed material might emerge as dead things, as fragments of self that have been "dead" to our conscious persona. Because suppressed material is "frozen" into inaction, it may appear as characters encased in ice. *"I dreamed that some friends and I wanted to go sailing, but when we arrived at the lake we realized that the lake was frozen and our boat was encased in ice under the surface."* Isolating yourself emotionally from a situation can also appear as being encased in ice. *"I dreamed my daughter was lying dead on a pile of ice cubes."*

As our ego consciousness becomes more self-aware and comfortable with the inner self, the unconscious elements may appear as beautiful, dramatic and exciting. Black becomes a beautiful shiny black; discoveries become joyful and things of value appear, such as gems, gold and silver; unknown characters become guiding god-like entities. Jung indicated that dreams "differentiate the undifferentiated portions of the personality," i.e., they bring forth and identify one's inner hidden potential and help bring about the evolution of the greater Self.[4] This evolving inner potential can emerge as fascinating dramatic natural elements (volcanoes or tornadoes) or as beautiful nature imagery such as the tree (or tree of life), crystal waters of life, symbols of rebirth, or the new, yet wise child: *"We were admiring my new baby girl, her face was not that of an infant but was almost the face of a middle-aged woman – very mature and wise looking."*

The organizing forces, as mentioned previously, may appear as center-oriented geometric patterns or integrations of opposites. As the ego-self fears or resists the unconscious, the inner Self will try to compensate, by showing its beauty, guiding us gently or not so gently, or with symbolic compensating statements as in the "waters of the unconscious" dream: *"the water is your unconscious, jump in and you will be fine."*

Conscious Personality

The conscious realm of the psyche, or personality, contains: personal memories; the ego-self and its various states and behaviors; and your personal mythic structure. The characters we know in our dreams usually represent characteristics we recognize from our waking experience, and are thus from the conscious realm. The roles we play, as the dreamer in our dreams, are also part of our conscious personality. The friendly, cooperative or well-defined characters may also represent fragments, behaviors and states of the ego-self that we are familiar with. We may use objects in the dream (vehicles, cars, airplanes, other tools) that represent how we are progressing or achieving our objectives in our waking lives.

Our personal mythology may represent itself in the story of the dream. In the "ice cave" dream discussed in chapter 2, the dreamer spent most of the night confined in a boat lost on a journey through endless caves and tunnels: *"I dreamed all night that I was on a long journey as a passenger in an enclosed boat going nowhere, just aimlessly moving through tunnels and underground caves."* This only resolved itself when the ego-self abandoned the myth, in this case the myth of being a "helpless passenger in life." *" At one point in the journey a shadow-like character urged me to take charge of the boat's direction. When I did, the boat emerged from a white ice cave onto a crystal stream in a beautiful, sunlit colorful land with trees and mountains and singing in the air."* The unconscious compensating force (the shadow-like character) presented another option to the conscious ego-self, and reinforced this "take charge" counter-myth with the celebration of a successful ending. As Jung stated, it is the ego-self that must involve itself in the process of accepting the new myth into the consciousness personality.

Directionality

Jung discussed right-left orientation of dream imagery in relationship to conscious and unconscious material respectively, as it emerges in the dreamscape. He observed a tendency for conscious or transcending material to appear on the right and above, and for unconscious material to appear to the left, below or into the background in dreams [4]. He also discussed directionality as it related to movement in the dream, and as it is associated with the spiral: leftward or counterclockwise motion as being toward the unconscious; and rightward or clockwise motion as being toward consciousness [28].

There may be biological factors influencing the left-right orientation in dreams. Dream orientation has a curious correlation with the eye's left and right visual fields being separately processed by the right and left brain hemispheres respectively. It is known that these two brain hemispheres process information differently. Might it be that the left and right orientations in the dreamscape are representative of these processing differences?

There is evidence that information-processing differences may be associated with left and right field of vision. Penfield and Roberts found that stimulation of certain portions of the right hemisphere produced eye shifts to the left, and vice versa.[cited in 10] Day found that direction of eye movement is fairly consistent for each individual, when shifting from a passive to an active mode (e.g., when answering a question or writing).[cited in 45] A person will generally look at a speaker when asked a question, but generally look away when answering. Some research has shown that those who look away to the left are generally those who are "right brain" dominant, and those that look to the right have greater "left brain" involvement in overall functioning.[10]

If directionality in dreams has something to do with hemispheric processing, then the characters and images that are to the left in dreams should exhibit a relationship to the characteristics of right hemisphere processing. Referring to table 3-2, the dream elements that emerge from the left (right brain processing) should relate to: anomalous experiences that don't fit the inner model; unprocessed or unresolved emotional and social situations including repressed threatening emotional memories and traumas; representations in the form of analogies and metaphor; value representations; insights and forces that attempt integration in a holistic, synthetic manner as well as the reference image (the Gestalt) for the whole self. This sounds similar to the imagery and forces referred to by Jung as emerging from the unconscious (left) in dreams.

Likewise images to the right in dreams should relate to left hemisphere processes. Thus dream elements that emerge from the right should relate to: storylines and compensating events which take the ego through a time sequential deductive learning process; things that can be named; consciously accessible memories; spoken or written words; and behaviors or information with which we are comfortable because it fits our "rational" model of self and reality. These are very close to the characteristics attributed by Jung to the conscious realm and the right orientation in dreams.

Also, as material is accepted into and recognized by our rational consciousness, it would make sense that it would move "into the left hemisphere" and thus toward the right field of vision in dreams. The "jokester" dream in chapter 2 illustrated right-oriented movement when a new part of self was accepted into the personality: *"a shadowy character entered from my left and argued that this jokester had been quite useful and that we should give him a chance. After some discussion I agreed, and the jokester character was told he would be given a chance to prove himself. At that point he walked off to the right down a sunlit path."*

This right-left orientation was also illustrated in the "office party" dream, in which right and light were associated with the conscious ego-self, and left was associated with fragments of the personality left behind: *My job was to bring each of the groups through the woods into a lighted area on the right to join in a circle dance. After bringing the first group to the circle, I got so caught up in the self-importance of my role as leader, that I dallied. By the time I got back to the other three houses, most of the people had left and gone home. They exited into the darkness on the left.*

Note that conscious and unconscious differentiation in dreams is not exclusively seen as left/right, East/West horizontal orientation. Often a vertical organization such as above/below, North/South or ascending/descending represents the duality of conscious and unconscious. Consciousness is often seen as in front or ahead, while unconscious elements may appear from behind, as illustrated in the "foreign invader" dream: *"Someone behind me says, 'no, you're OK'."* Ascending and moving North can often relate to bringing something into consciousness. *"I dreamed I was flying"* is a common escape dream often related to conscious control over the elements or a fantasy. Conscious elements often come from above. In this "Latin priest" dream, the airplane appears to represent new conscious concepts threatening old myths: *"I was in an airplane which landed in a spiral motion on the rim of a large circle in a Latin American village. In the center of the circle was a priest dressed in black, with a gun, protecting the village. The priest threatened to shoot me if I returned back to the plane."* Work on this dream revealed that some new spiritual concepts that the man was adopting (airplane) were in conflict with his childhood religious upbringing (priest in black that was protecting the village – protecting the existing myth around which the ego presently revolved). The threat was that the dreamer would return to the air in the plane – consciously (up) adopt the new concepts (airplane).

Unconscious material is often seen as below, under water, underground, or metaphorically below consciousness: *"I was following some people into a cave near the woods, when I looked down to see a deep hole with a swift swirling vortex of crystal water rushing in, leading to an underground river."* Suppression, or emergence of suppressed material, is often observed to be associated with imagery from below. The following dream, which we will discuss further in chapter 9, came to a woman who was suppressing a desire to go out and have fun (the red hat): *"In the dream I was one of three women, and was wearing a red hat. We were going into town, walking along a road, when suddenly we sank into the ground."*

Illumination

Illumination in dreams also appears to relate to awareness and consciousness, or conscious acceptance. Just as the cartoon metaphor represents an idea with a light bulb, our dreams do much the same. The conscious realm is represented by the brighter, illuminated regions in our dreams. When a new concept is accepted into awareness, the dreaming brain literally "illuminates" that concept. In the "jokester" dream, when the character was accepted by the dream ego, he moved to the right and into the light. In the "office party" dream, the characters that were brought into the circle dance by the dreamer were brought into the lighted area. As we learned earlier, Hamilton[105] noted dramatic increases in light as a dreamer achieved higher levels of consciousness and self-awareness during a transformation experience. On the other hand, the unconscious elements of the psyche are not "illuminated" by the conscious mind and thus they may appear in the areas of darkness in dreams. For example, in the "office party" dream, the unconscious elements, those persons left behind, remained in the darkness.

In the dream examples above, there was a definite distinction between light and dark, usually aligned with left and right. In the "office party" dream, the characters that joined the circle dance went to the right into the light, and the people that remained were to the left in the dark. In the "jokester" dream, the guiding shadow character came from the left and the jokester, once accepted, moved to the right into the light.

Encountering the Self

In dreams, we encounter ourselves: our ego-self (who we believe we are), the non-integrated and alienated fragments of our personality (parts we are not comfortable with), plus the non-actualized parts of our greater Self (who we could become).

The Ego-self

The ego is a term that might be used to describe the "you" that you identify with, all that you perceive yourself to be at the moment. It is therefore natural that you or a character with whom you identify would often play the role of the ego in the dream. Sometimes you will be a non-present observer, watching yourself in the dream. Sometimes you will maintain this strong sense of self throughout the dream, and simply interact with the other parts. Often you will play multiple roles at the same time, having the thoughts of more than one character. This appropriately illustrates that our inner self has many aspects that can exist simultaneously. Therefore, who we are at any point in time is a matter of focus.

Our dream ego aligns itself with the same personal myths that drive our behavior in waking life. In the "Taco Bell" dream discussed previously, the dreamer played the role of the ego just as in waking life, being torn between the stimulation of his ambitions and power (the whip), and the desire for finding his true value (the wallet south of the border).

You may sometimes switch roles and become one of the other players, or even become one or more at the same time. This may be the dream's way of allowing you to experience and integrate the myth and counter-myth or other parts of self. *"I dreamed I was arguing with a friend and was trying to convince him to go ahead and drive the bus. However, I also knew that I "was" that friend, that I was capable, but was struggling to let go of a small scrap of paper I was holding onto."* Here the dream tries to resolve the misconceptions of the ego by placing dreamer in both the role of being aligned with the myth (the lack of a credentials thus the small piece of paper) and being aligned with the counter-myth ("you know how to do it - so just get into the drivers seat and drive").

The Inner, Higher Order Self

Jung defined the Self (capital S) as the regulating center that brings about a constant extension and maturation of the personality. He considered it the organizing principle of the personality[23] that could only be grasped through the investigation of one's own dreams.[4] Perls referred to this as a representation of our non-actualized potential. The Self can emerge as a superior male figure (Cosmic Man, the wise old man, guardian) in a man's dream or superior woman (priestess, sorceress, earth mother) in a woman's dream. In the "book of truth" dream, the dreamer encountered the inner Self while searching for truth: *"I was wandering all over town looking for the book of truth. No one could tell me where it was. Suddenly I saw a wise old man sitting on the left, who pointed down a descending wooden spiral staircase. He said that truth lies down there."* In waking life, after having experienced an abundance of seminars, books and experts, the dreamer still felt unsatisfied in his search for truth. After experiencing the dream, the dreamer immediately understood the message or metaphor that the "truth lies within."

Jung also indicated that the Self could appear in many other forms in our dreams, including balanced geometric forms such as the mandala or a great circle divided by four. One of the most frequent symbols of the Self is the stone. Such a symbol appeared in the transformational "ice cave" dream discussed earlier: *"We landed by a large rock which, when I struck it, rang like a bell."* The rock appears as a representation of the inner Self that the dreamer is now beginning to resonate with.

The stone motif often appears as a shiny black stone, but can also appear as any number of shiny deep black objects in dreams. Shiny black stones appeared in this dream of a young man at the point of breaking from a parent and gaining his independence and own sense of self: *I was sitting on a slope by a stream with my father. There were rectangular indentions in the stream bed filled with polished brightly colored, yellow, green and red stones. When I picked them up I noticed some were a very beautiful shiny black. I threw them in the air, watching the beautiful colors as the sun hit them. My dad said "Don't do that. You could hit me with the rocks."* The son was discovering his own non-actualized Self in the black stones, and was dazzled by the delightful emotions (colors) that this discovery stimulated as he brought it into consciousness (the sunlight). This threatened the existing sense of self that his Father had instilled within him.

The Shadow-self

Jung indicated that one of the initial images encountered in the process of "individuation" is that of the shadow,[22] perhaps to convince the dreamer to "accept what seems to be criticism from the unconscious."[4] The Shadow is an instinctive, lesser-known side of the personality, typically appearing as a shadowy figure of the same sex.

It can often appear in a rejected, unhealthy, repulsive, frightening or threatening role, as it represents characteristics that you may have rejected within yourself. You may find yourself running from the shadow, unable to get away – in essence unable get away from yourself. If you become lucid enough in the dream to turn around and face the shadow, you may see it visibly transform into something less frightening: *"I have had this recurring dream for years where I am running away in fear from some unknown person. One night, when I recognized that I was back in the same dream, I turned around and faced the person. It was me!"*

The shadow can also play a positive, insightful, guiding role and initiate the process of compensation and integration. In the "jokester" dream, it was the shadow-like character that guided and negotiated with the dream ego: *"...an influential shadowy character entered from my left and argued that this jokester had been quite useful and that we should give him a chance. After some discussion I agreed, and the jokester was told he would be given a chance to prove himself."*

The Animal Motif

While Jung attributed an instinctive nature to our Shadow, he also described how the animal motif represents our deeper primitive instinctual nature, the autonomous emotions erupting from the unconscious.[4] This is illustrated in the following dream of a woman caught in a negative relationship with her mother in-law: *"My husband threw my artwork out onto a huge tree which moved downward and disappeared into the ground, into a rectangular area shaped like a grave. As the tree disappeared, a furry form rose up from the grave and grew into a large creature with a woman's face that had that triumphant self-satisfied look that my mother-in-law always has when she makes trouble for someone."*

Jung also considered animals to be our connection with our natural surroundings and some animals, such as the bird, to symbolize the goal of transcendence.[4] Human cultures have also historically represented their gods in the form of animals. Jung commented on this as a possible relationship between the worship of the divine and the instinctive nature of humans. Biologically, it makes sense that animals represent the instinctive influence of the more primitive parts of our brain, which we have in common with the rest of the animal kingdom.

Our personal and instinctive associations with (or reactions to) the animals that we see in our dreams, seems to define what they represent in our dreams. For example, this "four cats" dream represented a situation in which the dreamer was trying to contain her emotions: *"I dreamed my four cats were running all over and I was trying to get them inside the fence."* Primitive animals can be a motif for parts of ourselves that have not fully evolved: *"I dreamed of a big red amoeba."* Sometimes the animals will represent the characteristics we attribute to them in our culture or experience, i.e., faithful dog, warm fuzzy feelings of a kitten.

Some animals may be associated with deeper instincts or fears. I have observed that this is the case with snake imagery, which often relates to an unidentified fear, or an instinctive reaction or drive that is emerging from the unconscious. The following dream is an example of this, in which the snake seemed to represent a fear of the unknown that was surfacing within the dreamer, something that was "trying to get out of the basket." *"I dreamed of a black and white snake with two heads that was trying to get out of the basket it was in."* In mythology, snakes have also been associated with creation of the world of form, and the awakening of the Kundalini.

Sometimes the animal represents the element they live in, for example birds and fish. Birds often represent a "flight of ideas," feelings of freedom, spiritual aspirations – things of the mind and the spirit – metaphorically "of the air." Fish naturally relate to water, which to Jung was symbolic of the life-giving forces within the unconscious. In the following "brown fish" dream, the fish related to the emergence of an instinctive fear (a flight response). It was a fear of "being out of her element," as the dreamer moved into a new and exciting job situation: *"I dreamed it had rained so hard that a pond overflowed*

and <u>brown</u> fish were floundering on shore. I was trying to get the fish back in the pond."
The dream continued with the image of gray kitten playing with a snake, which was further associated with her fear of the unknown, in venturing into unfamiliar areas.

Release

Jung regarded any strong movement, exemplifying release, as a symbol of transcendence.[4] When something is suppressed over long periods of time, the energy build-up can result in explosive releases which appear in our dreams as explosive imagery: *"The woman threw a large pillar of stone into the painting, and the cloth of the painting flew up around the base of the pillar exploding in bright red and black."* As unrealized potential and non-actualized parts of ourselves begin to surface, they can appear in dreams as natural eruptions from within the earth, often accompanied by bright colors: *"Suddenly a volcano exploded in bright pastel colors."* Unconscious forces, in general, can appear as natural forces in turmoil, storms, twisters, or rushing water. In the four segment "tornado" dream from chapter 4, the dream began with unconscious forces emerging as a destructive force: *"I dreamed there was a spirit that came up from a creek, destroying trees in its path, like a tornado."* Here the dreamer is encountering a new emerging sense of self as a tornado spirit that was tearing at the old roots, the old trees.

Imagery of Compensation

The natural compensating force within the psyche appears in many forms in the dream story. It appears in order to reveal the misconceptions and inappropriate myths that have bound us in conflict, to provide an alternative path or reversal in our thinking in the dream, and to lead us in the direction of transformation and release.

Guiding Characters

We discussed the Self above as a major inner guiding force and thus a force that often compensates for misconceptions of the ego-self. It might appear as the guide that speaks with authority, or the wise old guardian pointing the way as in the "book of truth" dream previously discussed: *"I was wandering all over town looking for the book of truth. No one could tell me where it was. Suddenly I saw a wise looking old man who pointed down a descending wooden spiral. He said it is down there."*

The compensating character often appears as an unknown companion, challenging figure, or shadow-like character. In the "jokester" dream we discussed earlier, it was a shadow character that challenged and negotiated with the dream ego. The shadow can also represent unknown or non-actualized attributes of self. In the following "rusty car" dream, the shadow was the compensating element, appearing as a companion and urging the dreamer to not give up on himself so quickly: *"I was wandering through a desert setting and saw an old rusty car. Upon looking inside, I found a man who was not moving. I was going to give him up for dead, but my companion (a somewhat shadowy unknown male) urged me to wake the man. I argued that it was useless, but reluctantly gave in and shook the man. When I did, both the man and the car came to life and began to transform into a newer car."* The dreamer had given up on some talents and capabilities he once had, that he had permitted to go "rusty." The dream compensated by giving them a little shove and bringing them to life again.

Voice or Words

Jung identified the appearance of the voice in dreams as the compensating intervention of the Self. It may come in the form of a voice or written words. This was the case in the "invaded village" dream where the dreamer was told *"you are OK"* and in the "rising water of the subconscious" dream where the voice stated *"the water just represents the subconscious, jump in and you will be fine."*

For the most part, the words spoken by the voice in the dream are metaphors and need to be understood in the context of the dream and what it relates to. Some messages can be quite literal, but only if you consider them in the context of the dream, as was the case in the "exorcism" dream example discussed earlier: *"I dreamed that a person I disliked was alive again and realized an "entity" was at work. I went through a ritual of exorcism, but the sky only became darker. Suddenly a voice said, 'stop you are only making it worse'."* Here the message made little sense until the dreamer recognized the entity and darkening sky as part of herself that she considered evil and was trying to suppress. The compensating voice then became quite literal, warning her that repeated attempts at suppressing that part of self would only add to its energy, making matters worse.

Humor

Compensating with humor is a frequent experience in the dream. It can appear as an actual joke created within the dream story, a silly way of portraying yourself in the dream, or a silly mixture of imagery. The dream of cartoon characters can be the mind's way of illustrating the "silly" way in which you are viewing things, such as in the "old shoe" dream. The dream will make you laugh, often at something that is not funny upon awakening, but indeed meaningful in the context of your view of life. *"I dreamed I was in front of a crowd, about to give a speech, when I was introduced to a man named 'Willy Pisstoff.' I was trying to control myself to keep from laughing."* The dream focused on a situation the day before that made the dreamer really angry. In the dream, the dreamer's angry self was portrayed as "Willy Pistoff." The dream provided the opportunity for the dreamer to laugh at himself and release a little of that tension.

Surprising Mixture of Imagery

Often the compensation shows up as a strange or illogical mixture of imagery, whereby one part of the image is the expected element, and the other part the unexpected compensating element. *"I have a recurrent dream of being terribly angry with my husband, who I am running away from. These dreams continued until one night I turned around and faced my husband and looked at his face – it was my father's face."* The dreams stopped once she realized that it was early issues with her father she was dealing with, which she had clearly projected on her husband. The strange combination of the father's face on her husband's body was the compensating imagery. Sometimes the color of the image provides the compensating message. When we learn more about color in chapter 9, you will see that the color of an image can reveal conflicting emotions or a compensating view, which is not obvious from working on the visual image alone.

Guidance by Example and Positive Endings

Dreams compensate by their very nature. They do this by testing scenarios, urging us to go in new directions, and projecting the result. They also do this by revealing surprise outcomes and letting us experience the results of our actions: *"I dreamed I wanted this warm fuzzy puppy. I placed the puppy on my husband's back and it pissed on him and then all over the floor. I said, I don't know if I really want it, because it will just make a mess of things."* The fuzzy puppy related to the warm fuzzy feelings surrounding a tempting but messy opportunity. In this case, the dream made obvious what the potential outcome might be; a burden on her husband and making a mess in their home life.

Often the dream will reinforce the compensation by carrying the scenario to a positive ending, sometimes a surprise ending, and celebrating that ending in some way. This was the case in the "ice cave" dream that I discussed in chapter 5: *"At one point in the journey, a shadow-like character urged me to take charge of the boat's direction. When I did, the boat emerged from a white ice cave onto a crystal stream in a beautiful, sunlit colorful land with trees and mountains and singing in the air."*

Figure 10
Collective Imagery
Geometric and Number Patterns
(based primarily on the works of Jung)

❑ **One, the Circle, Circular Shape**

■ **Unification of the Whole Self, of a collective unconscious origin (feminine quality)**

❑ **Two, Duality and Pairs**

■ **Pairs of Equals (twin images, same sex) = Conflict and Indecision or 2 equal forces in conflict for dominance**

■ **Pairs of Opposites (male/female, black/white, gold/silver, left/right patterns, cross) = unification of opposites, integration of conscious + unconscious; relationship and connection**

❑ **Three**

■ **Unified Three (equilateral harmony) = creative force, evolving new state of order; revelation, self-discovery, spirit, goal-directed**

■ **3 becoming 4 (shape or grouping of four with one element missing, eg. 2 males + 1 female) = a search for something that is missing and necessary for completion, a need for closure, an anxious state**

❑ **Four or Four-ness**

■ **Square pattern, grouping of four, quartering of a circle, four primary colors, numbers of wholeness = completion or stable state of a conscious nature (masculine quality)**

Patterns of Integration

Look over your dream records, and if you prepared fairly detailed records, you may notice something interesting among your dreams – geometric shapes and perhaps curious combinations of numbers. Jung discussed these geometric shapes and the number patterns that accompany them (particularly four-ness and circular or center-oriented shapes and the mandala), as evidence of a compensating force or focusing image, that appear at times of psychic dissociation or disorientation.[28] They appear as a natural attempt at self-healing, or a formal aspect of instinct. He found a fundamental conformity in mandalas, regardless of their origin in time, geography and culture.

Circular or Center-Oriented Imagery

Jung spoke of the circular motif in terms of the totality of the human psyche and the relationship with all of nature. It represents a completion, the ultimate wholeness, and the natural centering force within the psyche. This motif appears as a circle, the sphere, or a circular mandala. It may also appear as a center-oriented motif, to represent the new center as it comes into consciousness,[29] perhaps as a circle with an object in the center such as a tree, character or representation of the inner Self.

The centering force may also appear as images moving in a circular or spiral pattern, drawing the ego towards the center. This might include walking around a path in a clockwise or counter-clockwise direction, or descending or ascending a spiral stair. Note that in the "office party" dream, the dreamer stated "*my job was to bring each of the groups through the woods into a lighted area to join in a circle dance,*" which symbolically represents bringing all the guests (the fragments of the personality) into a circle dance of integration. Jung considered the spiral motif to be a pattern of new creation and new ways of thinking that spontaneously arise from the unconscious. The spiral has also been related, by anthropologist Angeles Arrien,[102] to growth and evolution. It is an evolutionary pattern often associated with spirit, that can lead into the unconscious, or bring forth new creation from the unconscious. Within this new creation, the older pattern returns on a higher level. I find the spiral often appears in dreams as a tornado, i.e. a storm of natural forces from the unconscious that brings forth new concepts. This was the case of the four-part "tornado" dream discussed previously "*I dreamed there was a spirit that came up from a creek destroying trees in its path, like a tornado.*" In the following case, the dreamer was experiencing an upwelling of anxiety and unidentified fears as she was thrust into a legal situation: "*I saw a wall of wind coming toward me, with dozens of gray counter-clockwise spiral cloud forms in it. I felt it hit me and push me back.*"

At times, the object in the center can be a central theme around which the fragments of the personality are orienting. It might appear as a symbol of inner growth, such as a tree, or perhaps as a character clearly associated with the conflict or myth with which the dream is dealing. This appeared to be the case in the "Latin priest" dream discussed earlier: *"I was in an airplane which landed in a spiral motion on the rim of a large circle in a Latin American village. In the center of the circle was a priest dressed in black with a gun, protecting the village."* At the center of the conflict were the childhood religious concepts (the old myth) represented by the Latin priest.

The circle or unity-of-one motif also appears in the form of the number 0 (likely due to its circular shape), or more frequently as the number 1 (as symbolic of unity). It is common to see patterns of 10, or more often 100 (or its quartering in the number 25), as representing this state of ultimate wholeness.

Four-ness and the Square

Jung[4] noted that the motif of four or four-ness appears in dreams as related to the process of individuation, a state of completion, the four stages of evolution, or as a pattern of order, stability, completeness or closure. Arrien[102] further indicates that the square takes on the aspects of stability, solidity and security. It takes on a masculine quality. Jung discussed the four as representing the four functions of consciousness (thought, feeling, intuition and sensation), which equips humans to deal with the impressions of the world received from within and without. Whereas he considered the circle as a symbol of the psyche, the square symbolized stable concepts or creations within earthbound consciousness or reality. While the circle relates to the whole self or the greater Self, the square or four represents a state of closure, balance or completion within the conscious personality. He also made distinctions between the number five, as associated with the physical body of man, and number four as associated with conscious totality.[28]

I find four-ness to be one of the most prolific and important pattern images in dreams. The square shape, it's derivatives (rectangle), or groupings of four (dream characters or associated objects), appear in a great majority of our dreams. Recognizing how dream characters and elements interplay within a group or pattern of four can be of great help in understanding what is going on in a dream. I will discuss this further in the next chapter. Four seems to appear when creation is involved (emergence of a new concept or ego-state), when a pattern of stability and order is needed at a time of change or stress, or when a pattern of completion is required to establish closure. It appears as a reference for completion when the ego-self is fragmented by some traumatic event, as was the case in the "foreign invader" dream: *"the leader announced, 'everyone that lives beyond four, tense up."* A large group is tensing up and the remaining move away to the right, toward* *the windows. I am confused, not knowing what the command means or what I should do, since I don't know if I live "within four" or outside of it. I tense my fists."*

I have observed that the state of completion represented by four-ness often accompanies stress reduction, as it did in the "maze" dream: *"There was a liquid crystal rectangular game of four squares that I had to find my way through. The squares were made up of three colors (red, yellow and green) that were constantly changing at a hectic pace. Finally, it appeared that I solved it, as things seemingly fell in place by themselves and the colors covered the entire surface of the now [vertical] rectangular game. The colored shapes now changed at a calmer pace. I now felt relaxed, that there was no longer a need to control the puzzle."*

The four motif appears frequently in dreams as square or rectangular shapes and objects, such as the shape of a room, a building, or a table. In Jung's writings, he often equated conscious forces (thinking) to the horizontal and unconscious forces (feelings) to the vertical.[29] The appearance of a rectangle, as opposed to a square, would therefore represent an imbalance in unconscious or conscious forces, or thinking versus feeling. In the "maze" dream, the balanced pattern of the square seemed impossible to control, due to the rapidly changing colors. A calm state was achieved only by abandoning the need to control the situation, and by adopting a cooperative attitude. Perhaps this was why the square became a vertical rectangle – feelings dominating over thinking or control.

The four-ness motif can appear in dreams as four similar objects (as it did with the four houses in the "office party" dream), a family of four (father, mother, sibling and the dreamer); a group or mixture of male and female characters, or as a square pattern or square object (as in the "color maze" dream above). Four-ness will appear as the number 4 or 40, as derivatives of the number 4 (as in 1/4, 1/2, 3/4, 25, 50), and as the quartering of the circle or the whole (perhaps a cross inside a circle). In one dream this quartering of the circle appeared as a game with quarter coins: *" I dreamed I was with a bunch of friends and we were playing a game of pitching quarters into a large circle."*

As mentioned in chapter 4, the four-ness motif can appear in what Jung and Perls called the four psychological "primaries." The balanced grouping of the four colors (red, yellow, blue and green) is illustrated in this "blue sphere" dream: *"I dreamed of a blue sphere which was part of a group of four spheres colored red, yellow, blue and green that formed the dial on a pay-phone. The blue sphere separated and landed on my finger like a "magic" ring that I perceived would give me the power to solve all my problems."* In this dream, the color blue became the more active color. The four "primaries" were also present in the "maze" dream above. However, in that case blue was the missing color. Often when the "primaries" are present with one color active or missing, it is that active or missing element that is the key to what is needed for balance or closure.

I have talked about four-ness here as a balanced state. However, this is true only when there is a proper balance of the elements making up that four. An over-abundance of one element over another in a grouping of four can often be as revealing as a missing element, in understanding what must be adjusted in order to achieve balance and completion. For example, in the following "four women" dream, the appearance of more women than men appears to represent an overbalance of feminine forces acting on the situation: *"I dreamed that I had hired three other women to run my restaurant, which we had purchased from the owner who was the man from the last dream."* In this case, the dreamer was establishing herself as a dream worker, and had been dealing with how best to go about it, by either pursuing the more structured approach in which she had just been trained (the man she bought the store from), or by sticking with the more intuitive approach she was most comfortable with (the three women she had hired). Her struggle in this dream, and many subsequent dreams, was over how to integrate the structured work with the intuitive dreamwork method. As she worked her way through the dilemma over many months, her dreams contained varying mixtures of male and female populations, generally gathered in groups of four. Noticing this pattern provided a valuable clue to working on important balancing factors in her waking life.

Three Becoming Four

I have frequently observed an interesting derivative of the four-ness motif, that I call "three becoming four." It seems to appear when the dream is dealing with completion and searching for the missing element that will bring about a solution for closure. Jung related it to the incomplete state of existence, with 3:4 relating to the relationship between the incomplete and the complete state.[28]

If the mind contains a natural tendency toward completion, then dreams would contain imagery representing that tendency; perhaps emerging shapes, partial constructs, or incomplete patterns with a missing element. You may dream of walking partway around a circular or square path, or an unbalanced grouping of three people (perhaps yourself with two people of the opposite sex), or numbers and patterns as illustrated in figure 10.

The incomplete four was seen in the "office party" dream which began in four houses, but only three of the houses were distinct. The fourth appeared incomplete or shadowy in nature. This motif of 3:4 can appear in circular form as well, such as a circle with a quarter missing as in this dream: *"I dreamed we were trying to swing a large satellite dish antenna around to receive communications, but it would not work. One quarter segment of the antenna was missing."*

It is important to note this pattern in your dreams, since the missing element in the grouping may be associated in some way with the missing element required for resolution in your waking life. This pattern is important in how you structure your dreamwork. If the missing part is obvious (such as a missing color, person or object), you may try making that missing element the subject of your imagery work in order to determine how that missing piece relates to what is missing in your waking life. The dream story might allude to the problem caused by the missing element, as in the communications antenna dream above, which was dealing with a "communications problem" in the dreamer's life.

The Triad

I discussed "three" appearing in dreams as a representation of the incomplete state. But what's happening when a seemingly balanced pattern of "three" (such as an equilateral triangular shape) appears to be a complete pattern within itself? Jung states that the incomplete state of existence is expressed by the triadic system,[28] and that completion can retain the triadic geometry, but perhaps as two penetrating triangles.[4] He indicated that traditionally "three" was related to the masculine, "six" to creation and evolution, the conjunction of "two" and "three" to the even and odd, and the female and male.[28] Thus the balanced triad may indeed be a pre-disposing pattern of evolution, or representative of the pure creative force, leading to a new state of order. Anthropologist Angeles Arrien[102] indicates that the triangle carries the theme of self-discovery and revelation, and can represent goals and visions. I have often observed that the balanced triad in dreams takes on a theme of revelation and discovery, often in a religious, spiritual or "outside force" context. Revelation and self-discovery was the case in the "Santa Claus trinity" dream: *"I dreamed that it was the end of the world and Christ was coming in the sky as the Holy Trinity."* The spiritual revelation theme was present in the "triangular sign" dream from chapter 2: *"I was being shown a huge brightly lit triangular-shaped sign with red lettering which said, 'make yourself a perfect channel and wait, and all things will be given to you'."*

Duality and the Unity of Opposites

Unification often appears in dreams as a unity of opposites, the integration of opposing imagery, the yin and yang. As we learned in chapters 4 and 5, dualities form as our conscious personality evolves and individualizes. The basic process of evolving as a conscious personality separates your conscious self from your unconscious or un-realized Self. The experiences of your conscious self, that form your ego and differentiate you from others, create further splits. I referred to these as the "me" and the "not-me" side of self, or the personal mythic structure with its opposing counter-myths. Thus, within the psyche is a constant battle between becoming an individual and becoming an integrated whole. This battle appears in our dreams as interactions between equal or opposite dream elements. Cook[14] proposes what might be a biological reason for the appearance of opposing imagery, that our experiences create complementary information in the two halves of the brain.

Jung spoke of the unity of the masculine and feminine in dreams as a symbol of unification between conscious and unconscious.[4] These are symbolized by marriage, sex, or other imagery relating to the joining of the two opposite sexes. Jung used the term Anima to describe the motif of the woman within man, the female personification of his unconscious. He used the term Animus to describe the motif of the man within woman, the male personification of her unconscious.

When the sexual partner is an unknown person, they usually relate to the masculine or feminine force. When that partner is someone you know, however, you may be borrowing them to represent something that you are integrating with: *"I dreamed I was having a sexual encounter with a woman at work to whom I have never really been attracted."* In this case, the dreamer was beginning to get in touch with how much he really enjoyed his career, and used the woman to represent the emotional aspects of his work environment. At times, it can simply be a sex dream, a reflection of unresolved urges or an unrealized attraction.

Jung indicated that although the Anima and Animus are influenced by our relationships with our parents (or parental figures), they also put us in tune with inner values that balance those of the ego. In the "book of truth" dream discussed earlier, the dream continued as follows: *"I followed the advice of the wise old man and went down into the tunnel with the wooden spiral staircase. When I got to the bottom, all I could see around me was a shopping mall. Again I felt lost among all the options. I looked back at the steps and there stood a beautiful woman. She pointed out that just behind me, right where I was standing, was a pedestal, and on it was a golden book – the book of truth."* In this case, the dreamer had accepted the urging of the Self that "truth lies within" and began the inner exploration. But again, he was looking for conscious constructs (things he could "buy" metaphorically speaking). It was only when the inner female (the Anima) guided him to the intuitive self, that he saw where truth was actually located.

A geometric pattern of opposing pairs is generally a positive sign of the natural balancing and unifying forces at work. Geometric opposites may appear as left versus right or horizontal versus vertical shapes, such as in a cross. Jung spoke of the horizontal and vertical as an integration of conscious and unconscious respectively. Arrien[102] indicates that the cross universally symbolizes the process of relationship and integration, and a tendency toward connection. Opposing pairs, representing the integration of conscious and unconscious, often appear as black and white patterns: *"I dreamed I was in a house and the floor was a checkerboard pattern of black and white;"* or *"The dress I was wearing was white with black polka dots; or "I dreamed of swirling clouds of black and white patterns."* The motif of black and white, plus left and right, appeared in the "two headed snake" dream discussed earlier: *"I dreamed of a black and white snake with two heads, that was trying to get out of the basket it was in."* The opposing black and white, left and right heads of the snake, appeared as conflict (pulling in two directions), but also as a powerful sign of unification of conscious and unconscious forces at play. The dreamer was involving herself in a new creative venture in her life, which caused some instinctive fears to arise about venturing into the unknown. The compensating message in this image was that although this fear was emerging "snake getting out of the basket," it was leading to an integration within herself (an evolution of unrealized potential into consciousness).

Duality and Opposing Forces

When imagery pairs contain identical elements, this often relates to a conflict rather than a unification, between equal opposing forces. These might be forces of equal strength such as conflicting fears, or the conflict between myth and counter-myth. The condition can appear as a pairing of two identical objects, a pairing of characters of the same sex, perhaps geometric shapes such as parallel lines and the number 2, or number pairs or patterns such as 11. The parallel pattern appeared in this dream for example: *"I dreamed all night of train tracks, and that I was on a train that I could not control."*

The appearance of a male pair or a female pair in the dream may reflect an imbalance of masculine or feminine qualities in dealing with a situation, which can move the dreamer in a direction that provides no basis for unity. For example, in the following "clever dog," dream the conflict involved a pair of males: *"Two unknown men were trying to convince us to let them kill a dog they considered aggressive and threatening. The dog suddenly decided to roll over and play dead in order to spare its life."* I will talk more about this dream later, but the dreamer was dealing with a conflict involving male aggressiveness and how to act in a social environment in a way that would not always result in getting hurt and rejected.

Four-ness - the Alchemical Elements

At one point in our history, the elements of our physical universe were classified in alchemical terms. There were four basic elements: earth, fire, air and water. Jung often related the practices of alchemy to the integration motifs in our dreams. I will discuss some of the common associations attributed to these elements, but remember that personal associations and cultural beliefs strongly influence the meaning they may hold for you in your dream.

Earth

Jung [4] associated many earth symbols, earth-altars, trees, stone and stone structures, with symbols of the Self to which we must submit in the process of individuation (becoming an individual). He discussed the stone motif as related to the new center of the personality, the Self,[28] or in simpler terms, our unrealized potential emerging from the unconscious. Earth imagery, such as caves, trees, rocks, and ground can relate to the unconscious origin from which our conscious personality evolved. Trees and natural wood imagery often relate to growth of the psyche, emerging from the inner Self (as opposed to growth of our instinctive self which is represented by animals). Entering or emerging from caves has often been associated with exploring and entering into, or material emerging from, our unconscious origins.

Fire

Fire is a mythological and alchemical symbol of transformation. Fire may also be associated with the conflagration of our emotions, and explosive anxiety or anger. Often it can be a sign of self-emergence as it combines with an earth symbol. Both motifs are illustrated in this volcano dream: *"All of a sudden a volcano exploded and we were running from the lava. The red of the lava seemed significant."* In this dream, it related to both an emotional upheaval (the emergence of emotions and desires associated with redness) and the emergence of a more assertive side of self. As we saw in chapter 2, fire can appears as a metaphor for "inflammation" when there is an injury: *"I dreamed of a skull with red fire coming out of a section above the eye."*

Air

Air symbols such as wind, flying, and birds are often associated with mind and spirit. In the "Latin priest" dream, for example, the airplane related to new concepts that were being considered. Birds or airplanes can represent thoughts, concepts, goals and aspirations, but as with any dream image, you need to work on the personal associations with the flying object to understand its true nature. Flying unassisted is an unnatural act, and therefore most often represents fantasies or feelings of control or overcoming a situation by getting "above it all." When questioning younger people with frequent flying dreams, I find they admit to a fair amount of daydreaming. Flying can also be associated with lucid dreaming as described earlier.

Water

Water has a long history of mythical and evolutionary associations that may account for its many forms in our dreams. It can symbolize the "life force" in dreams relating to rebirth and growth. Water may represent the depths of the unconscious, as you may recall from the "waters of the unconscious" dream: *"Suddenly a voice said 'the water is your unconscious, jump in and you will be fine'."* Most often water appears as an emotional force, particularly when the water affects the dreamer (drowning, swimming, rain, floods). In chapter 9, figure 15, we will discuss a dream containing flood imagery: *"Later a flood came by. I tried to save my dog which was in the water, but he would not let go of a piece of wood held tight in his teeth."* In this dream, the flood represented a flood of emotions in which the dreamer would drown if they let go of something they were holding on to.

Water has been seen in dreams relating to pregnancy, and can relate to blockages if the water is stagnant or the flow impeded. As a metaphor, rough water can relate to emotional turmoil; dark, deep water to matters concerning the unconscious; frozen water to suppressed emotion or parts of self; bright, flowing or bubbling water to healthy excited or sensual emotions; crystal water to the source of inner life; and dirty "muddy" water to illness or emotional uncertainty. In any case it is always best to test your own personal associations with the water image in order to understand what it means for you.

Imagery of Transformation
Symbolic Death and Rebirth

As discussed in chapter 5 human transformation can be characterized as a four stage process: 1) death of the ego; 2) journey and encounter; 3) transformation and rebirth and 4) actualization of the new self in waking life. Jung discussed this death and rebirth motif as relating to the passage from youth to maturity. He observed this cycle in the works of alchemy, as well as in human mythology. It appears in the myth of the hero cast out into darkness, proceeding on a long journey, encountering and overcoming many challenges, collecting something of value from each challenge and finally, transformed, emerging and returning to preside over his place of origin. The motif of death, and rebirth or renewal, also appears in nature in the four seasons (Fall, Winter, Spring And Summer) and even in our daily cycles (sunset, night, sunrise and day). These seasons and times of day are often incorporated into our dreams to symbolize the stages of transformation. The cycle may also appear in dreams as submergence, search and re-emergence, or as images of death followed by rebirth imagery such as pregnancy or a little child.

Hamilton[105] observed that individuals going through a psycho-spiritual transformation also experience increased levels of consciousness that are reflected in the dream imagery they report. In the earliest stages of their journey, where they turn inward to face their shadow self, he noted dream themes of darkness, fear, worldly concerns, animals and elements of an instinctual nature. As the individual progressed to higher levels of self-awareness, the dream imagery would evolve, evidencing fewer instinctual elements and more creativity and clarity, plus an increase in light, color, beauty, natural landscapes and mythological imagery. There would be encounters and conflict between opposing sides of self. Eventual integrations would be accompanied by celebration, joy and rebirth imagery. With further levels of transcendence, spiritual imagery begins to appear with qualities of peacefulness, sacredness and splendor. Finally, as the pure Self is experienced, imagery of purity (such as whiteness and snow) and integration (such as marriage) was observed. During the daily progression toward higher levels of consciousness, he observed a corresponding and dramatic increase in color and light in the dreams, with appearances of multiple colors often combined with white, and the appearance of "clear light" at the highest levels.

Symbolic Death

Symbolic death occurs as the ego-self gives way to the impending unconscious forces or counter-myth, and begins the process of transformation. Essentially, the ego-self must die so that the new self can be born. It may submerge itself in the dark, unknown realms of the unconscious in search of a new self.

The theme and imagery of death in dreams may have a biological basis. Edelman and his colleagues, in their theory of "neuronal group selection," [cited in 38] state that neuron groups in the brain that benefit our survival thrive and develop strong interconnections, while those that are unused actually die (as might be the case with the discarded personality fragments and behaviors). Could such cellular awareness exist in the brain that the "death" of neuron groups can be literally translated into "death" imagery in dreams?

Sometimes the death phase appears as destruction of the world as we know it. This was the case in the "waters of the unconscious dream: *I dreamed it was the end of the world and water was rising all around me. Suddenly a voice said 'the water is your unconscious, jump in and you will be fine'.*" In this case, the compensating voice was encouraging the ego to take that "death of the ego" step into the unconscious.

Figure 11
Imagery of Transformation - The "Death/Rebirth" Cycle

Death of the Ego   Search for Self

Actualization   Rebirth

The destruction of the world motif also appeared in the "Santa Claus Christ" dream: *"I dreamed that it was the end of the world and Christ was coming in the sky as the Holy Trinity. But Christ appeared as a trinity of Santa Clauses, who merged as one and began pouring gifts of love from an urn. They were invisible but I felt the gifts hit me, so I ran."* In this dream, there was a destruction of the existing myth of a Santa Claus Christ that delivers physical gifts if you are good.

The Journey

Jung stated that the individuation process is often symbolized by a voyage of discovery into unknown lands. If the ego has been severely damaged, or has accepted the need for change, substance must be found to replace the parts that have symbolically died. At this point in waking life, the dreamer might feel a sense of being lost or at an impasse. If nothing is apparent in the environment to re-create and sustain a new healthy sense of self, the dream story may evolve into a journey or search. You probably recognize the journey motif in the "ice cave" dream: *"I dreamed all night that I was on a long journey as a passenger in an enclosed boat going nowhere, just aimlessly moving through tunnels and underground caves."* The Journey might take the form of searching for a solution, solving a puzzle, wandering through a maze, or trying to solve an un-solvable problem as illustrated by the "colored maze" dream. It may become a search for one's lost sense of worth: *"I dreamed I lost my purse and was searching everywhere for it."*

When the conscious world does not contain the solution, the search might venture into the unknown aspects of the psyche, the unconscious side. The dreams may journey into the darkness or into foreign unexplored lands where dangers lurk. *"I was on a large yacht in the far east where we were being pursued and shot at by enemy planes."* This side of the psyche is also seen as dark and below. Therefore the journey may take you into dark places, changes from daytime to nighttime scenes, and venturing into caves, basements, down steps, into underground tunnels or under water. The "yacht" dream above continued with a journey under the water: *"The captain sank the boat, explaining that the boat could go underwater as a diversionary tactic."* The "ice cave" dream above began in the journey phase in an underground tunnel. The "book of truth" dream discussed earlier was a search that took the dreamer down a spiral wooden staircase to further search and eventual discovery in an underground mall. In those cases, the dream continued to a potential discovery and rebirth phase, but in many cases the dream will end at the onset of the search: *"At the end of the dream, I found myself going down a flight of stairs into a dark basement area, and then I awoke."*

Symbolic Rebirth

As the psyche searches for a means to re-establish the self, the journey may eventually continue to a point of resolution. Compensating and integrating forces may enter in and demonstrate right action that can lead to a solution or rebirth of self, and celebrate those solutions with bright, joyful, emergent imagery. As you might recall, this rebirth motif was apparent in the "ice cave" dream: *"At one point in the journey a shadow-like character urged me to take charge of the boat's direction. When I did, the boat emerged from a white ice cave onto a crystal stream in a beautiful, sunlit colorful land with trees and mountains and singing in the air."* The dream projected a solution and took the dreamer through the joyful experience of emergence. It literally demonstrated to the dreamer that if he changed his behavior, from that of being a passive "passenger in life" at the mercy of events around him, to that of taking charge, he would emerge into a world of harmony. The dream celebrated this new behavior.

Jung indicated that it is the ego that is involved in this rebirth, and that "lights up" the entire system, allowing it to become consciously realized. As discussed previously, this may be literally shown in dreams as illumination. We know from neural scans that when a part of the brain becomes active, blood flow and electrical activity in that part increases. In other words, that part of the brain literally "lights up." An analogy to this appears to be observed in dreams. At the point of change, transformation, awareness and acceptance, it has been observed that the dream imagery involved becomes illuminated (by a light bulb, lightning, sunshine, etc.) or the environment of the whole dream brightens. As mentioned earlier, Hamilton[105] also observed this phenomenon in dreams of persons going through psycho-spiritual transformation and a period of transcendence.

We saw earlier that in the "jokester" dream, when the jokester fragment was accepted into the personality, it moved into a sunlit area. This was also the case in the "clever dog" dream mentioned earlier. When a new concept was accepted, the dream illuminated the scene: *"Two unknown men were trying to convince us to let them kill a dog they considered aggressive and threatening. The dog suddenly decided to roll over and play dead in order to spare its life. At that point the dog turned into a cute puppy, and the men stopped, convinced that the dog was no longer a threat. The dog was suddenly illuminated by a street lamp overhead."* This dream was about dealing with emotional threats. A new way of acting, that of "playing dead," was being tested and was subsequently accepted by the ego as a workable solution. At the point of acceptance a street lamp illuminated the scene.

Actualization

As discussed in chapter 5, the resolution of a dream may not be solidly incorporated into the psyche unless it is actualized, or placed into action. For this reason, the dreamworking approaches recommended in the following chapters include much more than simply understanding the dream. The first step, understanding the dream, must be followed by understanding yourself in relation to the dream, as well as attaining a deeper understanding of the inappropriate myths, beliefs and fears that impede resolution or transformation. The dream, or a dream series, can then be used to develop a solution or new myth, but the solution will not establish strong neural connections until put into practice and successfully experienced in waking life.

Exercise - Recognizing Collective Patterns

Look through a few of your more lengthy and interesting dream records. See if you can spot the following collective patterns:

a) The Realm of the Conscious Personality

Setting: Illuminated or sunny; the right field of view, above or ahead.

Ego: Generally you in the dream, or a character you identify with.

Characters and Imagery: Known or identifiable.

Symbols of acceptance: Movement to right, becoming illuminated.

b) The Realm of the Unconscious

Setting: Dark or black; imagery and places to the left, below, behind.

Characters and Imagery: Unknown, black, dark or shadowy; a non-specific male or female character. Symbols of the inner Self such as unknown guiding, wise god/goddess-like characters. Primitive creatures. Gold/silver metals, crystals, stone, shiny black. Frightening or disturbing imagery. Archetypes (see Jung).

Suppression/Rejection: Movement to left, under, behind, darkness, frozen, dead.

c) Impasse and Conflict:

Story lines: Stuck, trapped, afraid, lost, prevented from proceeding to your goal

Characters and Imagery: Something (character, situation, fear, barrier, separation, crossing) you must overcome to progress to your goal. A pair of equal elements (conflict between equal forces) = parallel lines and numbers (11, 22 etc.), a male pair or a female pair.

Release (breaking through the barrier): Explosions; volcanoes or earthquakes.

d) Forces of Unification and Transformation:

Unifying forces: Center-oriented motifs such as circular or spiral shapes or motion. Numbers relating to unity or wholeness such as 1, 0 or combinations thereof (10, 100). Four-ness motifs representing completion, such as the square, number 4, groupings of 4 objects or pairs of opposites (2 males and 2 females), squaring of the circle (circle in quarters or with a cross in the center).

Compensation: Companions or beings that guide or influence us. Verbal or written words. Events that change our thinking or direction. Revealing or surprising events. Strange but revealing combinations of imagery. Humor.

Transformation:

    Death Cycle: Death related imagery, loss, darkening, fall or sunset, descending.

    Journey or Search: Lost, searching, trying to return or go home, frozen, winter.

    Rebirth Cycle: emerging, discovery, becoming light, spring, fire of transformation.

CHAPTER 8
WORKING WITH PERSONAL IMAGERY

Really become that thing – whatever it is in a dream – really become it – Fritz Perls[15]

In dreams, you "borrow" objects and characters from your waking life to represent emotional associations and memories, or fragments of your own personality. As we learned in chapter 3, the waking life identity or naming of a character or object has little to do with its meaning in the dream. The part of the brain active in dreams internalizes these characters and objects, based on your experiences, memories and associations with them. This is often the case, even when the character in your dream is a person you know. In chapter 6, I introduced four approaches for working with the personal associations from which your dream imagery is created. I will address these four techniques in more detail in this chapter.

Exploring Personal Imagery

As table 8-1 implies, dreamwork involves various levels of exploration, beginning first with metaphors in the dream narrative and concluding with deeper exploration of emotional content within the dream imagery. The objective is to discover the personal associations that originally created the dream image. One common element in these four approaches is that they all are based on recognizing metaphor, i.e., figurative phrases that are verbalized by the dreamer when applying each of the four methods to the dream and the dream elements. Whether the dreamer is telling the dream, or describing associations with a dream element, the words used are explored to see how they might also be making a statement about the dreamer's waking life situation. Understanding the metaphor is not always necessary for the dream to have a positive impact on the dreamer. However, I find it to be the most useful way to establish a relationship between the dream story and the life story.

Table 8-1
Working with Personal Imagery

Work with the Dream Image using the Dream "Language"		Compare the Words with Your Waking Situation
- Metaphor		- Words also Describe Waking Situation
- Memory		- Past Experiences
- Define		- Personal Associations
- Role-Play		- Emotional Statements

Importance of the Dreamer's Response

The 'Aha' Response

The accuracy of a suspected metaphor or figure of speech can be determined by the dreamer and their reaction to it. If a meaningful connection is made, it almost always stimulates a spontaneous recognition response, an "aha" with the dreamer. If it doesn't create that "aha" response with the dreamer, leave it alone and move on. It is either an incorrect association, or it will trigger a response later as the dreamer dwells on it.

Non-Verbal Clues

If you are helping someone work on their dream, watch for body language as they tell the dream story. Notice such things as defensive posturing during one part of the narrative, or a nervous twitch during another, or revealing facial expressions and hand gestures. Don't try to analyze the body language, just use it to explore that part of the dream. For example, a dreamer was relating the following dream: *"I am walking down a path with a companion, and we have been walking for a while when we pass by an old mill. I did not want to stop there, so we continued on."* When he described passing by the old mill, he crossed his arms, and then again relaxed as he moved on down the path. This seemed like a sign that he might have been emotionally defending himself against something inside of that dream image of the old mill. Dreamwork on the old mill revealed that this was the case.

Emotional Response

Dreamwork will often create a spontaneous emotional response, frequently grief, sorrow or anxiety. Sometimes the response will come forth without the dreamer understanding either the emotion or its source. At that point, it is best to stop the work for a minute (or discontinue altogether if in a non-professional setting) and let the dreamer recover a bit. In a professional setting, the source of the sorrow and associated memories would be explored and the dream element that was being worked on at the time further explored to determine the associations it represents. The following dream is an example. *"I dreamed I was alone on a beach, and noticed a vase lying in the sand. I awoke feeling upset."* When I asked her to "become" the vase she did not say a word but began crying. She did not know why she was crying until she reflected further on the image of the vase, and recognized it as the one that her husband, who had just passed away, gave her on their wedding day.

The First Step – Metaphors in the Dream Story

Working with metaphors in the dream story is often the quickest way to relate the dream to your waking life situation. For that reason, I recommend that you first scan the dream narrative for obvious metaphors.

Recognizing Metaphors

In chapter 3, I discussed how metaphors are culturally-derived figurative phrases used in everyday speech, which we substitute as simple analogies for more complex concepts. I also described how metaphor might appear in the dream story or dream narrative. In this chapter, I will discuss how to work with them. Recognizing metaphors is a process of looking for activities in the dream, or phrases or figures of speech in the dream narrative, that also describe feelings or events in the dreamer's waking life situation. Sometimes phrases in the narrative are unmistakable ("I dropped the ball" for example), but at other times it is the activity in the dream story from which we draw analogies. When orienting yourself to a dream, underline phrases that seem to be figurative or potentially descriptive of an experience in the dreamer's waking life at the time.

Figurative Speech in the Dream Narrative

When telling the dream, or reading a dream narrative, look for phrases that might have a double meaning, i.e., phrases that not only describe the dream story but also in a figurative way, describe the waking life situation. Statements such as *" I am in rut," "I put him down," or "I am holding things up,"* are examples of common figures of speech which might have double meaning.

The Picture Language of the Dream Story

As we learned in chapter 3, figurative analogies can be drawn between dream stories and our waking life stories. For example, the following dream was related to a frustrating situation in which the dreamer was trying to negotiate a business deal with a client: *"I dreamed I was a dentist and one of my business clients was in the chair. I was pulling as hard as I could, but could not get the tooth out."* This dream activity also figuratively described the waking life situation: *"it is like pulling teeth trying to get anything out of the client."* Look for role similarity. Define your role in the dream, and then ask how that is similar to your role in waking life. For example: being lost and seeking your way in the dream may be a reflection of a waking life situation where you feel "lost" and unable to work things out. Being trapped or stuck, undecided or unable to move in the dream may be analogous to your inability to progress, or to a feeling of being stuck, trapped or undecided in waking life.

Picture Words

Since the dreaming brain can't express itself by combining letters or words into meaningful sentences, it does so by combining imagery fragments in meaningful ways. Combining a slide-rule with a thermometer (illustrated in figure 4) to pictorially spell out "engineering degree" is an example of this. Ann Faraday's book *Dream Game*[24] gives many such examples of what she terms "wordplay," in which dream imagery literally sounds like or spells out a meaningful word or phrase. She gives one example where the image of "jeans" appeared to represent "genes." The "hide 45" dream we discussed earlier is also such an example, where the words HIDE 45 combined with a license plate image to represent the dreamer's desire to find a "license" to hide her age.

Slips-Of-The-Tongue

When telling a dream, it is important to pay attention to slips of the tongue. For example, in the following dream the dreamer had a 35mm projector that he was trying to return to the university. He stated: *"I have a 'rejecter,' I mean projector, that I am trying to take back."* It became clear with this slip-of-the-tongue that the dream was about rejection. The dreamer had made a statement the day before that was causing him to feel rejection, and he was trying to "take it back."

Working with Metaphors in the Dream Story

Successful work with metaphors depends on properly telling your dream. It works best if you tell or record the dream in the first person, as if you are re-experiencing it, in a spontaneous way, recording the stream of words as they come to you. Use the present tense, first person, such as "I am dreaming that .. ," "in front of me is …," "we are …. ," "it is ….. ," "suddenly I see…". It is also important to never correct a misspelling or slip-of-the-tongue. These, as you will learn later, can be valuable clues to associating the dream story to your life story.

Ullman[72] indicated that, as we experience our dream story at night, feelings are evoked in the dream which can be accessed and re-experienced through proper dreamwork. He pioneered a group approach to dreamwork (often referred to as group projective dreamwork), whereby members of the group recognize possible metaphors in the dream story and project their own associations on these metaphors as "if it were my dream." The objective is that the group associations might also trigger personal associations with the dreamer. A secondary benefit is that the group members often get something of personal value out of discussing the dream in this manner. The approach must be used with the clear understanding that the projections of group members are their own, and that the ultimate meaning of the dream remains with the dreamer. More on this and other group approaches will be discussed in chapter 10.

The Ullman approach was studied at Saybrook Institute by Kautner[75] on a group of nine seniors in eight weekly sessions. After each session, the dreamer and a group participant were interviewed. A phenomenological approach was used to systematically analyze the data from the perspective of the subject's own insights. Overall, each participant came away from the groups gaining new awareness and/or insights into their dreams and the dreams of others. One of the commonalities was a realization of the similarity of the human experience, as several participants would come forward with similar associations.

Working at the metaphoric level with the dream story, therefore, provides valuable insight in a relatively fun and safe manner. However, working with metaphors in the dream story alone has limitations. Although strong emotions sometimes surface, working at this level rarely probes deeply into the personal feelings, decisions and conflicts that are the primary stimulus of the dream. Also, a casual group setting is often not conducive to deeper work. In the above study it was found that several of the participants held back from expressing projections and associations relating to important, life-altering periods in their lives. They saved these insights until their individual interviews with the researcher, when they must have felt a greater sense of safety. A different approach is required for more serious dreamwork, one that permits the dreamer to understand and deal with some of the deeper issues that stimulated the dream.

The Next Step – Exploring Associations

Working with metaphors in the dream story generally reveals a connection between waking life events and the dream, but often not much more. It rarely reveals what lies within a dream element, which may contain the deeper emotional connections to the waking life story. A common approach to working with the content within a dream element is association. The deepest approach is role-play, which we will discuss in the next section. Association does not go as deep as role-play in revealing the inner story of the dreamer, but association is useful for working with dreamers who have a difficult time role-playing a dream image. These approaches are healthy because they rely on associations from the dreamer and avoid projections from others.

Memory Association

Sometimes, a particular dream element or event can bring to mind emotional memories of a past event from your waking life. Such memory association may provide valuable connections between the dream and your waking life situation. The "vase" dream mentioned above is an example. A dream about one's parent, long after they have passed away, is another. Such dreams can provide valuable information if there are still unresolved issues regarding people in your past. Memory associations may be an expedient approach to getting at that information.

Free Association

Another associative approach is to freely associate words with the dream element. Marcia Emery, PhD, in her book *The Intuitive Healer*[76] describes two free association approaches for working with dream imagery, which she calls "amplification" and "word association."

One or two key images, perhaps the central image, are selected from the dream story. Using the "amplification" approach, the dreamer freely associates words with that specific dream image until an "aha" or connection is made with a situation in their waking life. The "word association" approach is more serial in nature. A dream image is selected and the dreamer associates a word with it. The dreamer then associations another word with that prior word association. This continues until an "aha" or connection is made with a situation in their waking life. With both techniques, those connections are then further explored as they relate to the dream and the waking life situation.

Defining the Dream Element

One clever technique used to reveal the personal associations within the dream imagery, is an approach called Dream Interviewing used by Delaney & Flowers.[55] In this approach, the dreamer is asked to describe the image as if describing it to an interviewer who has come from another planet and is unfamiliar with life on Earth. The dreamer is encouraged to give concrete descriptions and include his or her judgments and feelings about the image. The interviewer asks a series of specific questions from the alien's point of view, such as "What is George Bush like? Pretend I have never heard of him before." Or, "What are cats like in general? We don't have them on Mars. What is the specific cat in your dream like?" The interviewer asks a modifiable series of questions tailored to elicit concise, and not too detailed descriptions of each of the major dream elements, including settings, people, animals, objects, feelings, actions/plots. The dreamer's associations arise spontaneously and are kept to a workable minimum. Throughout the process, interviewers are not to ask the dreamer any leading questions, and must keep their own associations and interpretations to themselves. Instead, the interviewer recapitulates each description to the dreamer, and asks if it reminds them of anyone, anything, or any part of themselves. This is the interpretation question that lets the dreamer identify the metaphoric bridge between the dream image and the dreamer's life experience.

Defining the Function or Purpose

As we learned in chapter 3, the verbal language center of our left hemisphere is inactive in the dream state, but those centers in our right hemisphere, which recognize things by their contextual nature and their function or purpose, remain active. As we learned from the "door" exercise, a simple trick for understanding your personal associations with a dream image is to define the purpose or function of that image.

Working with the Associations

Stanley Krippner[79] presents a valuable approach for using the personal associations within the context of the dream, to create a new dream story that might reveal direct connections with the events in the dreamer's waking life story. In essence, it re-creates the dream story in the language of the dreaming brain, because it substitutes associations for the elements in the dream story. You begin the work by circling the main elements in your dream record. Although Stanley used a short version of the definition technique in the work I was exposed to, any of the above methods can be used to create associations with each dream element. It may work best if someone else records the associations for the dreamer. If you are working with your own dream, you may want to record and list the associations or definitions on a separate page if you need more room. Once the list is complete, review the associations and note (perhaps underline) the phrases or parts of each association that seem important, in that they might relate to something in the dreamer's waking life. Go back to the dream record and in place of the original dream element, insert the association in a way that creates a coherent new story. Read the new story and reflect on how it might relate to your waking life story. An example of this technique will be given later in this chapter. Another example, which includes color and collective associations as well, is given in chapter 12.

Going Deeper - Image Activation Dreamwork

I prefer an approach that uses some of the techniques above for initial exploration, but then permits deeper exploration of the underlying emotional content using a technique that stimulates emotional expression. I call this method "Image Activation Dreamwork." I apply it to an exploration of both the personal content within the dream image and the emotional associations within dream color.   At the core of the personal content exploration is a role-play technique, which permits the dream image to "speak" and express its own content at a deeper emotional level. Speaking as the image evokes metaphors that can relate to underlying conflicts and personal mythic elements. It is a healthy approach to dreamwork, since the meaning of the dream comes entirely from the dreamer. While Image Activation reveals direct connections with the waking life story, it also relates the dream story to the dreamer's inner story.

The Importance of Exploring Emotions

Justina Lasley,[101] in her book *Honoring the Dream: A Handbook for Dream Group Leaders*, supports one of the basic premises of Image Activation dreamwork, i.e. that it is important to identify the emotions of the dream and bring that awareness to waking life. We act and react out of our emotions, so it is helpful for the dreamer to be conscious of the emotions at work in waking life. In her book, she features my role-play approach and offers several other exercises to help the dreamer become aware of emotions. She states that it is helpful to move the dreamer to the basic emotions of MAD, SAD, GLAD, and AFRAID. This is important, because we often use words such as 'frustrated' and 'confused' in a way that covers up the basic emotion, making it more difficult to understand what is actually being felt and how to deal with it effectively. She does not regard emotions as negative, but considers an honestly-felt emotion to be positive. Only unexpressed or misdirected emotions have a negative impact. She encourages the dreamer to make notes in their dream journal regarding the emotions in each dream they record, and to relate those to emotions of their day.

Role-Play - Let the Image Speak

Image Activation Dreamwork adapts a role-play technique derived from Gestalt therapy.[15] A true Gestalt session is usually intended for therapy, and involves intense and prolonged dialogue with hidden or conflicting parts of self. The method can go deep very quickly. A therapy session might involve what is known as a "double chair" technique, in which the subject engages in a dialogue between conflicting images or characters in the dream, perhaps to bring a point of impasse and a possible path to resolution to the surface.

This degree of Gestalt work is more than is required for casual or general dreamwork. Therefore, I adopted part of the technique, but did so by formulating a tightly scripted, step-by-step set of 6 questions, designed to reveal deep content in a way that avoids probing too deeply. It is scripted in a way that can easily be understood and used for beginning dream workers as well as professionals. The approach can thus be used for personal dreamwork, or in a professional setting can be taken deeper as deemed appropriate by the therapist.

The content of a dream image is revealed by what the dreamer states, feels and/or experiences when imagining him or herself as the dream image. This is validated when the dreamer has a "connection" or an "ah-ha" response, as they make a dream-to-waking life association. As with the prior approaches, recognizing metaphor and figurative speech is a key element. However, in this case, you will be looking for the figurative speech in the dreamer's statements while they speak as the dream image.

Perhaps the best way to illustrate the power of role-play is through an example. *" I dreamed that I was standing in a sweet potato patch separated from my boss who was on the other side of a barbed wire fence."* In waking life, the dreamer was having trouble with his new female boss. He saw himself as a capable worker but, when around her, he could never seem to do things to her satisfaction. He needed her approval, but his "male ego" made it difficult to admit to himself that he was in the position of "needing approval from this woman!" When we worked on the dream at the metaphoric and associative level, his associations to the barbed wire were "it hurts when I approach her," and "her barbed conversation." This linked the dream with the situation, but did little to reveal the underlying emotions and conflicts.

Figure 12
Dream Images can be "Decoded"
if we "Let them Speak"

Analogy with Waking Life Feelings

Following Perl's guidance, that every image in a dream is meaningful, and that the most alienated fragments of the personality might lie within the least human imagery, I wondered what might lie inside the lowly sweet potato. Certainly it was there for a reason! I therefore asked the dreamer to "become" the sweet potato and tell me about himself. He immediately stated, *"I am a sweet potato, butter me up and I'll be good."* This was an immediate "aha" to the dreamer, and a precise statement of the conflicted feelings that he was having about his need to be buttered up by his boss in order to do a good job. The sweet potato was a fragment of himself the dreamer was ashamed of (the failures on the job and the need to be buttered up), and which had been alienated and reduced to the form of the lowly sweet potato in the dream. As lowly as it was, it contained the most powerful content.

The 6 "Magic" Questions

The scripted role-play technique consists of six questions or statements that I call the "6 magic questions." There is nothing necessarily "magic" about them, but I found that giving the technique a clever name made it easier for people to remember. On the other hand, the questions are very carefully designed to target emotional memories, reveal conflicts and impasses, and discover fears and myths that might feed those conflicts and impasses. Over the years, I have found that these six questions best reveal the key personal association within a dream image. Scripting the dreamwork into six specific questions also avoids dwelling on any line of questioning too long. In a professional therapeutic setting, focusing on a particular line of questioning may be necessary. But for basic dreamwork, these six usually provide more than enough information. Whereas role-play can also be used to work on dream elements other than images (such as actions, feelings and sensations), the questions are designed more for the visual elements. Feel free to be a bit creative with the phrasing of the questions in order to try them on non-visual dream elements.

The six questions are listed in the procedure below. They are designed specifically to target and reveal the following content within a dream image. Asking the dream image to describe itself is intended to evoke a free "I am" association statement that will hopefully reveal a similarity with waking life roles or feelings. Asking the image to describe it's function or purpose is designed to reveal right brain contextual associations. It is interesting to note that defining the function or purpose during role-play evokes a much deeper and more emotionally meaningful response than is achieved through the cognitive association exercise described in the prior section. The "what do you like and dislike" question pair is designed to reveal potentially conflicting emotions or beliefs that lie within the dream image. The "what do you fear and desire" question pair is designed to further understand and reveal the emotional forces and belief systems that might be driving the conflict. The "I desire" statement may at times reveal an unrealistic focus that contributes to the conflict, but at other times may point to a reasonable outcome that can be helpful in formulating a waking life solution.

As discussed previously, alienated fragments of our personality lie within a dream image. Using the "6 magic questions" reveals that some of the conflicts and impasses, responsible for the fragmentation, also lie within the dream image. Both the fear and its imagined consequences, and the desire and its imagined rewards, are beliefs or myths that may have resulted from decisions made during an emotional event sometime in our past. We tend to generalize earlier crisis decisions, creating myths that may be totally inappropriate to the current situation. Understanding the inappropriate personal myth at the core of a conflict is the first step toward transforming it.

If you are not an experienced dreamworker, take care when using the approach on other people's dreams, either individually or in a group. Role-play of an extended nature should only be done with professionals present who can help you work through any open wounds. Stick to the scripted questions and do not dwell on a particular line of questioning, in order to avoid opening the dreamer to hurtful or threatening content. Ask the dreamer to answer the questions with one or two sentences each. Then go onto the next question. At the first sign of a strong emotional reaction, stop and allow the dreamer to choose whether or not to continue with the exercise. Investigate the emotions with the dreamer before continuing, to make sure that doors are not being opened that can't be closed. Most of the information needed to associate the dream to a waking life situation can be obtained from simple statements, without going too deeply.

The Role-Play Procedure

Below is a four-step procedure for role-playing a dream image. Step three contains the "6 magic questions," which are statements that you speak while imagining that you are the dream image. It is important with role-play to go back into the dream and pretend or imagine yourself as the dream image, to "become" that dream image. If this is too difficult, then alternatively you can re-enter the dream as the dreamer, bring the image to mind, see it in your mind's eye, and ask the six questions to the dream image. Then speak and answer as the image might answer; imagining what the dream image might say. Since it is most effective when you really get involved in "becoming" the dream image, it is best done with either a voice recorder or in the presence of a person who can write down your statements and feed them back to you. If circumstances don't permit this, then write your statements down in your dream record, as spontaneously as you can, without selectively filtering the words you use.

1) Pick a Dream Image or Character

Pick an important dream image (object, nature image or character). Select one that seems important to you, that has emotional impact, or one you are most curious about. Also include the inanimate objects or non-human creatures, because they may hold the most interesting content, or as Perls would say, "the most alienated fragments." You might try an image that is in color, since it may contain more emotional intensity. Picking a colored image also helps if you want to later work on image using the color questionnaire in chapter 9.

2) Become the Dream Image:

Close your eyes, go back into the dream and bring the dream image or dream character into view. Now take a few deep breaths, relax, and with each breath slowly move into the image and "become" the image - feel its essence - feel it become you. You might position your body into the shape or orientation of the image if it helps, and look out at the dream from the "eyes" of the image or dream character. When you feel you are there, proceed with the next step.

3) Let the Image Speak (the 6 "magic" questions)
Have a person with you ask the questions below or, if you are alone, read them, and record your statements. Speak as if you are the image in the present tense, answering these questions in the first person using "I am" and/or "I feel" statements.

1) As the image, who or what are you (name and freely describe yourself and perhaps how you feel as the dream image): "I am _____ and I feel ___ ."

2) What is your purpose or function? "My purpose is to _____"

3) What do you like about who you are and what you do? "I like _____"

4) What do you dislike about who you are and what you do? "I dislike _____"

5) What do you fear the most? "As the image what I fear most is _____".

6) What do you desire most? "What I want most is to _____"

Known Person? If the dream character is someone you know in waking life, substitute this question for question #1 above:
1b) Become that person and: describe your personality _____ ;
In what ways you are like the dreamer _____
In what ways you are different from the dreamer _____

4) Play Back & Look for a Life Situation Analogy: Read back, play back or have another person feed back the role-play statements. Do one or more of the statements sound like something you feel or would like to say about a situation in your waking life? Describe one specific situation in which you felt that way and define your feelings at the time. Now reflect on the role-play statements:

a) Do the "I am" or "My purpose or function" statements sound like a way you are feeling, a role you are playing, or a situation in your waking life?

b) Do the "I like" versus "I dislike" statements sound like a conflict going on inside you regarding some waking life situation?

c) Do the "I fear" and "I desire" statements sound like fears and desires you have regarding that situation, perhaps fears and desires that feed the conflict? Does the "I desire" statement reveal a realistic or an unreasonable outcome?

Known Person? If the dream character is a person you know, does some aspect of this character's personality relate to a manner in which you are approaching the waking life situation, or alternatively does this dream character have a personality trait that you admire or wish you had more of in order to better handle this waking life situation?

Example – Working with Personal Imagery

Below is a dream example that will demonstrate the various personal imagery techniques I discussed above. I underlined the possible metaphors and key elements but omitted the color descriptors at this point, since we will discuss that in a later chapter. Note how each technique goes slightly deeper. The metaphor work with the dream story relates the dream story to a waking life situation, but it does not reveal much about the underlying emotions. The association work and the element definitions explore the connections a little further. Role-play finally reveals the deeper emotions, conflicts and personal myths underlying the situation.

The Dream

I am <u>walking</u> in a red <u>sandstone desert</u> and I look down into a <u>crystal clear stream</u>. There is a red <u>bird</u> with a green tail, like a <u>parrot, moving under the water</u>. I take a <u>stick</u> and <u>poke</u> at the <u>bird</u>. It is then that I realize that it is <u>dead</u>. The <u>water</u> was <u>poisoned</u>, and the <u>bird died</u> when it tried to get a <u>drink</u>. I realize <u>the very substance that was to give it life killed it</u>. I then look up at the bank and notice that the water is <u>undercutting the whole foundation</u> of the valley. I feel a need to warn my <u>friends</u> to get out.

Technique #1 - Recognizing Metaphors in the Dream Story

Possible metaphors are double underlined above. Exploring the metaphors led to the following associations with the dreamer: *"'The very substance that was to give it life killed it' also describes my waking life situation where I am trying to sell a new project that is a key part of a larger strategy. The very organization that I thought would benefit from it and thus sponsor it, was killing it. Even worse is that if they killed the project, it would affect my larger strategy, i.e., 'undercut the whole foundation'."* Note that at this level of work, the dream can be related to waking life events and some of the feelings with which the dream may be dealing. Little is revealed about the deeper emotional issues involved, however.

Technique #2 - Association

Examples of the four approaches for establishing personal associations with dream imagery are given below to illustrate the various association techniques. These exercises will usually trigger strong connections with something in your waking life (that "aha" experience). You may feel that those connections are adequate to explain the relationship between the dream story and your waking life story. If, however, you want to explore a more complete relationship between the dream story and events in your life, you can insert these associations into the original dream narrative to create a new dream story.

Inserting the associations into the dream story can be interesting, since it provides a surprisingly effective way of directly relating the entire dream story to waking life events. On the other hand, it can be a bit time-consuming and generally remains at a cognitive level, dealing only with the events in waking life rather than the deeper emotional issues. When using this approach, I personally find that a short definition of the image (including defining its function or purpose) is adequate. I find memory association to be useful as well, but only when a memory is spontaneous or forthcoming. Later on (in the chapter 12 example) you will see how color and collective associations can be added to the mix.

For most dreamwork, rather than use the more involved Association approach, I go directly to role-play for imagery association. Role-play inherently includes association, and is more direct at quickly getting to the deep inner issues.

Memory Associations

Walking in a red sandstone desert = *"I am reminded of an occasion when we hiked in the desert, dealing with the heat and stress, in order to get to the goal at the end, which was a campsite - this sounds like dealing with the heat and stress at work in order to achieve the goal on the project."*

Moving under water = *"reminds me of trying to walk under water, I struggle and flail my arms and legs, but make little progress – similar to the way the lack of progress feels on the project."*

Free Association

Amplification: Parrot = *colorful, attractive, agile, talkative, clever, <u>fly away</u> (wanting to leave the situation strikes a chord)*

Word Association: *Parrot > beautiful >sunset > night time> <u>unable to see where I am going</u> (not knowing where this situation is going strikes a chord)*

Defining the Dream Element

Sandstone = *"not fully solidified. It has taken shape but can be easily destroyed."*
Desert = *"a place that is hard to live in unless you can adapt to the heat"*
Die = *"a state where you no longer have life, no future, you can't function or move; it's all over for good"*
Poison = *" something that, when it enters a system, kills it"*
Friends = *"those who support me"*
Valley = *"the larger surrounding area of which this is a part"*

Defining the Function or Purpose

Walk = *"to progress slowly one step at a time"*
Crystal Clear Stream = *"the purpose of a stream in the desert is to be a source of life"*
Bird = *"the function of a bird is to escape it's enemies by flying away"*
Parrot = *"the purpose of a parrot is to survive by remaining agile and attracting others with its color and language ability"*
Drink = *"to provide life"*
Stick = *"enables you to move something from a distance"*
Poke = *"to investigate or move something along by giving it a push"*
Foundation = *"to establish a basis or support mechanism"*

Rewriting the Dream

A more complete understanding of the relationship of events in the dream narrative to events in waking life is achieved by rewriting the dream story, by replacing the underlined words in the narrative with the definition and memory association statements above. Note that color and collective associations (which we will learn about later) can be substituted as well. The rewritten dream below incorporates the above associations:

I am <u>progressing slowly, on step at a time,</u> on <u>something that is just taking shape but can easily be destroyed.</u> The environment is <u>hard to live in unless you can adapt to the heat.</u> I am dealing with the heat and stress, in order to get to the goal. I see a <u>source of life</u>

where there is <u>a way to survive by remaining agile and attracting others with language ability</u> but I <u>struggle and flail my arms making little progress.</u> While <u>keeping my distance,</u> I try to <u>investigate the situation and move it along by giving it a little push.</u> It is then that I realize that it <u>no longer has life, no future. Something has entered that which was attractive and has killed it.</u> It died at the <u>source that was to give it <u>life.</u> I realize <u>the very substance that was to give it life killed it.</u> I then realized that that which was to give it life is now undercutting the whole <u>basis and support mechanism</u> for the <u>larger area of which this is part.</u> I feel a need to warn <u>those who support me</u> to get out.

This new dream story now has a clearer connection to the waking life situation that stimulated the dream. The new dream story reflects a new project that was "just taking shape and could easily be destroyed" that the dreamer was "progressing slowly on, one step at a time." It was a tough management environment "dealing with the heat and stress in order to get to the goal." The dreamer saw a "source of life" for the project in a particular organization that he was certain would support it. The dreamer saw himself like the parrot, agile and able to make the project attractive to that organization with his presentation capability, i.e., "language ability." When he tried to "move it along by giving it a little push" at an important meeting (the day before the dream) he realized that something (the poison) had entered into the situation such that "the very organization that was to give it life killed it." Further he realized that killing this project would undercut the support for the larger strategy, "the larger area of which this was a part." He felt a need to warn "those who supported him" to pull out.

Technique #3 - Role-Play

Note that each of the associations above, as well as the new dream story that was created, related directly to the events of the waking life situation. Although it revealed some of the feelings, frustrations and experiences in the associated life story, it did not penetrate into the deeper conflicts within the dreamer, the threats to the dreamer's self-image, or the impact and role of the dreamer's personal mythology in the situation. It is this sort of information that is valuable in creating an inner perspective so that the dreamer can better deal with the external events. Applying the "6 magic questions" to the dream resulted in the following:

1) "***I am*** *a dead bird under water and I feel cheated and tricked by the water."*
2) "***My purpose is*** *to get to where I want to go by flying.*
3) "*As the bird* ***I like*** *being able to amaze people with my language abilities and to be attractive to people and to other birds when I present my unique colors."*
4) "*As the bird* ***I dislike*** *being so small and vulnerable, and so easily tricked."*
5) "*As the bird* ***what I fear most*** *is that this is the final blow, I am dead, that we all are dead, and I can't fly away from this one."*
6) "***What I desire most*** *is to fly out and above it all and be admired for the bird I am."*

Play Back the Statements and Compare with Your Waking Life Situation

Note that, in contrast to the association technique, the role-play personalized the statements in terms of the deeper feelings evoked by the situation. There was a feeling of being tricked and cheated that did not come out in the word associations. The "my purpose" statement revealed an anticipation of progressing quickly (in contrast to the slow plodding manner of walking). The "I like" statement revealed that he felt proud of his own presentation abilities to attract and sell the organization on what he was presenting. The "I dislike" statement revealed the devastating impact of the meeting on his self-image, and that he now felt small and vulnerable. This new image of self threatens the proud bird myth that he could simply flit around and attract success with his presentation skills. The "I fear" statement illustrates not only his fears about the program being killed, but the blow to the ego as well, in that he sees himself "no longer able to fly." The "I desire" statement reinforces this, showing that what he wants most is to be able to rise above it all and be admired (perhaps an unrealistic focus at this point). He is caught in the conflict of wanting to be admired for what he thought were strengths that would always allow him to succeed (his myth), and having those very strengths fail him, resulting in feeling small and vulnerable.

Note that by using the role-play technique, not only is the associated waking life situation revealed more rapidly (only one dream image and six statements were used in this example), but the associations go much deeper into the personal conflicts, threats, and fears that the dreamer needs to deal with. It also initiates an important step into exploring the personal myth and transforming any inappropriate beliefs therein.

CHAPTER 9
WORKING WITH COLOR IN DREAMS

Every night for a hundred years the angel of dreams came to the town and splashed the walls with bright colors that stayed until the first light of day – Brian Andreas [67]

What does it mean to dream in color? A search for the answer to this question led me through a ten-year investigation into the nature of color in dreams. My investigation was initially targeted at determining whether color had symbolic significance, as does other imagery in a dream. What I discovered was that individual colors not only had symbolic significance, but that dream color contained emotional content, which it added to the personal meaning of the dream image. [65]

Perhaps the most important thing I discovered relates to the nature of the emotional associations represented by dream color. Whereas our associations with color can have strong personal and cultural biases, for the most part it appears that color associations occur at a deeper unconscious and instinctual level. This is supported (as discussed below) by research indicating that the human limbic and autonomic nervous systems respond directly, and in a fairly predictable manner, to various color illuminations.

In chapter 7, I introduced the findings that most dreams are in color, but recall of color diminishes dramatically upon waking. As with any dream image, the more emotionally charged color may be recalled more easily than the rest. I mentioned earlier that this selective recall of color may have a benefit in focusing our dreamwork on colors that contain the most emotionally significant content. For example, it might be significant that a green wall is the only colored image you recall. Your more emotionally-charged dreams may be your more colorful dreams. My own observations, and those of Hamilton, [105] are that color also tends to increase in dreams related to transformation.

The Significance of Color in Dreams

Unfortunately, color is one area that has been given little attention by dream researchers. The work of Jung, as well as that of Perls, contained some discussion on color as it related to what were considered the four "psychological primaries," a color grouping of red, yellow, blue and green. Their notion was that these were the four colors that our mind considered "primary," or distinct from any color combination. Jung and Perls regarded the presence of a balanced pattern of these four colors in a dream as an evolving state of completion within the personality.[4, 28, 15] Jung associated the "primaries" with what he called the four orienting functions of consciousness: feeling (red), intuition (yellow), thinking (blue) and sensation (green). Jung also referred to a symbolic significance of black and white; with blackness representing the unconscious realm, and white or light representing consciousness or new material emerging into consciousness.

Perception of the full color spectrum can be created from only three primary colors - red, green and blue. Research[106] also tells us that our eyes have three color receptors (3 types of cones) with peak sensitivities near the color wavelengths of yellow-red, green and blue-violet. Research also indicates that the brain processes what the eye senses, based on the relative presence of four colors (Red, Yellow, Blue and Green), plus black and white (known as the opponent-process theory).[106] The concept of "psychological primaries" therefore may have some relation to the way we process color, even though our basic sensory equipment seems to be structured for three wavelengths.

When I began doing content analysis research on color reports from dreams, I observed a very curious and exciting result. The colors most frequently reported in dreams seemed to support Jung's theories on the symbolic meaning of certain colors in dreams! Figure 13 illustrates 6,237 colors recalled from 15,245 dream reports collected from the UCSC dream bank database.[73] It was derived from a broad (but primarily US and European) base of dreamers, including individuals who kept long term journals, girls aged four through nine, persons in high school, college women and men, college graduates, persons in their 40s and 50s, artists, scientists, factory workers, psychologists, physiologists, and a group representing the Hall and Van de Castle norms. No attempt was made to equalize the reports by category. However, a similar study done on a database of roughly 8,000 dreams from 5 dreamers, collected in a separate database by the author and Curtiss Hoffman, PhD,[66] resulted in an almost identical result (within a few percentage points).

As a result of these two nearly identical results, it appears that these two studies represent dream color recall percentages in the general population (or at least the Western population). Red, yellow, blue and green were present in nearly the same relative amounts as in the first study (red dominating, then blue, yellow and green), varying between 9% and 14% of the total colors reported. As with the first study, a nearly equal pairing of black and white also dominated the second study, accounting for a similar 17 to 20% of the colors reported (although the relationship of black to white was reversed with black slightly higher than white).

Figure 13 – Color Recall from 15,000 Dream Reports

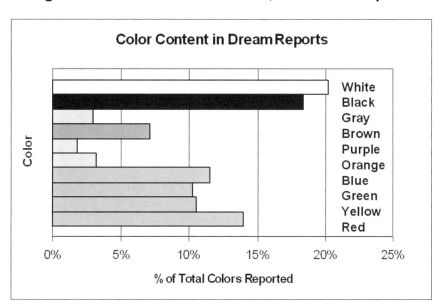

One might expect our dreaming brains to present a dominance of these colors, if our eye-brain visual system processes color based on the opponent-process theory (the relative presence of blue versus yellow, red versus green and black versus white). As we learned in chapters 3 and 6, our amygdala assigns emotional associations to color. Combining these findings provides some support for the Jungian concept that there are four "psychological primaries" plus black and white, and that they contain important symbolic meaning in dreams.

It is quite striking that the most dominant colors reported in dreams, by a ratio of two to one, were a balanced occurrence of black and white. Jung contends that the integration of the unconscious and conscious is one of the most basic processes taking place in dreams, and that it is often symbolized by equal patterns of black and white. The next most dominant colors reported in dreams, by a factor of four or five over lesser colors, were the nearly equivalent grouping of red, yellow, blue and green (although red was slightly dominant). If, as Jung and Perls indicated, this grouping of "primaries" relates to a state of balance in the conscious personality, then one might expect those four colors to be dominant in dream reports and to appear in equivalent percentages, on average, across the population.

I was surprised by the low frequency of gray. As you will later learn, color psychologists consider gray as a color one is attracted to when they are trying to shield themselves from emotional stimulation. My own observations of gray imagery in dreams supports this, as it often contains emotions or personality characteristics that the dreamer wishes to reject or shield themselves from. The emotional shielding related to gray seems to be a frequent theme in dreams, but it is an infrequently reported color. It may be that people don't typically consider gray a color and don't report it, but this remains uncertain.

The Human Association with Color

Although content analysis provides some curious insight as to the significance of color in dreams, the lack of further dream research data led my investigation toward the waking human response to color. In this area, there is more test data and some established tools for working with color. The question to be answered was: if color stimulates emotion in the waking state, do emotions stimulate color in the dream state? I speculated that if I could establish a link between the human waking response to color and color imagery in dreams, then I could better understand the color content in dreams.

Over the last 50 years or so there has been a small, but notable, degree of work in the human response to color.[15,16, 25-27, 30-35, 99] This color psychology research has had a visible influence on advertising, food packaging, art, style, decorating and more. Much of the research indicates that color evokes a somewhat common, unconscious, physiological and psychological response in human subjects. For example, red illumination excites the autonomic nervous system, while blue illumination calms the autonomic nervous system. All of this happens below our threshold of awareness. As mentioned earlier, this is likely linked to a function of the limbic system (operating in conjunction with the autonomic nervous system) which assigns emotion to the sensory input we receive, including color. Because this part of the brain is highly active in the dream process, it is likely that it plays a role in assigning color to the emotions that surface in the dream. My research to date, summarized herein, supports this notion.

Table 9-1, the result of a literature search, illustrates some of the more common human associations with color. For the most part, these associations were based on small variations around the pure hues of each color. Note that associations can change from those listed, as the brightness, or the tint and shade (addition of white or black), is altered. One resource, which discusses the effect of color mix and variation on mood, is Sutton and Whelan.[99] The table includes the physiological and psychological associations from various research sources, Jungian theory, various cultural and philosophical sources, and the associations upon which the Luscher Color Test is based. The Luscher Test is a psychological profiling tool, based on color preference, that I will discuss later in the chapter.

Note that in general, there appears to be a reasonable correlation between the reported physiological responses, the psychological associations, and a majority of the Luscher associations. There is a wider variance between these and the cultural and metaphysical associations. There is also a wide variance among the cultural associations themselves. This may be attributed to the fact that learning and experience have greater influence on cultural and metaphysical associations, whereas the more common instinctive and autonomic factors (our common human evolution) influence physiological and psychological associations. I will further discuss the cultural factors in the next section.

Table 9-1
Human Response to and Associations with Color

Color	Source	Response and/or Associations
Red	Luscher [25] associations	An energy expending physiological condition. Desire in all forms including sexual drive as well as intensity of experience and a fullness of life. Represents force of will. Is outwardly focused, active, aggressive, autonomous, competitive, operative. Driven to win and succeed. Its affective aspects are: excitability, domination.
	Emotional response [35]	Disruption, thrown out and attracted to outer world, activity, aggression, excitation and emotionally determined action.
	Psycho-logical [99]	Power, excitement, speed, joy, danger, passion, attracts attention, feelings of warmth. Crimson and Burgundy reds feel rich, regal, strong, exclusive.
	Physio-logical [25, 33]	Stimulating effect, increases blood pressure, heartbeat, respiration. Excites sympathetic branch of autonomic nervous system.
	Sensory [25]	Sensory Perception = Appetite
	Jung [4,28]	Feeling, Affectivity, Passion
	Nature	Blood associated with aggression and anger; twilight.
	Cultural	Christian = Charity, Martyrdom, Hell, Blood of Christ; Cabala = strength; Judaism = love and sacrifice, sin and salvation, fire; Lakota = East; Chinese = fire; Cherokee = success, triumph [26]. Chinese = good luck [99]
	Chakra	Base [64] or Root [78] = principles of survival, earth energy, drives.
	Aura [64]	Passion, strong feelings, anger.
Orange	Psycho-logical [99]	Friendly and outgoing, energizing, vital, adventurous, appetizing, warm, exotic, creative, enthusiastic, active, playful and maybe a bit irresponsible.
	Physiological [99]	High visibility (use on warning signs); encourages oxygen intake to the brain; stimulates the appetite.
	Learning	Improves social behavior. [34] Increased learning ability with children. [34]
	Nature	Sunset. Campfire for social gathering. Fall harvest. Clay pottery for food.
	Chakra	Sacral [64] or reproductive system. Creativity. [78]
	Aura [64]	Red-Orange: Ambition, sexual passion.

Color	Source	Response and/or Associations
Yellow	Luscher [25] associations	Cheerful, happy, stimulating and spontaneous. Directed toward the future, toward new experiences, the developing. Hope and a desire to escape from existing difficulties. Expectancy and projection of the outcome. Outwardly focused, active, projective, heteronymous, expanding, aspiring, investigative. Its affective aspects are: variability, expectancy, originality, exhilaration. Change, a loosening or relaxation, uninhibited expansiveness, spontaneous enjoyment of action.
	Psycho-logical [99]	Joy, optimism, vitality, moving, warmth; most noticeable color (packaging and signs); overexposure can be unsettling; pale hues best for socializing.
	Physio-logical	Increases blood pressure, respiration rate but in a less stable way than red.[25] Highest visual acuity.[32] Alerting and arousal.[33]
	Learning	Yellow and yellow-green increased learning ability with children.[34] Stimulates clear thinking, black print on yellow aids memory retention. [99]
	Sensory [25]	Sensory Perception = Piquancy
	Jung [28]	Intuition
	Nature	Daytime, sun and daylight, outward activity.
	Cultural	Christian (yellow or gold) = power and glory, gates of heaven; Judaism = air; Chinese = Earth; Lakota = South[26]. Relates to prosperity and power in some cultures.[99]
	Chakra	Solar Plexus.[4] Power [78]
	Aura [64]	Yellow = Intellect; Gold = connectedness to God, love and service.
Green	Luscher [25] associations	Will in operation. Concentric, autonomous, passive, defensive, retentive, possessive, immutable. Tenacity, firmness, constancy, pride, logic, control, persistence, tension, ambition. It's affective aspects are: persistence, self-assertion, obstinacy, self-esteem. A high value is placed on self and increasing self-value by: self-assertion, holding on to an idealized picture of self, or acknowledgment by others of one's wealth or superiority. Wants one's own opinions to prevail. A need for recognition and prestige. A quest for better conditions such as health.
	Emotional Response [35]	Withdrawal from the outer world, retreat to one's own center, condition of meditation and exact fulfillment of the task.
	Psycho-logical [99]	If a vibrant green it can relate to nature, life, youthful energy. Darker green relates more to stability, growth, economic status and success. Dependability. Green is a global symbol for safety.
	Sensory [25]	Sensory Perception = Astringency
	Jung [28]	Sensation. Growth as it may be associated with the natural self.
	Nature [99]	Spring, life, the security of food and an alive environment. Dark green is associated with maturity.
	Cultural [26]	Christian = faith, immortality, eternal life, contemplation; Cabala = victory; Chinese = health & family.
	Charka	Heart, [64] Love [75]
	Aura [64]	Healing, healer, nurturer

Color	Source	Response and/or Associations
Blue	Luscher[25] associations	Complete calm, contentment, fulfillment, depth of feeling, meditative awareness. Unification and a sense of belonging or loyalty. Concentric, passive, incorporative, heteronymous, sensitive, perceptive, unifying. Affective aspects = tranquility, contentment, tenderness, love and affection. Increased emotional sensitivity.
	Psycho-logical[99]	Best liked color, positive and uplifting, peaceful. Navy blue – loyalty, trustworthy, fidelity, integrity. Space appears larger.
	Physio-logical	Blood pressure, heart rate, breathing reduced. Calming effect on parasympathetic branch of autonomic nervous system.[25] Lowest visual acuity, hard for eye to focus in blue illumination.[32] Brain response is relaxation.[33] Productivity increases.[99]
	Learning[34]	Light blue environment increased learning ability.
	Sensory[25, 99]	Sensory Perception = Sweetness
	Jung[4]	Thinking; "Lapis, the Philosophers stone"
	Nature	Color of sky, realm of the gods to early people, the ethereal, air and thus spirit; Clear water, thus calm and a source of life.
	Cultural	Christian = spirit, love of divine works, piety, hope, sincerity, peace, heaven, the Virgin Mary, serene conscience; Lakota = west; Cabala = mercy; Judaism = the Lord's hue; Cherokee = tribulation & defeat.[26] Opulence in some cultures, protection in others.[99]
	Chakra	Throat[64] = expression and colors of aqua and turquoise[78]
	Aura[64]	Sensitivity, teacher
Violet	Luscher[25] associations	Identification, mystic union, sensitive intimacy leading to fusion between subject and object. A magical or wish-fulfilling state. A desire to fascinate, charm and delight others. Intimate, erotic, intuitive and sensitive understanding. Unrealistic.
	Psycho-logical[99]	Power, class, passion, sensuality, luxury, higher-ranking. Deeper plum - spiritual, mysterious, magic, noble. Lavender – romantic, nostalgic.
	Learning[99]	Not conducive to performance since it encourages daydreaming.
	Cultural[26]	Christian = suffering, endurance & repentance; Cabala = foundation; Judaism = Lord's divine splendor and dignity.
	Chakra	Indigo = Head chakra,[64] Third eye = transcendence,[78] Violet = Crown chakra[64] and unity[78]
	Aura[64]	Purple = deeper connection with spirit; Lavender = spirit;
Brown	Luscher[25] associations	Sensation related to the body and the senses. Relates to physical ease and sensuous contentment. Physical discomfort and disease. Importance placed on "roots," on home, and the company of one's own kind and security of the family.
	Psycho-logical[99]	Comfort, warm, home, natural. It grounds us. Approachable, reliable, sincere, hardworking. Lacks authority. A rugged masculine quality.
	Jung[4]	A Nature symbol relating to our instinctive origins.
	Learning[34]	Brown room caused decrease in learning ability.
	Nature	Earth and Trees = dwelling place (family) and our physical origin.

Color	Source	Response and/or Associations
Gray	Luscher [25] associations	Uncommitted and non-involved. A shielding, separation, isolation from direct participation. No emotional involvement, mechanically watches self go through the motions. Compensatory and perhaps self-deceiving.
	Psycho-logical [99]	Neutral, non-involvement. Dignified and conservative authority, wisdom, maturity. Lacks warmth, solemn, gloomy. Discourage lively conversation. Metallic gray or silver – speed, motion, technical advancement.
	Nature	Color of fog – inability to see, detachment from the environment.
	Cultural [26]	Christian-blend divine light of creation + darkness of sin/death; Cabala=wisdom.
Black	Luscher [25] associations	Nothingness, extinction, renunciation, ultimate surrender, relinquishment. Compensation of an extreme nature. A protest against existing conditions. Nothing is as it should be. Revolt against fate.
	Psycho-logical [99]	Authoritative, foreboding, intimidating, aggressive, mysterious, seductive. Conservative, dignified, solemn, formal. Increases perception of weight and depth. Death.
	Learning [34]	Caused decrease in learning.
	Jung [4]	The unconscious; dark primal or shadow self. Death of the ego.
	Nature	Dark, night, depths of the earth, fear of the unseen, sleep, death
	Cultural	Christian = death and regeneration; Cabala = understanding; Chinese = water; Cherokee = night, death; Lakota = west [26]. Symbol of grief. [99]
	Aura [64]	Absence of light, profound forgetting, thwarted ambition, disease
White	Luscher [25]	Virgin page on which the story has yet to be written. A beginning.
	Psycho-logical	Purity, innocence, peace, goodness, truth, simplicity, sterility, safety; cooler associations; a subdued or calming effect in some combinations. [99] Bright light and white (often mixed with other colors) appears during periods of heightened self-awareness & psycho-spiritual transformation. [105]
	Jung [4]	Light – awareness & consciousness. White = God-like & divine.
	Nature	Daytime, ability to see, thus awareness. Ice and snow, thus cool.
	Cultural [26]	Christian = chastity, innocence, purity; Cabala = the Crown.; Lakota = North; Judaism = purity, joy and victory; Cherokee = peace and happiness. International call for truce. [99] Death in India, China and Japan. [99]
	Aura [64]	Truth
	Chakra [94]	White associates with Crown chakra in some systems.
Pink	Psycho-logical [99]	Arouses the interest and excitement of red but in a softer, quieter way. Romantic, passive, sensitive, nurturing, compassionate, gentle. Promotes affability and discourages aggression. Calms, soothes. Feminine.
	Physiological	Aids digestion, tranquilizing, slows heart beat. [99]
	Aura [64]	Rose color - love
Gold & Silver	Jung [23,28]	**Gold:** Associations include the divine, the sun, value, the masculine, conscious; (may exhibit some of the emotional themes of yellow). **Silver:** Associations include the moon, mercury (quicksilver), the feminine, the unconscious (may exhibit some of the themes of gray and white).
	Transform-ation [105]	**Gold & Silver** = Often appears in dreams as an integration of opposites during psycho-spiritual transformation.

In figure 14, I have aligned some of the non-cultural associations from the table, adjacent to the chromatic and achromatic color spectrums. Note that as we move from the red toward the blue end of the spectrum we move from what we typically associate with the "warmer" emotions to the "cooler" emotions. Also, as we move from black to white, we move from non-awareness and unconsciousness to awareness and renewal, with gray seeming to be the barrier or separation state.

Figure 14 – Associations and the Color Spectrum

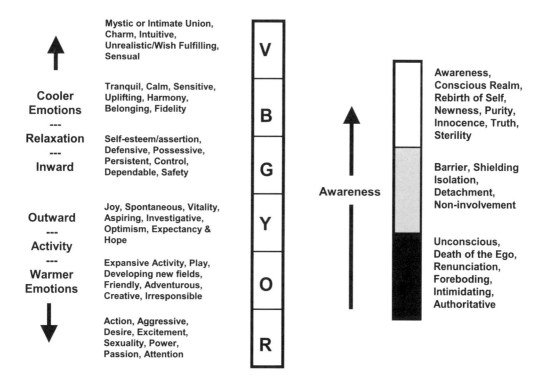

Cultural Factors

I have not attempted to do an in-depth study of cultural factors in this book, but have included a few cultural associations in order to illustrate that culture and perceptual beliefs do influence our personal associations with color. Luscher[25] made a distinction between what he called the "objective" response to color, our physiological and basic instinctive emotional response, and the "functional" meaning of color, or our attitudes and personal associations with a color. It makes sense that such a condition exists. Our instinctive response to a stimulus such as color occurs in a different part of the brain and nervous system, than does our learned, personal and cultural associations. Our personal association and attitude toward a color is linked to our personal associations and attitude toward the emotion evoked by that the color. Red may stimulate the same excitement, increased heart rate and energy in all of us, but each of us will have a different personal attitude toward that energy. One person may thrive on that energy, using it to succeed and achieve, while another may loathe the energy, feeling they are already spreading themselves too thin. These "objective" versus "functional" differences form the basis of both the Luscher test and our approach to working with dream color.

The "functional" associations are influenced by cultural factors. Using red as an example, the energy stimulated by red may be associated with winning and assertiveness in the West, whereas in China that same energy may be associated with good luck. The history of a color within a culture, as well as the mythology of that culture, can affect our associations with it. Sutton and Whelan[99] point out that colors such as purple and white are commonly associated with wealth, not for any physiological reason, but because these colors during much of our history were so difficult to create or maintain, that only the most wealthy could afford them.

Perhaps the most striking cross-cultural difference lies in the naming of color. Research by Debi Roberson, PhD, of the University of Essex[92] found that while humans establish a continuum of color terminology the same way around the world (in keeping with the structure of our visual system), the specific names we call these colors are learned relative to language and culture. Certain cultures name colors and color groups very differently than others. For example, Roberson studied the Himba tribe in northern Namibia in Africa that uses only five terms for colors, whereas the English language uses at least 11 basic color terms, plus many more for shades and mixtures. She found that the Himba use one word "serandu" to describe what English speakers call red, orange and pink. They likewise group dark colors such as dark blue, dark green, dark brown, dark purple, dark red and black into one group, using the word "zoozu." She also found that the link between color memory and color language increases as the cultural names for the colors are learned, strongly suggesting that color names are learned and not innate. This language factor does not necessarily affect our "objective" (instinctive and physiological) response to color, but it definitely would affect our personal or "functional" associations with the names we give colors.

The motif of four color "primaries," spoken of by Jung, does seem to appear in many cultures in relation to primary elements or cardinal direction. The specific colors that each culture adopts as "primaries," and even the number of "primaries," may vary by culture however. Jewish historian Josephus associates white with earth, purple with water, red with fire and yellow with air. Leonardo da Vinci associated yellow with earth, green with water, red with fire, and blue with air. Birren[26] indicates that: the mythology in Tibet describes north as yellow, south as blue, east as white and west as red; in China, north is associated with black, south with red, east with green and west with white; and one Navajo Indian fable considered white (day) to be east, yellow (twilight) to be west, black (night) to be north and blue (dawn) to be south. An alchemical process, symbolically related to human transformation by Jung, is a four-stage metal purification and coloring process involving the colors black, white, yellow and red.[107] In Chinese lore, they recognized five elements, with yellow relating to earth, black to water, red to fire, green to wood and white to metal.[26]

While the naming of colors, and our personal associations with specific colors (the "functional" factors) are heavily influenced by culture, our physiological and instinctive responses (the "objective" response) may be dictated more by our common evolution. More cross-cultural research is required, but it appears to be the case that there are similar physiological responses across cultures. This is observed in the fairly common findings of laboratory results, color psychology findings and the Luscher associations in table 9-1. Even this data was primarily developed from Western populations, however, so there remains some uncertainty regarding its pertinence to Eastern populations.

Our Physiological Response to Color

The response of the eye itself may determine much about our "objective" instinctual association with color. A study of the physical structure of the eye leads many scientists to believe that blue and yellow color vision evolved first (these colors are sensed at the extremes of the retinal structure near the more primitive receptors).[106] We exhibit the highest visual acuity for yellow illumination, and the lowest for deep blue (making it difficult for the eye to focus).[31,32] Yellow illumination thus makes activity more possible, whereas blue illumination makes it less so. As a function of our optical receptors alone, the human instinctual association with yellow would lean more toward outward activity, and with blue toward the more passive or limited physical activity.

Furthermore, the human physiological response to color can be tested. Colors have an observed effect on the various parts of the autonomic nervous system. This system is concerned with functions that take place below the threshold of awareness. Blue has been observed to have a calming effect on the parasympathetic branch that regulates automatic, involuntary functions such as heartbeat, breathing, and digestion.[25] The color red has been observed to have the affect of exciting the sympathetic branch, and causing certain processes such as heartbeat and breathing to speed up.[25] The experiments of Barbara Brown,[33] which were designed to understand the associations between color and brain wave activity, supported these findings. She determined that the brain's electrical response to red is one of alerting and arousal, whereas the response to blue is that of relaxation.

Our Psychological Response to Color

The field of color psychology has had a great impact on our advertising, packaging, food, clothing, and decorating industries, since it appears that color influences our moods and appetites.[99]   Research on our psychological response to color supports the notion that humans respond emotionally to color. As indicated above, this is likely linked to the function of our limbic system, which assigns emotion to sensory input.

Goldstein[35] found that red stimulation corresponds with the experience of being disrupted, thrown out, attracted to the outer world, and being incited to activity, aggression, excitation and emotionally determined action. Goldstein concluded that the color green corresponds with withdrawal from the outer world and retreat to one's own center, to a condition of meditation and exact fulfillment of the task. Henner Ertel[34] conducted a 3-year study on room color and its effect on learning with children. He found that yellow, yellow-green, orange and light blue increased learning while white, black and brown caused a decrease in learning; and orange improved social behavior.

Color response has also been used in the development of some early personality testing tools. The Rorschach test, for example, uses associative scoring based on the various ways that a subject names or projects colors, on color and monochrome test cards. Dr. Max Luscher, Professor of Psychology at the University of Basel, created another psychological testing tool, that more directly associates color with emotional experience. His work led to the introduction in 1947 of a testing tool based on color preference, called the Luscher Color Test.[25] It was first based on work by Hering, who established a link between responses in the eye-brain system to color contrast. As mentioned above, Luscher made a distinction between the "objective" (physiological and instinctive) and the "functional" meaning of color (whether we are drawn to it, indifferent toward it or find it distasteful). To Luscher, a person's choice of color, in a particular circumstance, was based on both psychological preference and physiological need.

While the Luscher Test is not used much today, it was widely used in the 1950's and 60's in the fields of medicine and psychology, and even in industry (where it was often used as a screening tool for job applicants). Reference 25 contains a listing of over 140 clinical investigations and papers supporting the test, primarily across populations on the European continent. The full Luscher test is based on making 43 choices, from seventy-three different colors, of twenty-five different hues and shades.

In my investigations, I used a version with only eight colors. The tool establishes an emotional profile based on a person's selection of colors in a preferred sequence. I found that the Color Test correlated to a basic degree with color research, other color psychology literature, and appeared to be the only widely used test tool that related color to the human waking emotional response. I did not attempt to validate the Color Test further, but rather decided to proceed with my dream research on the premise that it represents a reasonable characterization of the human waking response to color.

The Research

I designed my investigation to determine if there is a relationship between the dreamer's association with colored imagery in dreams, and the waking response to color as represented by the Color Test. I hoped to demonstrate that dream color contained emotional content that was important to the overall "meaning" of the dream image with which it combines. In order to establish the emotional content of the dream image, I used the scripted Gestalt role-play technique (the 6 questions), which had proven effective in revealing emotional content within dream imagery. This technique was also appropriate because of the standardized scripting. I then compared the role-play responses with the Luscher Color Test associations for color preference. The correlation was then confirmed with the dreamer as to how it related to an associated waking life situation.

The result was that the Color Test correlated well with the dream image role-play statements, as well as the dream-related waking life experiences.[65] A few examples from this investigation are given in the next section. They support the notion that color in dreams relates to emotions contained within the colored dream image. The research further provides some interesting and surprising insight into how colors combine with dream imagery to present a fuller meaning to the composite dream image.

How Color Relates to Dream Imagery

As we discussed above, when an image in a dream is a certain color, it can be treated as a condensation of two symbols, one being the color and the other being the image. For example, a red hat would be more expressive of energy and vibrancy than a colorless hat. Interpreting the results in terms of this condensation principle helps to more fully understand the role color plays in a dream. In the investigation, I found that the condensation of color and imagery appears to occur in at least four primary ways as illustrated in figure 15:

Figure 15
How Color Combines with Imagery

COLOR "AMPLIFIES" THE IMAGE

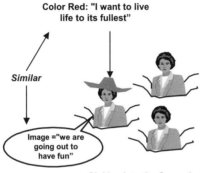

Color Red: "I want to live life to its fullest"

Similar

Image = "we are going out to have fun"

Sinking into the Ground = suppressing part of self

COLOR "COMPLEMENTS" THE IMAGE

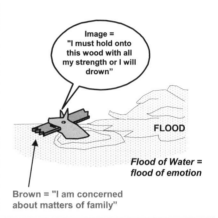

Image = "I must hold onto this wood with all my strength or I will drown"

FLOOD

Flood of Water = flood of emotion

Brown = "I am concerned about matters of family"

COLOR "COMPENSATES"

GRAY = "I want to shield myself from the feelings"

Compensation

"I feel powerful and assertive"

GRAY 4 Wheel Drive Truck

GROUPING OF "PRIMARIES"

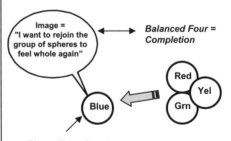

Image = "I want to rejoin the group of spheres to feel whole again"

Balanced Four = Completion

Red

Yel

Grn

Blue

Blue = "I need rest, peace and a chance to recuperate"

1) **Amplifies:** Often, the color associations and role-play statements are nearly alike. In this case, the content within the color appears to "amplify" the content within the image. Perhaps the color and the image are stimulated by the same emotion.

2) **Complements:** Frequently the color associations add new information to the associations within the dream image. Color completes the story and thus "complements" the content within image. Perhaps the dream color and the dream image are stimulated by separate but associated emotional memories.

3) **Compensates:** At times, the color associations reveals a hidden meaning within the image that is not revealed in the image work alone. The color might reveal a rejection of something that the dreamer associates with the image. The color may reveal how the dreamer reacts or feels toward the situation represented by the image. Perhaps the image is stimulated by one set of associations, and the color is stimulated by an emotional reaction to those associations. In this case, color may be performing an important compensating function in the dream.

4) **Color as a Symbol:** Sometimes colors appear alone, without a specific object attachment. For example it may appear as the grouping of color "primaries," or as part of the dream setting. Here it may be setting the emotional tone for the dream scene.

Color "Amplifies" the Image

If the color of an image, and the image itself, emerge in the dream from the same emotional stimuli, then their associations should be similar. In this case, the emotional associations from the color tables would match the statements and feelings expressed during role-play of the dream image.

Case 1a - "woman in red hat"
(illustrated in the top left panel of figure 15)

Dream: *"In the dream I was one of three women, and was wearing a red hat. We were going into town, walking along a road, when suddenly we sank into the ground."*

Personal Content within the Dream Image: Role-play of the woman in the red hat revealed: *"we're just going out for the evening to have fun,"*- *"I feel vibrant."* The body language of the dreamer at this point was revealing as well. She became suddenly lively and animated as she became the woman wearing the red hat.

Emotional Content within the Color: When the dreamer reviewed the Luscher associations for red, the one she responded most to was: *"Intense vital and animated, taking delight in action. Desire to live life to the fullest."*

Confirmation - Waking Situation: In this case, both statements supported the same emotional state, that of being animated and going out to have fun and living life to the fullest. Thus the color and the image appeared to support or "amplify" each other. As the dreamer reviewed these statements, she indicated that this is a way she had not felt for a very long time, as she had suppressed her social life and desires in order to take care of a personal situation. Note that the action in the dream of sinking into the ground, or disappearing below, is a common metaphor or motif for suppression.

Color "Complements" the Image to Reveal the Whole Story

Sometimes the color and the image complement each other and must be understood together to provide a complete understanding of the dream image. The role-play imagery work might reveal one set of emotional associations or conflicts, while the color work might reveal a different but related set of associations. A check against the waking life situation usually makes the complementary relationship or correlation obvious.   One example is the continuation of the dream in case 1a.

Case 1b - "holding onto brown wood"
(illustrated in the top right panel of figure 15)

The Dream in 1a continued: *"Later a flood came by. I tried to save my dog which was in the water, but he would not let go of a piece of wood held tight in his teeth. The only color was the brown wood."*

Personal Content within the Dream Image: Role-play of the dog with the wood revealed: *"I must hold on to this wood with all my strength or I will drown."*

Emotional Content within the Color: In this case I used the color association table 9-2. The statement for brown that the dreamer most resonated with was: *"Concern about matters of family, home, or one's roots"*.

Confirmation - Waking Life Situation: The dreamer revealed that in her situation she was indeed suppressing her own needs, due to trying to support a family member who was in trouble. She feared that if she "let go" and had fun, and did not "hold on tight" to this family member, that person would leave her and she would "drown in a flood" of emotions. Here the color brown added the missing element, that of the concern for a family member at the core of the conflict. The dog (her motherly instinct?) was holding on tight to this family member (brown). The fear of letting go and drowning in emotion was contained within the dog, but the object of the struggle, the concern for a family member, was contained within the color.

Case 2a - "brown fish"

Dream: *"I dreamed it had rained so hard that a pond overflowed and <u>brown</u> fish were floundering on shore. I was trying to get the fish back in the pond."*

Personal Content within the Dream Image: Role-play on the brown fish revealed: *"I feel I am out of my element."*

Emotional Content within the Color: The Luscher statement for brown that the dreamer most resonated with was: *"seeking freedom from problems and a secure state of physical comfort in which to relax and recover."*

Confirmation - Waking Situation: I asked the dreamer about the feelings of "being out of her element." She revealed that at work she had mixed feelings about a recent promotion. She felt that she was being asked to do too many things (too much rain) with which she was unfamiliar (out of her element). She felt a need to reestablish a more familiar, comfortable state where she felt secure (similar to her association with brown). The role-play identified her fear of being out of her element (a need to put the fish back in the water), and the color further establishes her reaction to that fear, of wanting to reestablish that familiar sense of security where she could relax.

Color "Compensates"

Sometimes, the dreamer's associations with the image and with the color reveal a meaningful contrast. The nature of that contrast can vary. Sometimes, associations with the image and associations with the color reveal a meaningful conflict – the words relate to opposing fears, desires or myths, that in turn relate to a conflict the dreamer is struggling with in waking life. Sometimes the color performs a compensating function. In this case, the dreamer's associations with the color can reveals hidden feelings or reactions to the emotional memories within the dream image. The color essentially "paints" the image with the dreamer's emotional response to it. I find this to be particularly true of gray, which is a color of shielding and non-involvement. Gray can often "paint over" a dream image to reveal how the dreamer is shielding themselves from the associations or emotions within.

Case 3 - "gray trucks"
(illustrated in the left lower quadrant of figure 15)

This dream illustrates how gray can "paint over" a dream image, to shield the dreamer from a behavioral style within the image that they are afraid to exhibit.

Dream: *"I dreamed of looking down on a sandy beach area where there were three gray 4-wheel drive trucks."*

Personal Content within the Image: During role-play of the trucks, the dreamer became animated, appeared to enjoy the role, and made statements about feeling powerful and assertive.

Content within the Color: Luscher relates gray to a barrier or *"wanting to remain shielded or separated from the situation or associated feelings."*

Confirmation with Waking Life: After observing the animated response, I assumed the dreamer really enjoyed expressing the assertive side of herself, but when I asked what she liked about being gray trucks, she surprisingly answered: *"Nothing - I don't like being that way, people wouldn't like me, I would drive them away."* Here was a case where the truck image represented the characteristics of assertiveness and power (that she seemed to enjoy experiencing), but the gray indicated a conflict with behaving in that manner. She felt a need to shield herself from that behavior, for fear it would "drive others away" (also an interesting metaphor for the function of a truck). Here the dream appeared to be "painting over" the dreamer's powerful assertive side with a mood of noninvolvement, in order to avoid expressing that side of herself.

Case 2b - "gray kitten"
(dream segment that followed 2a about the brown fish)

The brown fish dream continued: *"As I reached for one of the fish, I was threatened by a snake. I reached anyway and the snake turned into a gray kitten."*

Personal Content within the Image: Role-play of the kitten revealed positive associations with the energy the dreamer planned to invest in this new role at work. The snake, however, revealed expressions of fear about taking on too much that was unfamiliar, and fear of the unknown.

Emotional Content within the Color: The Luscher association with gray which the dreamer most identified was: *"remains emotionally uninvolved, mechanically going through the motions."*

Confirmation with Waking Life: In this case, the dream evolved a bit from the previous sequence. It again revealed her instinctive fear of the unknown (the snake) but, in this case, she diverted her attention from that fear (reached away) and toward the excitement she felt for the job and the warm fuzzy feelings about her promotion (the kitten). There is a concern here, however, since the kitten was (gray). She seemed to be shielding herself from the conflict between fear and excitement, and was unemotionally "going through the motions" just to get through the situation.

Color as a Symbol in Itself

Color Patterns (Conflict and Integration)

Sometimes color appears by itself, unattached to any other imagery, to set an emotional tone or represent an emotional memory. Color can appear as a color pattern or form (as in the "maze" dream), a color shape (sphere, box, square or such), or as color illumination or background. Two-color patterns or combinations will often appear by themselves, or as part of a dream image, in order to represent an integration or conflict regarding the emotions represented by each color. When working with color combinations, use the statements in table 9-2 for each color to explore possible conflicts between two emotional states. Then use table 9-3 to trigger and explore personal associations associated with the combination of the two colors.

Case 4 - "red/blue instrument"

Dream: *"I dreamed I was looking all over a large facility for a work associate, who had been very uncooperative with me in waking life. I wanted to find him and convince him to work with me as a team player. I entered a building where I sat down on a pile of some unidentifiable shapes in the corner painted red and blue. I was then confronted by four members of a band, and was offered the choice of an instrument to play. I finally picked one, but then woke from the dream."*

Emotional Content within the Color – Luscher: The two colors represented in the background of this dream were red and blue. The initial step was to explore these colors as a possible set of conflicting emotions, using table 9-2. The association for red with which the dreamer connected was: *"desire to win, succeed, achieve."* His association with blue on the other hand was: *"needing a relationship free from contention where he can trust and be trusted; a need for harmony."* The dreamer confirmed that this was a conflict related to the situation. I then tried table 9-3 for the color pair red/blue (which was derived from the Luscher test-scoring procedure for color pairs). The statement the dreamer connected with was: *"I seek harmony and cooperation with my associates for our mutual benefit."*

Confirmation with Waking Life: The dreamer's main anxiety in the dream seemed to be a replay of the conflict in which he found himself the day before. He needed to "succeed and achieve" on a management assignment he was responsible for, but this required him to find a way to convince his co-workers - particularly the one in the dream - to work with him in harmony as a team. The dreamer's associations with blue, as well as the red/blue pairing, were an exact statement of how the dreamer felt about the situation. The metaphor of "choosing an instrument," related to his attempt to choose a means by which he could convince his coworkers to "play in harmony."

The Psychological "Primaries"

As discussed earlier, the grouping of Red, Yellow, Blue and Green (that Jung, Perls and Luscher called the psychological "primaries") often appears in dreams, representing a pattern for completion and balance. When working with the "primaries," look for the appearance of the four colors (or three out of the four) in some sort of geometric grouping. Generally, there is little work to do with a geometric color grouping, other than to note its presence, unless one of the colors is active or missing. Work on the missing or active color as if it is the key to understanding what is required for closure or balance, or that which is disturbing the balance.

Case 5 - "blue sphere"
(lower right panel of figure 15)

In this dream, the four colors appeared in balance at first, but then one of the four colors (blue) becomes activated.

Dream: *"I dreamed of a blue sphere which was part of a group of four spheres colored red, yellow, blue and green that formed the dial on a pay-phone. The blue sphere separated and landed on my finger like a "magic" ring that I perceived would give me the power to solve all my problems."*

Personal Content within the Dream Image: Although a sphere is a collective image, we attempted the role-play anyway. As the blue sphere the dreamer stated: *"I am a* *blue sphere, part of group of spheres, and I just want to rejoin the group to feel whole again."* As suspected, the sphere expressed a desire for unification, which Jung attributes to this grouping of the four "primaries."

Emotional Content within the Color: The dreamer's association with blue from table 9-2 was: *"I need rest, peace and a chance to recuperate."*

Confirmation with Waking Life: The dream occurred on the first day of a much-needed vacation, and the dreamer stated that he was upset about things in his life and indeed needed rest, peace and a chance to recuperate. Assuming that Jung is correct about the four "primaries," the four colored spheres together would represent a state of stability and balance. Thus, the separation of blue from that grouping would represent what was needed by the dreamer to reestablish balance - the need for rest.

Case 6 - "blue man/red man"

This case, from a group session at the IASD conference in Leiden,[100] illustrates an appearance of only three of the "primaries" in a group, with one color active and one color missing. In this example, I worked on both the most active color and the missing color, to see whether there was a connection. Blue was the most active color and red was missing.

Dream: *"I dreamed that 2 other men and I, all dressed in green and yellow, were being chased by a blue man".*

Emotion within the Image: Role-play on the blue man revealed: *"I want to belong"* and *"my purpose is to keep us united."*

Emotional Content within the Color: The statement in table 9-2 with which the dreamer connected was: *"I need a peaceful state of harmony and a sense of belonging."* Green and yellow on the other hand (table 9-3) related to: *"I want to impress others and be popular and admired"* and *"I am trying to establish a better relationship with others."*

Confirmation with Waking Life: The dreamer indicated that these statements described feelings which dominated his waking life behavior. He holds back from expressing himself "in order to bridge the gap between himself and others" because he "wants to belong, to be popular and admired." The statement "keeping us united" also seemed to relate to the principle of the "primaries," which was to bring all parts of self together.

Further Work on the Missing Color: Speculating that "redness" was the element needed for balance, I asked that he role-play a man dressed in red. As the red man, he suddenly became more animated, assertive, vital, and expressed a feeling of *"being alive again."* This correlated with the Luscher associations for red of: *"intense, vital, animated, a desire to live life to the fullest."* These were feelings that he admitted were missing in his life. He was reluctant to express them because he feared rejection, and that he would scare his friends away. As a result of the dreamwork, he recognized the need to let the red man side of self come forth. People in the group, who observed the session, reinforced how much they liked seeing him as the red man. An interesting footnote was that he appeared at the IASD costume dream ball that evening, dressed completely in red, swinging a red wooden sword, definitely "feeling alive" again.

Does Color Recall
Relate to Waking Emotional Events?

If the color of a dream image contains emotional content that relates to a persons waking life situation, then it would follow that the colors most often recalled from a person's dreams at any point in their life should reflect the dominant emotional events taking place at that time. This premise was quite a stretch, but I decided to focus a second phase of my research on determining whether dream color recall can be observed to relate to waking emotional events. Dr. Curtiss Hoffman[94] joined me in the investigation. In total, we collected color frequency samples from roughly 8,000 dreams. The results were reported at the International Association for the Study of Dreams 2004 conference in Copenhagen[66] and in *DreamTime*[108].

The dream journals of the subjects were scanned for mention of color. Color names from the dream reports were grouped to correlate with the eight colors in the Luscher Test. Color frequency reports were sorted into monthly or yearly aggregates, based on the correlation being tested for. These monthly and yearly aggregates were then profiled using the Luscher tool, and those profiles compared with specific emotional events experienced by the subjects during those time-frames. The aggregate total of all dream color reports for a subject were also converted to a baseline personality profile.

The Luscher Color Test derives an emotional profile based on a subject's selection of color in a sequence from highest preference to lowest preference. We applied the test to the color data, under the premise that the highest frequency of dream color reported might also relate to a greater color preference, and so on to the lowest frequency of color reported. Each resultant profile contained roughly 12 to 20 statements relating to emotional states or situations. The subject would then be asked to self-grade each statement in three categories, as to how well each fit what they perceived as their emotional state during the period being tested ("yes it fits"; "it sometimes fits, a partial fit, or it fits but not exactly as stated" or "it does not fit as a statement or theme").

The first analysis was performed on a subject that had collected 11 years of data and close to 4,800 dream reports containing color. A year-by-year Luscher profile was performed on the sequence of the total frequency of colors reported in the dreams each year. In this case, the subject challenged me to find the period of emotional turmoil during this time. When the results were compiled, the Luscher profile described this emotional period with an accuracy of 81%. In addition, a second event during these 11 years was described with a perfect 100% correlation. In the intervening periods, which were described by the dreamer as "not having a lot going on," the dream color profile was somewhat constant and closely matched (75% on average) the dreamer's baseline profile. This provided a promising indication that the colors we recall from our dreams might indeed be influenced by emotional events in our lives.

Does Recall of Dream Color Relate to Personality?

Extending this reasoning further, might the frequency of colors recalled over a lifetime (or long period of time) correlate to key traits in the dreamer's personality? For this work, we looked at 3 subjects who had recorded color in their dreams over many years. For each subject, the total recall frequency of each of eight colors was added up for the total period of their dream records. These were then ranked to create a color profile for that dreamer (most frequent color recalled to least frequent color). A Luscher personality profile was then performed on the color profile for each subject. The resulting Luscher personality profile was given back to each subject for self-grading to determine how accurately the resultant profile described their personality (or at least their perception of their personality).

The resulting color profiles and Luscher personality profiles were very different for each subject. The three subjects graded their resultant personality profiles as 75% accurate, 78% accurate and 91% accurate respectively. Much more work must be done in this area to be certain, but it appears promising that our personality might influence the colors we recall in our dreams. It would make sense that our personality would influence the emotional conditions to which we are sensitive, and thus the dream colors that reflect those emotional conditions. If we are drawn to colors that represent our emotional sensitivities in waking life (in how we dress or decorate), then it should follow that we would represent those same colors more frequently in our dreams.

The Color Questionnaire

The positive correlations between role-play associations and Luscher-based color associations, led me to believe that the Luscher Color Test might provide an interesting tool for enhancing personal dreamwork. The analytical nature of the Luscher test, however, did not lend itself well to dreamwork, because it could be too easily used as a color "dictionary" to interpret the "meaning" of color. The emotional themes represented by the color tables, however, appeared quite useful as triggers for a dreamer's own personal associations. Since they also agreed nicely with other color psychology literature and research, I decided to use the emotional themes in the Luscher tables as a baseline from which I created new statements. I also augmented those statements with other color psychology findings.[4, 25, 28, 32, 33, 35, 99] The objective was to create personalized statements, which describe emotional themes that have well-researched associations with color; statements that would not be seen as the "meaning" of color, but rather would be used to trigger the dreamer's own emotional associations. The results are tables 9-2 and 9-3.

Single Colors

Table 9-2 was derived from: the color themes in the eight-color Luscher test; associations from other color psychology literature; some of the principles of Jungian theory; and results from my own work with color. The Luscher test, and most color psychology sources, do not adequately capture the collective associations assigned by Jung to black and white. I therefore augmented the associations for black and white with the Jungian work. The statements within each color cell were created around an emotional theme. Within each theme can be both positive and negative emotions, and positive feelings and needs. Red, for example, can relate to feeling energetic as well as to a need for energy.

Pastels

The color table reflects work from various sources related to pastels (mixing a primary color with white). I have observed that, in dreams, white associates a "newness," often of a fantasy nature, or a renewal or transformation of the emotion represented by the color with which it combines. Likewise, Hamilton[105] observed that color combinations with white increased as higher states of self-awareness were achieved during a transformation experience. Sutton and Whelan[99] discuss the mixture of white with colors as related to a coolness or peacefulness, and associate many of the color combinations with white as a "cooling" of the color (and thus emotion) with which it mixes, making it less intense and more pleasant and friendly.

The "newness" or "rebirth" experience is illustrated in the following dream: *"I dreamed I was dressed in pink."* The dreamer looked through table 9-2 at the emotional themes associated with the color red. She indicated that assertiveness is a newly emerging condition within herself that she is only beginning to understand how to deal with. The mixture of newness (white) with the assertiveness (red) related to an emergence or rebirth of a repressed assertive part of self.

White sometimes adds an emergence theme, with a flair of fantasy or celebration, as in this dream: *"I dreamed I was on a huge white yacht that was being chased and bombed by old WWII aircraft. The captain said not to worry since the yacht was invincible. He fired the guns of the ship, which created a blaze of pastel rainbow colors. Later, when it turned out that the boat was not so invincible, we hid in a lagoon near a volcano which then erupted in similar pastel rainbow colors."* In waking life, the dreamer felt under attack in his career because of age (reference to WWII planes – the period when he was born). He had escaped into a new area of interest, not subject to career or age, which made him feel "invincible." The white yacht and white mixed with an explosion of rainbow colors, seemed to represent both an emergence of a new "invincible" self, as well as a transformation of his self-image (to one not limited by age or career). There was perhaps a fantasy nature to this thinking as well.

Color Pairs and Mixtures

When working with dream images that contain a color pair, I have often found that the pair represents a conflict between the two emotional states associated with the two colors. Such a conflict was illustrated in the "blue/red instrument" dream. It is also apparent in the following dream: *"I dreamed of a round gas station sign that was orange, with the number 76 in blue letters."* Although this is a commercial sign, the dreamer related it to a trip to Nepal in 1976, and stated that she was indeed conflicted between a *"desire to do more and expand her interests and activities"* (orange from table 9-2) and her "need for more gas" or *"needing rest, peace and a chance to recuperate"* (blue from table 9-2). I therefore generally explore the possibility of conflict using table 9-2 before proceeding with the color pair table 9-3.

The color pair can also represent an integration of the qualities of the two colors. The Luscher Color Test also provided a convenient way to understand emotional themes that result from color pairs. The scoring process assigns emotional associations to color pairs.[25] Table 9-3 is a result of applying the same principles I used in creating the single color table, but using Luscher color pair themes as a reference. This table can be useful for triggering your own emotional associations resulting from both color pairs and color mixtures in dreams (blue-green, yellow-green, red-violet, tan as brown-yellow, etc.).

The "change purse" dream from chapter 7 illustrates the use of the tables for color mixtures. *"My associate in the dream was a slightly rounded but rectangular shaped zippered change purse, red on the top-side and a green-brown color on the under-side. I kept flip-flopping it over in my hands, trying to decide which side and color I liked best."* In this case, the dream presented the two sides as an indecision or conflict between the emotions represented by the red side and the emotions represented by the green-brown color pair on the underside. Using table 9-2, the dreamer connected with the red statement: *"I want to win, succeed and achieve."* When he reviewed the color pair table 9-3 for the green-brown mixture, he connected with the statement: *"I want to overcome difficulties and establish myself, even though I am tired and feel too much is being asked of me."* His conflict was between pursuing a goal of "winning," in what he saw as an upcoming "battle" with his colleagues, and the desire to "not to take on too much," which, in this case, would be the result of winning.

Proper Use of the Questionnaire

The statements do NOT represent the "meaning" of a dream color and should not be used as a dictionary of color meaning. It does not work that way. They contain emotional themes reportedly associated with color. The statements are designed to trigger your own personal associations with a situation the dream might be dealing with. When you use the table, you may find that only one or two statements within a color cell relate to your specific situation, whereas the others do not. This is exactly how it was designed. The statements are variations around an emotional theme found to be associated with that color. The statements are also designed to provide a spectrum of emotions, from being "filled with the emotion," to needing more of that emotional stimulus. Your own particular situation would naturally be limited to just a few statements, and may not be described exactly by the wording of the statement. You may also find that none of the statements trigger an association. That is possible since the statements were derived from a limited set of common human associations, and are limited to those associated with basic color hues. So don't depend totally on the tables for answers. They are intended only as an aid to trigger your own associations. If the tables do not trigger associations, then you may want to try freely associating with your feelings, as you envision being illuminated by the color of interest in the dream.

When working with the tables, pick the statement(s) that really stands out, that provides the greatest "aha" or connection with your waking life situation. Then set aside the table and use your own words to describe your situation and relate it to the dream story.

1) **Select the colored images from your dream** that you feel are the most important, that you feel most drawn to, or have the greatest emotional reaction to. It is best to work with something that is not a commonly colored object (like green grass), unless it stands out. Work with a colored image on which the color is optional (such as a red hat, a blue car, an orange dress). Look for a grouping of the four "primaries," and work on the color that is most active if there is one. Look for a grouping of three of the four "primaries," in which a color is missing. Work on the missing color, as if it is something you need, in order to bring about closure or harmony in your life.

2) **Pick the color** or color combination in tables 9-2 or 9-3 that best matches the color(s) of the dream image. Don't worry if there is not a perfect match. The tables are not intended to reveal the meaning of the color. They are intended to trigger your own associations from the emotional themes represented.

   - **Single Color:** use table 9-2 to select the closest matching color.

   - **Color Pair:** Explore the possibility that the two colors might represent conflicting emotions by using table 9-2 on each color separately. Explore the possibility of an integration of color and emotion with table 9-3. First pick the row with the dominant color, then select the secondary color from the column, and read the statements at the intersection of the two.

   - **Color Mixtures:** Table 9-3 also seems to work well with mixed colors, for example reddish-brown, blue-green, etc. Again, match the dominant hue in the mix with the colors in the rows first, then the secondary color in the columns.

3) **Read each expression** for that color (or better yet have someone else read them while you listen) **and ask yourself:** "Does this statement relate to a way I have felt recently or describe a situation in my waking life?"

4) **Recall:** Pick the one or two statement(s) that create the strongest "aha" response or "connection," that best relate to a waking life situation or conflict. Describe the situation, and the feelings at the time, in your own words.

5) **Compare:** How might the situation or feelings relate to the dream? How might the color statement relate to, or better clarify, the dream and/or the work you may have done with the dream imagery? Does the color work help to complete the relationship between the dream story and the waking life story?

Table 9-2 SINGLE COLOR EMOTIONAL THEMES
(Statements are Designed to Trigger Personal Associations)

COLOR	ASSOCIATED EMOTIONAL THEMES
RED	1) I feel intense, vital or animated. 2) I feel transformed. 3) I feel assertive, forceful. 4) I feel creative. 5) I want to live life to its fullest. 6) I want to win, succeed, achieve. 7) I feel sexy or have strong sexual urges. 8) I have a driving desire. 9) I need something to make me feel alive again. 10) I need to be more assertive and forceful. 11) I need to get out and enjoy myself. *12) If it appears as blood or inflammation - it could indicate sickness or injury.*
ORANGE	1) I want to expand my interests and develop new activities. 2) I want a wider sphere of influence. 3) I feel friendly and welcoming. 4) I want more contact with others. 5) I feel enthusiastic, outgoing and adventurous. 6) I am driven by desires and hopes toward the new, undiscovered and satisfying. 7) I feel driven but need to overcome my doubts or fear of failure. 8) I must avoid spreading myself too thin.
YELLOW	1) I feel a sense of joy and optimism. 2) I am seeking a solution that will open up new and better possibilities and allow my hopes to be fulfilled. 3) I feel the new direction I am taking will bring happiness in my future. 4) I am hopeful. 5) I need to find a way out of this circumstance or relationship. 6) I need a change. 7) I may be compensating for something. 8) I am acting compulsively.
GREEN	1) I need to establish myself, my self-esteem, my independence. 2) I want recognition. 3) I need to increase the certainty of my own value and status, through acknowledgment by others of my achievements or my possessions. 4) Hard work and drive will gain me recognition and self esteem. 5) My opinion must prevail. 6) I must hold on to this view in order to maintain my self-esteem. 7) I want what I am due. 8) I must maintain control of the events. 9) Things must not change. 10) Detail and logic are important here. 11) I need to increase my sense of security. 12) I need more money to feel secure. 13) I need healing or better health.
BLUE	1) I feel tranquil, peaceful and content. 2) I feel a sense of harmony. 3) I feel a meditative awareness or unity. 4) I feel a sense of belonging. 5) I need rest, peace or a chance to recuperate. 6) I need a relationship free from contention where I can trust and be trusted. 7) I need a peaceful state of harmony offering contentment and a sense of belonging.
VIOLET	1) I like to win others over with my charm. 2) I feel an identification, an almost "mystic" union. 3) I have a deep intuitive understanding of the situation. 4) I feel a sense of intimacy. 5) The feeling is erotic. 6) I seek a magical state where wishes are fulfilled. 7) I yearn for a "magical" relationship of romance and tenderness. 8) I seek to identify with something or someone. 9) I need intimacy. 10) I engage in fantasy a bit to compensate for my feelings of insecurity.

Table 9-2 SINGLE COLOR EMOTIONAL THEMES
(continued)

COLOR	ASSOCIATED EMOTIONAL THEMES
BROWN	1) I seek a secure state where I can be physically comfortable and relax or recover. 2) I am uneasy and insecure in the existing situation. 3) I need a more affectionate environment. 4) I need a situation imposing less physical strain. 5) I want to satisfy the physical senses (food, luxury, sex). *6) Natural wood brown: a) I am concerned about matters of family, home, or my "roots". b) I am concerned with a son or daughter. c) I am searching for my true self or natural state of being. 7) Dirty Brown could be physical problem or illness.*
GRAY (Free of Color)	1) I want to shield myself from those feelings. 2) I feel emotionally distant, only an observer. 3) It is as if I am standing aside, watching myself mechanically go through the motions. 4) I want to remain uncommitted, non-involved, shielded or separated from the situation. 5) I do not want to make a decision that will require my emotional involvement. 6) I have put up with too much and now wish to avoid any further emotional stimulation. 7) I am trying to escape an anxious situation. 8) I am compensating for something.
BLACK (Negation of Color)	The unconscious realm. Moving into darkness = suppression, "death of the ego" (first stage of transformation). Beautiful shiny black = a positive view of the unconscious from which a new self emerges. Try: 1) I am anxious and don't know why. 2) I am fearful of or intimidated by the situation. 3) I have been dealt an unacceptable blow. 4) Nothing is as it should be. 5) I refuse to allow it/them to influence my point of view. 6) I can't accept the situation and don't wish to be convinced otherwise. 7) I feel the need for extreme action, perhaps in revolt against or to compensate for the situation.
WHITE	1) This is a new experience. 2) I'm aware of new feelings. 3) I'm experiencing a new beginning, a reawakening, a transformation. 4) I have a new outlook, a new awareness. 5) I feel pure and/or innocent. 6) I feel open and accepting. 7) I feel unprepared. 8) I feel alone, isolated. 9) It feels cold or sterile.
PASTEL (Color + White)	White transforms the emotion associated with the color it mixes with. It can represent a newness, unfamiliarity with, innocence regarding, or renewal of that emotion; or a subdued coolness, calming and pacification of the emotion. White mixed with red (pink) for example might transform passion into romance or pacify the "red" emotions into nurturing and the discouraging of aggression.
COLOR GROUPS	**Red/Yel/Blu/Grn** – A grouping of the 4 "primaries" represents a state of completion or balance. An active or missing color may be associated with an emotional element missing from the dreamers life that is needed for closure. **Black & White** (patterns) - Forces of unification, an integration of conscious (white) and unconscious (black) from which a greater self emerges; a unity of opposites; an internal change. **Gold & Silver** - Integration of masculine & feminine, conscious & unconscious.

Table 9-3 COLOR PAIR - EMOTIONAL THEMES
(Statements are Designed to Trigger Personal Associations)

Color	Red	Yellow	Green	Blue
Red	I feel Intense, full of energy. I want to win and succeed. I feel driven by desire. I want to live life to its fullest. I want my will to prevail. I feel sexy or sexual urges.	I feel enthusiastic, outgoing and active. I want contact with others. I want to expand my interests and develop new activities. I want to overcome my doubts.	I am purposeful and controlling in pursuing my goals. I don't allow myself to be deflected. I want to overcome obstacles & achieve recognition from success.	I feel emotionally fulfilled. I want a relationship that provides emotional and/or sexual fulfillment. If I follow this course of action I will achieve harmony.
Yellow	I want a wider sphere of influence. I am driven by desire and hope for something new and satisfying. I like the new and undiscovered. I am seeking new fields of interest.	I need a change that will give me some relief. I am hopeful in my search for a solution that will bring happiness. I am interested in things that are new and developing.	I am ambitious. I want to prove myself and gain appreciation and recognition. I stay alert to opportunities that would allow greater freedom and bring recognition.	I feel emotionally dependent. I need affection and understanding. I am helping the group in hopes that I might be treated with warmth and understanding.
Green	I want to succeed to a position of authority and prestige. I want to overcome opposition and to make my own decisions. I don't want to depend on others. I want to be in control.	I am ambitious. I want appreciation and recognition. I want to impress others and be popular and admired. I am trying to establish a better relationship with others.	I need to establish myself, my self-esteem or my independence. I want recognition. I need security. I want my opinion to prevail. I need to control the events. Logic, detail & order are important.	I want to make a favorable impression and be admired and appreciated. I can be easily hurt if I am not noticed. I want to be proven right. I am a bit precise and can be bossy at times.
Blue	I seek harmony and cooperation with associates for our mutual benefit. I need emotional fulfillment. I seek an affectionate, intimate relationship of mutual trust.	I am emotionally dependent. I am enthusiastic. I seek a happy, affectionate, fulfilling relationship. I am helpful and willing to adapt in order to gain affection.	I need peace and freedom from stress and conflict. I am proceeding cautiously so as to control the situation. I am sensitive and exacting and can be fussy.	I need peace, harmony, and a sense of belonging. I need to rest, relax and recuperate. I am sensitive and have deep feelings. I feel content.
Violet	I can get preoccupied with exciting, erotic, stimulating things. want to be seen as exciting. I want to have a charming, impressive influence on others.	I thirst for adventure. My future must be exciting, stimulating and interesting. I want to be well liked and charming. I am over-imaginative and given to fantasy and daydreaming.	I use charm and clever tactics to influence or gain recognition, but I don't want to accept the responsibility of a close relationship. I want to be considered someone special.	Aesthetic or erotic things attract me. I seek a sympathetic relationship and a situation of ideal harmony. I feel a need to identify with something in an idealized way.

Table 9-3 COLOR PAIR - EMOTIONAL THEMES
(continued)

Color	Violet	Brown	Gray	Black
Red	I need stimulation. I desire fascinating and stimulating things. I like erotic or aesthetic things. I am acting so as to fascinate and charm others.	I am taking it easy and being a bit self – indulgent, gratifying my senses. I am choosing comfort and security over ambition and prestige at this point.	I am acting impulsively with little concern for the consequences. I don't want anything to get in the way of my having fun, which I hope will shield me from my problems.	I am living intensely to make up for what I have missed, and to escape from my burdens. My desires are exaggerated and I tend to over-dramatize.
Yellow	I love fantasy. I want a fantasy adventure. I express my hopes through my imagination and fantasies. I want to be admired for my charm. I find myself often daydreaming.	I want security and comfort. I seek a solution that will bring physical comfort and free me from fear and insecurity. I need relief from despair and a chance to recover.	I am stuck in indecision and lack of resolution. I want to commit to a solution but can't determine what to commit to. I escape the problem through vague illusionary hopes.	I am in crisis. I made a decision and I am sticking to it. There is no middle ground so I find myself making abrupt decisions and changes in order to find a solution.
Green	I am using clever tactics and a pleasant manner to win over others, but in a way that avoids commitment and responsibility. I keep a close watch on how others react in order to maintain control and measure my success.	I need physical comfort, security, recognition and fewer problems. I want to overcome difficulties and establish myself, even though I'm tired and feel I'm being asked to do too much.	I am defending my self-esteem, prestige or status. I want to impress others. I want to establish myself and make an impact despite unfavorable circumstances or a lack of appreciation.	I am closed to attempts by others to influence me. I want to prove that I am strong, superior and above all that, that it doesn't affect me. I can be a bit obstinate or self-righteous.
Blue	Beauty and taste is important in this situation. I consider peace and fulfillment to be achievable through beauty, aesthetic pursuits, or an ideal relationship.	I need to overcome my physical condition and to be treated with a lot of special care, in a conflict-free environment. I fear separation and the resulting emptiness and solitude.	I need a release from stress and a period of peace and tranquility which will give me a chance to recuperate.	I have an urgent need for peace and a chance to rest. I need to be lovingly understood. I feel I am treated with a lack of consideration. I want others to comply with my requests.
Violet	I want to identify or form a "mystic union" with something or someone. I want an intimate, romantic relationship - a magical wish-fulfilling state. I try to charm others to gain their support.	I am stimulated by sensual pleasures and luxurious surroundings.	I am sensitive to my environment, and want to protect it against any disturbing influence. I want to be understood with sensitivity and compassion. I need to protect myself against conflict and stress.	I have a compelling desire to unite or blend with something / someone I identify with. I want the bond to be sensually fulfilling but not to conflict with my convictions.

Table 9-3 COLOR PAIR (continued - Brown/Gray/Black)

Color	Red	Yellow	Green	Blue
Brown	I am being a bit self-indulgent. I need to satisfy my sensual desires or physical appetites.	I need total security. At this point I prefer physical relief over achievement of future goals. I am settling for a less active, problem-free existence with minimal demands.	I need physical relief & comfort. I am trying to maintain self-control so as to handle existing difficulties. I need a relaxed environment in order to recover and feel secure.	I desire a state of physical comfort with no conflict. I need to feel secure and fear loneliness and separation. I need to be handled gently.
Gray	I may seem cautious but I demand a lot out of life and want to impress others. I hide my intentions so that I won't be involved in, or committed to, the consequences of my actions.	I am looking for a way out of this intolerable situation, but feel there may be no solution. I can't even decide what to hope for, out of fear that a decision would mean commitment to a course of action.	I am in a hostile situation and am being cautious in order to protect my interests. I avoid getting too close with others who might undermine me. I hide my intentions so as not to stir opposition.	I am exhausted by conflict and need protection from it and time to recover in a peaceful environment. I will find peace if I can remain uncommitted. .
Black	I have exaggerated desires. My extreme dramatic behavior is driven by desire or revolt. Pent up emotions threaten to release in a passionate and impulsive way.	I need to escape from this crisis which may require extreme action and desperate measures. I am behaving recklessly and making abrupt headstrong decisions.	I defy restrictions or opposition. I refuse to be swayed from my point of view. I must not waiver if I am to prove myself righteous or independent.	I am in revolt against some situation which has devastated me, and I just want to be left in peace.

Color	Violet	Brown	Gray	Black
Brown	I feel sensuous. I want to be surrounded by luxury, and physical comforts - things which give bodily pleasure.	I want a secure and problem free situation in which to physically relax and recover. I want physical comfort. I want relief from a physical problem.	I am exhausted and my body is in need of rest, protection from distress, and a chance to recover. I desire to be secure and problem free.	I feel purposeless. I experienced a bitter disappointment and am rejecting all except physical pleasure. I need to forget/recover in a problem free state.
Gray	I am fascinated with something and want to identify with it but not openly. I am exploring it tentatively and cautiously so that I wont be discovered or overly committed.	I am exhausted. I need to shield myself from anything exhausting or tiring. I want physical comfort, security and freedom from disturbances.	I have put up with too much & am shielding myself from further feelings, stimulation or involvement. I remain uncommitted and uninvolved.	I want to remain separated and totally uninvolved. I feel betrayed and treated in an undeserving manner. I am in revolt against a situation that is disrespectful to me.
Black	I have a compelling desire to identify or blend with something / someone but I want the bond to be a perfect fit, without concession or compromise.	I set an idealistic goal that resulted in bitter disappointment and am revolting against it in self-disgust. I want to forget it all and recover in a problem free environment.	I want to remain totally isolated and non-involved. The situation is offensive or hopeless and I want nothing to do with it. I want to shield myself from the influence or irritation.	It feels mysterious, frightening, oppressive. This situation is over-demanding & offensive. Nothing is as it should be. I refuse to allow anything to influence my point of view.

Example - Working with Color

I will use the example from chapter 8 to further illustrate how one might explore the significant colors recalled from that dream. You might recall that the dreamer was trying to sell a new project, which was a part of a larger strategy he had tried to develop through a great amount of effort. The group that was most interested in the project, and that he thought for sure would support it, was about to kill it. He knew that if this happened, it would undermine the larger strategy.

The dream: *I am walking in a <u>red</u> sandstone desert and I look down into a crystal clear stream. There is a <u>red</u> bird with a <u>green</u> tail, like a parrot, moving under the water. I take a stick and poke at the bird. It is then that I realize that it is dead. The water was poisoned, and the bird died when it tried to get a drink. I realize the very substance that was to give it life killed it. I then look up at the bank and notice the water undercutting the whole foundation of the valley. I feel a need to warn my friends to get out.*

1) **Select and underline** the dream colors that you feel are unique and important.

2) **Pick the closest color or color combination in tables 9-2 or 9-3**: I first tested red and green as single colors using table 9-2 (to check for potential conflict) and then as a color pair using table 9-3.

3) **Read each expression and ask "which statement best relates to a waking life situation?"**
   Red (table 9-2) = *"I want to win, succeed, achieve."*
   Green (table 9-2) = *" I need to increase my sense of security;" " I must hold onto this existing view of self in order to maintain my self-esteem"*
   Red+Green (table 9-3) = *"I want to overcome obstacles & achieve recognition from success."*

4) **Recall a recent situation that the statement reminds you of, and compare to the imagery work:** The red desert through which the dreamer was walking related to the feelings, *"I want to win, succeed, achieve."* Note how this also relates to the red and green color pair statement for the parrot from table 9-3: *"I want to overcome obstacles & achieve recognition from success."* The dreamer confirmed that he indeed wanted to win and succeed, with the ultimate purpose of gaining recognition.

Next I checked whether there was a conflict or potential integration reflected by the opposing red and green tail colors. The statement for green is: *"I need to increase my sense of security."* If we view that statement in the context of the bird associations (from chapter 8) *"fly away from my enemies,"* they reveal a possible hidden desire to escape the project in order to maintain a sense of security (avoid being seen as a failure?). This was confirmed with the dreamer. Furthermore, this desire to escape the project was in conflict with the red associations - the desire to *"win and succeed"* with the project. There is an interesting correlation here as well with the red/green combination from table 9-3 *"desire to achieve recognition from success."* In the dream the red/green bird was dead. Thus, this option (represented by the integrated red and green) was no longer possible.

Note from step 3 above, the second association with green highlighted a deeper conflict: *"I must hold onto this existing view of self in order to maintain my self-esteem."* This reveals a deeper threat to the dreamer's self-image as he suddenly finds himself in this situation of failure, feeling diminished and vulnerable. It is likely that the dream metaphor *"the water undercutting the whole foundation of the valley"* is not simply referring to an undercutting of the strategy, but to a deeper emotional threat, the undercutting of the dreamer's sense of self, the existing myth.

CHAPTER 10
THE DREAMWORK PROCESS

To suffer one's own death and to be reborn again is not easy – Fritz Perls [15]

Dreamwork, or working with your dreams, can take on many forms. Many popular approaches aim at simply understanding the "meaning" of a dream. The better approaches relate the dream to feelings and situations in your waking life. Other approaches focus on experiencing the dream in various ways without cognitive understanding, including dance, body work, artistic expression, drawing the dream, or journaling. Others, which are aimed at therapy, take the dreamer deep within themselves to reveal emotional issues, conflicts and traumas that might lie at the source of the dream. I prefer a dreamwork approach which is aimed at understanding your dream in relationship to your waking life situation; an approach that establishes not only a relationship to a waking life event, but one that reveals some of the underlying emotions, emotional conflicts, beliefs and fears in a safe manner. Furthermore, I prefer an approach that establishes a means for using the dream to work through these underlying issues.

Aaron Rochlen and Clara Hill in the book *Dreamscaping*, co-edited by Stanley Krippner,[74] discuss an approach they call the cognitive-experiential model, that involves all of these processes. The therapeutic approach involves three stages: exploration, insight and action. In the Exploration stage, the client is encouraged to re-experience the dream as if it were happening in the present, and the various elements in the dream are examined. In doing so, the client accesses feelings, thoughts and experiences that are represented in the content of the dream. In the Insight stage, the client and therapist dialogue on the client's associations with each dream element in order to construct a new understanding of the dream, so that the client learns something new about himself or herself. In the Action stage, the therapist and client jointly figure out what changes the client might want to make, based on what he or she learned in the dream.

A healthy feature of this approach is that the therapist serves as a facilitator to aid the client in figuring out the meaning of the dream through collaboration. Thus, the content comes from the dreamer, not from the therapist. The critical assumption in this approach is that all three stages are needed for complete dream work. I mention this approach because it is a healthy approach, which is more complete than many others, in that it explores the dream in relationship to the dreamer's life, explores the life situation, and then uses the dream to help determine action steps toward personal transformation.

In chapter 6, I introduced the concept of Image Activation dreamwork as an approach for working at a deeper emotional level with the dream elements. The full Image Activation dreamwork procedure is similar to the cognitive-experiential model, in that it uses three stages of dreamwork containing 5 steps or modules (illustrated in figure 16). It permits the dreamer to explore his or her own dream in relationship to their waking life situation, and then uses the dream to create a solution that can be acted upon. It differs from the therapeutic method, however, in that the exploration of the dream contains some unique role-play and color work, designed to reveal the deeper emotional content within the dream elements without having to go too deeply into dialogue with the dreamer. It is useful in a therapeutic setting, but is highly scripted so that it can also be used for personal dreamwork when the guiding dialogue with a therapist is not available.

Figure 16
Image Activation Dreamwork

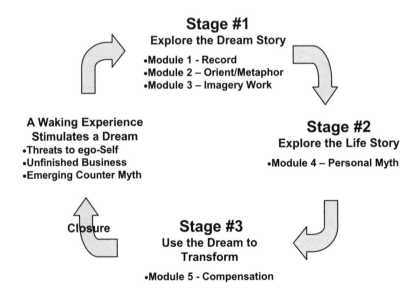

Stage #1
Explore the Dream Story

•Module 1 - Record
•Module 2 – Orient/Metaphor
•Module 3 – Imagery Work

A Waking Experience
Stimulates a Dream
•Threats to ego-Self
•Unfinished Business
•Emerging Counter Myth

Stage #2
Explore the Life Story

•Module 4 – Personal Myth

Closure

Stage #3
Use the Dream to Transform

•Module 5 - Compensation

Image Activation Dreamwork begins with recording and telling the dream, and then proceeds to Stage #1 – exploring the dream story and how it relates to your waking life story. The dreamwork can end here if the goal is simply to understand the dream, but the dream will usually reveal waking life emotional situations or conflicts that remain unresolved. Understanding the dream does not usually help you to resolve them. It may only reveal what you already know or feel inside.

Proceeding with Stage #2 – exploring your life story, helps you use the dream to understand some of the deeper fears, conflicts and personal myths that are preventing resolution and feeding waking life behaviors. Once understood, you will likely want to do something about it. In this regard, you may realize that a problem is serious or long-standing, and requires the supportive assistance of a professional. But for issues that might respond to self-help, you can proceed to Stage #3. This stage provides a method for using the dream to create alternatives and define action steps that might help bring about resolution.

At the core of Image Activation dreamwork are techniques for revealing the emotional content within a dream element or image. The role-play technique was introduced in chapter 8, and the use of the color questionnaire to trigger emotional associations was introduced in chapter 9. In this chapter I bring the various techniques together to create a comprehensive dreamworking approach. Since this chapter provides more depth than required for most dreamwork, I present the techniques as a series modules that can be selected, as appropriate to your desired level of dreamwork. I then provide examples in chapters 11 and 12 as to how the modules can be applied for everyday dreamwork (chapter 11), and in total, for working on every element of the dream (chapter 12). For the majority of your dreamwork, I highly recommend that you follow the procedure in chapter 11 that uses a simple subset of the modules. Chapter 12 illustrates how one might use the full set of modules for working on every element in a dream.

Individual and Group Dreamwork

The Image Activation procedure can be applied, with minor adjustments, to group dreamwork, even though the procedure below is written from the perspective of personal dreamwork. It can also be applied by professionals in a clinical setting for work with clients. It is often used in this setting by selecting and using the modules appropriate to the therapy being performed. Most therapists simply use module 3A (role-play) and sometimes add module 3B (color work), and apply it as an addition to their own therapeutic approach. In a clinical setting, the role-play is often expanded beyond the 6 questions, and the color work is used to trigger further questioning, in order to take the work in the desired direction.

When the procedure is applied to group work, I find it is best (for time consideration) to shorten it to just the modules 2A (metaphors in the dream story), 3A (the 6 magic questions) and 3B (color questionnaire), and work on only one or two key dream elements. Most dream groups will have already established an approach for working with metaphors. In this case, modules 3A and 3B (the 6 role-play questions and color questionnaire) can be inserted at the appropriate point in the group work, to trigger a deeper level of personal associations with the dream image the group is working on.

When doing group work outside of a clinical setting, with module 3A (the 6 magic questions), it is important to stick to the six questions and not pursue emotional associations too deeply. It is also important in a casual group setting to stop the dreamwork at that point, and not continue to the life exploration and transformation stages. Life exploration and transformation stages should only be used when the dreamer is comfortable and willing, and the dream group leader is experienced with doing deeper work. It should not be pursued in a group setting, if the associations from modules 3A and 3B bring forth deep emotional issues, unless it is a clinical setting with a professional leader.

Honoring the Dream and the Dreamer

Always approach dreamwork in a way that honors the dream and the dreamer. This means that the dreamer is considered the ultimate authority regarding the meaning of the dream. It requires that the group, dream worker, or therapist avoid imposing his or her own personal projections or connections with the dream in a manner that implies that those projections are the true meaning of the dream. This is best from an ethical standpoint as well.

I refer all readers to the ethics statement from the International Association for the Study of Dreams (IASD), as an excellent guide to proper dreamwork. Refer to **www.asdreams.org** for the complete statement. It states in part: *IASD celebrates the many benefits of dreamwork, yet recognizes that there are potential risks. IASD supports an approach to dreamwork and dream sharing that respects the dreamer's dignity and integrity, and which recognizes the dreamer as the decision-maker regarding the significance of the dream. Systems of dreamwork that assign authority or knowledge of the dream's meanings to someone other than the dreamer can be misleading, incorrect, and harmful. Ethical dreamwork helps the dreamer work with his/her own dream images, feelings, and associations, and guides the dreamer to more fully experience, appreciate,* *and understand the dream. Every dream may have multiple meanings, and different techniques may be reasonably employed to touch these multiple layers of significance.*

In order to honor the dream and the dreamer, avoid approaches which imply that someone in authority has the ability to fully understand and analyze the dream for the dreamer. Skilled practitioners and experienced dream workers may, indeed, have a greater understanding of dreams and dreamwork than the dreamer, but the practitioner should never treat the dream as if they understand its meaning for the dreamer. As you learned from the exercise with the image of the door in prior chapters, images contain personal associations that differ for each of us, and thus only the dreamer holds the key to the correct associations or meaning within a dream or dream image.

Guidelines for Group Dreamwork

It is prudent to follow a proven set of guidelines if you are contemplating group dreamwork. The guidelines below are derived in part from those offered by the Haden Institute,[95] a dream leader training institute for therapists, clergy and individuals who wish to lead dream groups or enhance their therapeutic skills (see the Resources appendix for details): 1) Participants should have some previous exposure to dreams and the leader should be versed in dreamwork and group process. 2) If anyone is seeing a therapist, they should consult with their therapist about participating in the group. 3) All should feel safe being there. The leader should address confidentiality at the beginning, by requesting that anything shared in the group is not discussed outside of the group. 4) Every gathering of the group should begin with a ritual, designed to bring about centering (silence, the ringing of a bell, a statement of intent or prayer invoking light or God's spirit etc., as appropriate to the beliefs of the group). 5) Spend 20 minutes or so checking in with each other and sharing something of your lives, to help build trust and life connections with your dreams. 6) At that point, there may be some general dream discussion and everyone who wishes may now share a dream (but without attempts at interpretation). Alternatively, you may move on to the next step. 7) The leader can now ask for a volunteer to share his or her dream for group work. 8) The person begins by sharing the dream, along with any pertinent information about their life at the time (but not their interpretation). 9) The group asks questions of clarification (not interpretation). 10) The protocol from that point depends on the approach adopted by the group. I will mention two below.

Group Projective Dreamwork ("if it were my dream")

Many organizations and dream workers use a group projective dreamwork technique, adopted from the Ullman approach.[cited in 95-98] With this approach, group members voice their own individual projections on the metaphors they perceive in the dream narrative. The objective is to trigger some connection within the dreamer, which the dreamer can then use to further explore the dream on their own. The group projection procedure used by the Haden Institute continues as follows from step 10 above: 11) The leader now asks the dreamer to give the dream to the group. 12) Projection: each member of the group who wishes to, now projects onto the dream using the words "if it were my dream, it would mean this to me…" (note: it is important to the process that the group adheres to this, so as to avoid any implications that the projections of the group are the meaning of the dream). 13) Checkout: after sufficient discussion, give the dream back to the dreamer for any comments (do not push for an interpretation; the dreamer will often offer feedback if one of the projections created a "connection"). 14) Thank the dreamer for sharing. 15) Conclude the meeting with a "feeling check" with the dreamer, and a closing ritual.

Group projection on a dream can be safe in the sense that it does not probe too deeply, yet it gives the dreamer the option to reveal connections or further discuss the dream. Working with projections on a dream also provides something of value to the individuals in the group, and to the community spirit of the group. Projection can become unsafe and discordant, however, if not managed as described in the above procedure. The group and the dreamer must understand that the dreamer is the ultimate authority on the meaning of the dream, and that projections are those of the individual group members, and in no way imply a meaning for the dreamer. All too often, while working with someone's dream, a figurative statement in the dream narrative may "strike a chord" with you, and you may suddenly feel certain you understand what the dream is all about. Sharing your insight with the dreamer as simply "my insight" or, "if it were my dream" is proper, assuming you intend it that way and state it that way. No matter how tempting it may be, it is not helpful to impose your interpretation as the likely meaning of the dream, particularly if the dreamer considers you an authority.

Care must also be taken that projections don't have the opposite effect of diluting the dreamwork. The dreamer may find it much more pleasant to latch onto a delightful projection from a group member or dream worker, than to delve into something fearful or disturbing that was triggered inside themselves.

Image Activation Group Work

In my own dream groups, I use the Image Activation approach, but select only the modules that make up the simpler "everyday dreamwork" approach you will see in chapter 11. After the dream is discussed in steps 9 and 10 above, 11) the dreamer is then asked to work on the dream image they feel is most important, has the most emotional impact or that stimulates the most curiosity. If there is a choice, I usually ask that they work on an image that has color associated with it. In group work, it is best to try to avoid working with archetypes. 12) The "6 magic questions" are applied to the dream image. In group work, the dreamer is asked to go back into the dream, bring the image to their mind's eye, take 3 deep breaths and, on the third breath, imagine him or herself as the dream image. 13) At this point the leader asks the dreamer the 6 questions, and six members of the group are assigned the task of recording the dreamers six statements (one each). 14) The six group members then feed the statements back to the dreamer, who dwells on each one in order to make connections with their waking life situation. 15) The dreamer then has the option of whether or not to share the connections with the group. 16) Next, if there is a colored image (or if the prior image was in color), the dreamer is asked to pick the closest color or color pair on the color questionnaire tables. 17) The group then divides the statements up by number, and each person in the group speaks one statement out loud, maintaining a pause between each one. 18) The dreamer dwells on the statement(s), noting the statement(s) that "connect" to their waking life situation. 19) The dreamer then has the option of sharing their "connections" and/or how the color work relates to the imagery work. 20) If the dreamer decides to share the experience and wants to dialogue with the group, the group may offer their observations, but should do so only based on what the dreamer has told them. They should take care that the observations are offered only as their own projections. 21) A "feeling check" is made with the dreamer and the dreamer is thanked.

If the dreamer feels comfortable and safe and wants to continue with stage 2 (exploring the life story) or stage 3 (using the dream for transformation), it should be performed only on a one-on-one basis between the dreamer and the group leader, who guides the process (and only if the leader is a professional or experienced in this level of work).

Combined Approach

The two approaches can be easily combined, thus introducing the deeper associations from Image Activation dreamwork into the group projective approach. In essence the group projective technique is used in place of module 2A to explore metaphors in the dream story. If it is determined during checkout that the dreamer would like to continue to work on an image or color, The Image Activation steps are simply inserted after the Checkout (step 13) in the Group Projective procedure. Note that although Image Activation dreamwork quickly reveals a deeper, personal level of association from the dreamer, privacy can be maintained. Just as with the dream, the Image Activation and color associations are spoken as metaphors, and if the dreamer wishes to keep their connections with those metaphors private, they can choose to do so.

STAGE #1
Exploring the Dream

Recording the Dream (Module 1)

How you tell the dream and record it are important for effective work on the dream. It is important to not only record the dream properly, but to also record the emotional situations happening in your life at the time. This is particularly the case if you are keeping a journal and want to look for dream patterns that relate to waking life patterns.

Begin by reviewing the entire dream as you record it, separating it into dream sequences. Note that a long dream may have a number of shorter sequences in it. These are shorter dream stories that appear coherent, but then end or fade out without a clear transition into the next sequence. Look for scene shifts. An example of scene shifting is seen in the four-part "tornado" dream from chapter 4: *"My dream had four parts: In the first I dreamed there was a spirit that came up from a creek destroying trees in its path, like a tornado. In the next I was in a classroom and I knew the teacher but could not identify her. I tried to volunteer to go out and survey the damage at the creek, but I was invisible so the teacher never recognized me. In the third, a very old friend I knew, who later became a missionary, was riding a tricycle down toward the creek. In the fourth, two men, including my friend, were struggling with the spirit which was invisible and neither good nor evil."* Note that the transition point is seen when the dreamer suddenly finds herself in a new setting, is suddenly with new people, or is engaged in a new and different activity that has no continuity with the prior activity. The scene shifts happened with a no reflection on how the dreamer got from one scene to the next.

Work on each sequence or "dreamlet" as a separate dream, then relate them to each other. The reason for doing this is that each segment generally views the same situation from a slightly different angle, perhaps learning something from the segment before.

Record the dream by telling it in the first person as if you are re-experiencing it (for example: "<u>I am</u> walking down a path…" or "Suddenly <u>I see</u> a person ahead …".). Many of the valuable metaphors may be lost if the dream is told in the past tense. Remember that the words you use, especially slips-of-the-tongue, are important metaphors. So don't try to correct your language. The idea is to try to permit the right brain to speak through the dream, and to provide the emotional associations and visualizations, without the filtering of our rational mind.

Sketch the dream. This permits you to see relationships between dream characters as well as patterns that provide important clues as to the processes taking place. Drawing the dream setting as if looking at a map from above is generally the best approach.

The dream story relates to our life story. Therefore, recording your life story at the time of the dream is also necessary. In particular, record emotional situations in your life, especially things that happened the day before which created some emotional discomfort, or that you did not want to, or could not, deal with at the time. It may not be possible at this point to determine and record the specific event that the dream is about, but it is good to provide a few waking life references.

Module 1 - Record the Dream

a) **Record the dream**: by telling it in the first person, as if you are re-experiencing it. Give the dream an imaginative title that captures its essence. Don't forget to date it. Separate the dream segments so you can work on them separately and compare them.

c) **Life Record:** Record emotional situations in your life at the time, especially things that happened the day before that you did not deal with at the time.

d) **Draw the Dream:** Draw the dream setting as if looking at a map from above. Sketch any unusual imagery.

Dream Orientation (Module 2)

The next step is to explore the personal content and associations with the various elements and imagery in the dream, in order to relate the dream story to the waking life story. Although some characters or events from waking life may appear in the dream, the actual event that stimulated the dream rarely appears as it was experienced in waking life (the reason for this was discussed in chapter 3). Look for the dream experience to be a story constructed from your associations with the waking life event, told in picture and metaphor, and stimulated by the unresolved emotions it evoked. It is more likely that the dream will reveal a past memory of a similar event, than the recent event as it occurred.

Figure 17
Dream Orientation

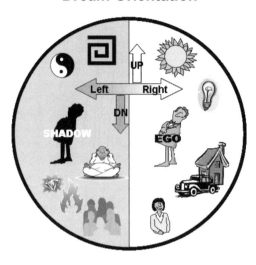

Module 2A – Metaphors in the Dream Story

Underline any phrase you used when telling the dream that sound like a figure of speech, or a statement which also describe a situation in your waking life at the time.

Module 2A – Metaphors in the Dream Story

1) **Look for Figurative Phrases:** Underline phrases in the narrative that sound like figurative descriptions of a situation in your waking life at the time. Look for:
   - **Dual Meaning and Figurative Speech:** puns or words that have a double meaning, that relate both to the dream story and to a waking life situation.
   - **Picture Language:** dream images, scenes, situations and activities that, when described, might also describe a waking life situation.
   - **Picture Words or Word-Play:** dream images and pictures that literally sound like or spell out what the dream is trying to say in picture words.
   - **Slips-Of-The-Tongue:** Mistakes in wording or spelling made while telling the dream are important keys to inner meaning.

2) **Compare with a Waking Life situation:** that fits the dream, that provides a "connection" or "aha" reaction. Describe the connection in the dream record.

Module 2B – The Dream Elements

The players in your dream, the characters and objects as well as the dream's general environment, all represent parts of you, emotional memories, or matters that you have internalized, as related to the situation that stimulated the dream.

a) **Characters:** Known and unknown persons, or an animated object that you interact with. Who are you in the dream: yourself; someone or something that you identify as you; or are you an observer? The known characters can contain valuable personality associations, and the unknown characters valuable collective clues.

b) **Object:** Note the objects in the dream, typically the inanimate man-made things. These often contain some of the most valuable content. Also note geometric shapes and numbers that might be important collective clues.

c) **Words and voices:** These can contain valuable compensating messages. The words, or dream messages, are almost always metaphors to be understood within the context of the dream story and its relationship to your life story.

d) **Nature Imagery:** Note the nature imagery, the plants or animals, or animal-like imagery. Also note the natural elements (example: earth, fire, air, water, rock, elemental metals, trees, etc.). These can contain personal associations, and a wealth of collective associations related to our instinctive animal nature and responses. The natural elements, such as earth, fire, air, water, rock, trees and elemental metals, can also contain collective associations related to growth of the psyche.

e) **Activity:** Note the actions and interactions that you and the other elements in the dream are engaged in. What are you trying to achieve in the dream? What is inhibiting your progress and how? The barrier to progress in a dream can relate to your own impasses or internal barriers to progress.

f) **Setting:** The description of the setting or environment of the dream might relate to the "place" you are in emotionally in waking life. For example: *" I am in a dark place"* might relate to a being in an emotionally "dark place" in waking life.

g) **Sensations:** Consider the importance of sensations such as touch and bodily feelings (cold, soft, hard, wet etc.). Some sensations may be externally induced (cold room, need to go to the bathroom, etc.) but often they can be emotionally significant or contain a useful metaphor (*"it felt warm and fuzzy"* for example).

h) Emotions: Note the feelings evoked by the dream when you are telling it, as well as the emotions that were felt in the dream, or when awakening.

i) Descriptors: How you describe a dream element may contain valuable metaphors. A crystal clear dream object might reveal something that has become "crystal clear" to you in waking life. Color is also a descriptor. Thus a red car can be more emotionally significant than a colorless one.

Module 2B – Note the Dream Elements

a) Characters: known or unknown persons, or animated object that you interact with.
b) Object: typically the inanimate man-made things.
c) Words and voices: can be valuable compensating elements in the dream.
d) Nature: plants, animals, earth, fire, air, water, rock, elemental metals, gems.
e) Activity: actions or interactions that you and the other elements are engaged in.
f) Setting: environment of the dream.
g) Sensations: touch and bodily feelings (cold, soft, hard, wet etc.).
h) Emotions: feelings that were present in the dream or when you awoke.
i) Descriptors: adjectives, adverbs and modifiers, including color.

Module 2c - Recognizing Collective Imagery

Due to its unconscious origins, collective imagery will generally not reveal personal associations. Recognizing collective imagery, however, is useful for helping to:
   a) make sense of the interactions and interrelationships in the dream story;
   b) choose the important image to work on;
   c) establish an inner intuitive or emotional sense for the influence of that collective image on the dream.

The significance of this imagery is described in chapters 6 and 7. Some of the more useful collective images to note in your dreamwork are related to patterns or forces at work in the dream, as listed in the module below.

Module 2c - Recognizing Collective Imagery

a) Conscious elements - illumination, right field of view, above, ahead.

b) Acceptance or awareness - movement to the right or becoming illuminated.

c) Unconscious elements - dark, the left field of view, underneath or behind; the unknown characters; the more frightening, elemental or primitive dream elements.

d) Suppression – movement of dream elements to the left, under or behind or into the darkness; frozen and dead imagery. Note, however, that the dreamer moving to the left, below or into the darkness can at times be a sign of exploring the unconscious side of self (going within), or a death-of-the-ego initiation, depending on the context. Also see transformation patterns (below).

e) Conflict - pairs of similar objects; a male pair or a female pair (perhaps representing an overly active or overly passive approach to the situation); parallel lines; numbers such as 2, 11 or similar dualities of the same element.

f) Impasse – something impeding progress which could be a character, a barrier, a separator, a crossing, or perhaps even a dream emotion such as a fear.

g) Compensation – a wise or guiding being or companion; an event or positive ending that reverses your direction or thinking; voices or words; surprises; surprising or bizarre images or image combinations; humor; certain color/image combinations.

h) Integrating Forces –Archetypes that guide us in the dream such as the Anima and Animus. Geometric forms and numbers relating to unification and wholeness such as: four or four-ness, the circle, a ring or the numbers 0 and 1, the spiral, the cross; circular or spiral movement (circle dance, a tornado, walking around a block, for example); pairs of opposites (balanced number of males and females in a pair or group, for example); unification of opposites such as black & white patterns, contrasting colors, marriage and sometimes sexual attraction.

i) Transformation patterns (death and rebirth cycle): **1. Death** - of an existing myth or ego-self may be experienced as death imagery, fear of death, loss, trapped, moving into darkness, storms, becoming dark, falling, descending, Fall or sunset. **2. Search:** Symbolic death is followed by a journey or period of searching for a new myth or new self. It can appear as a journey, a search, being lost, underground, or winter. **3. Rebirth:** Transformation and self-renewal may appear as a symbolic rebirth, discovery and release, coming into the light, growing illumination and color, springtime, beautiful water imagery, celebration, expansive or ascending imagery and activity. The new self can appear as a baby, child or pregnancy. Release imagery such as explosions, fire and earth upheavals such as earthquakes or volcanic action.

Imagery Work - Module 3

This section contains a procedural summary of the three approaches for working with dream imagery that were discussed in chapter 8: 1) role-play; 2) color work and 3) association. As the primary approach to working with dreams, I recommend applying role-play with color work to one or more key dream elements. I include the association technique as an option, however, since it is useful for gaining a basic understanding of the dream by those who have a difficult time with role-play, and imagining themselves speaking as a dream character or object. It is also an interesting, but rather lengthy, approach for translating the dream story into a new story that relates directly to the waking life events.

Selecting the Imagery to Work On

Each element in the dream is a meaningful creation. Each has some association with the waking life situation that created the dream. Some associations may be more important or emotionally impacting than others. You can choose to work on all of the dream elements, or just one or two, depending on your objective and which dream elements seem most important.

The associative approach (rewriting the dream story) requires work with all of the dream elements, so that the dream narrative can be rewritten. There is also an approach, which I will illustrate in chapter 12, that I call "Dream Mapping," which explores every element in the dream, including the collective elements. Image Activation dreamwork (role-play and color work) generally requires working on one or just a few dream elements, in order to effectively and quickly relate the dream story to your life story, and reveal the deeper issues involved. If you are using this approach, then you may want to be selective. You can follow some of the guidelines below in selecting the one or two dream element(s) to work on. In the end, however, there is no wrong way, and you will generally know which image to work on, based on your attraction to it, or curiosity or feelings about it.

a) **The Defining Image or Central Image**: Selecting the defining or "central image" of the dream is often rewarding. This could be the dream image that stood out, played the defining role in the dream, or had the most emotional impact on you.

b) **Archetypes**: Be aware when working with an archetype (Anima, Animus, etc.) that "becoming" that archetype will often result in a deep emotional experience relating to the essence of the archetype, but relatively few personal associations. The role-play statements will often relate to the characteristics that define that collective archetype.

It can be an unsettling yet rewarding experience, but be prepared for something that is more felt than explained.

c) **Collective Clues:** Recognizing collective patterns can provide clues as to the role of certain images. For example: twin images might identify an area of conflict. Working on the most active or obviously missing element in a group of four objects, people or colors, might reveal something needed for closure. An object or character in the middle of a circle might relate to a potential center around which the ego is revolving, thus the key issue the dream is dealing with. Working on a dream element that is suddenly illuminated or which moves to the right might reveal a concept that has been accepted. Working on a dream element that is moving down, to the left or into darkness may reveal suppressed material. Objects, characters and dream emotions that present barriers to progress in the dream might relate to impasses or barriers to progress in your waking life. Refer to chapters 6 and 7 for more details.

d) **Curious Imagery**: A bizarre combination of multiple images often contains an important combination of concepts or emotional memories. Cartoon-like images may contain a compensating message, viewing the "lighter side" of the situation.

e) **Inanimate Objects:** Although some of the characters in a dream may have the greatest presence, I find it useful to work on an inanimate object, since these can often contain some of the more interesting content. As Perls stated, the less humanized imagery may contain the more alienated or fragmented parts of the psyche, thus the most interesting information.

f) **Color**: Working on colored imagery gives you another dimension to work with that you can compare with the role-play work. Color often reveals something new and different about the emotional content of the dream image, that association and role-play alone may not. This works best with an image of one or two colors, and particularly for imagery where the color is not a common descriptor, such as green grass or blue sky. Also look for the grouping of red, yellow, blue and green, and work on the color that appears most active, or obviously missing from the group.

Module 3A – Role-Play (6 "Magic" Questions)

As I described in chapter 8, the most effective approach to exploring the underlying emotional issues, motivations and personal myths within the dream story, is to let the dream speak through role-play. This technique is at the core of what I term Image Activation dreamwork (the activation of the emotional content within a dream element). At this level of dreamwork, the dream story is related to the dreamer's inner story.

Module 3A – Role-Play (6 "Magic" Questions)

1) **Pick a Dream Image:** Pick one or a few important images in the dream (the central or defining image, one that had an emotional impact, curious or bizarre imagery).

2) **Speak as the Image (the 6 "magic" questions):** Close your eyes, go back into the dream and bring the dream image or dream character into view. Try one of the following: a) ask the image the 6 questions below and imagine what it would say; or b) close your eyes and take 3 deep breaths and with each breath move into and "become" the image. Then speak as if you are the image in the first person, present tense, answering these 6 questions:

1a) Who or **what are you**, and how do you feel in that role: "I am ____ "
1b) Alternatively, if the dream image is a person you know from waking life, then become that person and state:
- "my most notable characteristics are ____ "
- "The ways I am most like the dreamer are ____ "
- "The ways I am different than the dreamer are ___ "

2) As the image, what is your **purpose or function**: My purpose is to ____ "
3) What do you **like** about who you are and what you do? "I like ____ "
4) What do you **dislike** about who you are and what you do? "I dislike ____ "
5) As the image, what do you **fear** the most? "I fear ____ ".
6) As the image what do you **desire** most? "What I want most is to ____ "

3) **Relate these Statements to Waking Life:** Do any of the statements describe a situation or feeling in your waking life? Focus on one specific situation when you felt that way and define your feelings at the time. Then review the above statements:

a) Do the **"I am"** and **"My purpose is"** statements sound like a role you feel you are playing in waking life?
b) Do the **"I like"** versus **"I dislike"** statements sound similar to conflicting feelings, or an argument going on inside you, regarding a waking life situation?
c) Do the **"I fear"** and **"I desire"** statements sound like fears and desires you have regarding that situation, perhaps fears and desires that feed the conflict? Is the desire a reasonable outcome to pursue, or unrealistic in this situation?
d) If the dream character is a **known person,** does some aspect of their personality relate to a way that you are approaching the waking life situation related to the dream, or alternatively, does this dream character have a personality trait that you admire or wish you had more of within yourself, in order to better handle that waking life situation?

Module 3B – Color Work

If the dream image you are working on contains color, or if the dream has some key colors that seem important, then use the color questionnaire below in conjunction with the tables 9-2 and 9-3. These color tables in chapter 9 list emotional themes that have been commonly associated with color (based on research and color psychology literature). The theme statements in those tables are intended to trigger your own emotional associations with the dream and your waking life situation. In lieu of the tables, you can use association by asking yourself what feelings surface when you imagine yourself illuminated with the color. However, the tables will likely trigger some surprisingly deeper associations. Once the color-based emotional connections are made, compare them with the imagery work above to understand the complete content of a colored dream image.

Module 3B – Color Questionnaire

1) **Select colored dream images** that you feel are important, and in which the color is unique (not the common color for that object). Also look for a grouping of the 4 primary colors - red, yellow, blue and green. If one color seems to be most active, or is obviously missing (only 3 of the 4 present), work on that color.

2) **Pick the color** in table 9-2 that best matches the color of the dream image. If it is a mixed color or color pair, then use the color pair table 9-3. For color pairs, you might also try exploring the possibility that the two colors might represent a conflict between the two emotions (table 9-2) associated with each of the two colors.

3) **Read each expression** for that color in the table (or better yet have someone else read them to you) and sense your emotional reactions to each statement, while keeping in mind the following **questions**: a) Does this statement describe a situation or a way I have felt recently in waking life? b) If it is a color pair: do the statements for each color (in table 9-2) relate to conflicting emotions in my waking life?

4) **Recall:** Pick the one or two statement(s) that create the strongest "aha" response or "connection," that best relate to a waking life situation or conflict. Describe the situation, and the feelings at the time, in your own words.

5) **Compare:** Compare that waking life situation, and those feelings, to the dream story and the imagery work that you had completed previously. Does the color of the image add to your understanding of the dream as well as to your self-understanding?

Module 3C – Associative Dreamwork (optional)

This procedure does not go as deeply, or lend itself as well to working through underlying issues, as does role-play and color work. It is useful, however, for relating the entire dream story to events in waking life. It also provides useful associations when the dreamer has a difficult time imagining themselves as the dream image. In essence, it provides a means of translating each image and element in the dream story, into the original association that created it. It presents the dream story in a form that is closer to the original, non-verbal, right brain version.

Note that when using this approach, you will likely gain a clear understanding of how the dream relates directly to events in your waking life. However, this approach may not bring the deeper emotional issues and conflicts underlying that life story to the surface. Therefore if you want to continue the work with exploring the life situation (stage #2) and transformation (stage #3) below, it is highly recommended that you also try the role-play technique (module 3A) on what seems to be the dominant dream element.

Module 3C – Associative Dreamwork (optional)

1) **Dream Elements:** Circle or underline what appear to be the key dream elements in your written dream record, including characters, objects, words or voices, nature imagery, settings, actions, feelings, and sensations.

2) **Memory Association:** Note the dream elements and activities that freely trigger past memories and record the memories that come to mind.

3) **Define the Dream Element:** Define each dream element and its function or purpose. Note: define the dream element as if you were explaining what the dream element is to someone who never heard of it before.

4) **Rewrite the Dream Story:** Go back to the dream narrative, and in place of each dream element you circled or underlined, insert the above associations (memory and definitions) in a way that creates a coherent new dream story.

5) **Relate to the Life Story:** Read the new story, with the new associations in place, and reflect on how it might relate to the events in your waking life story.

STAGE #2
Exploring the Life Situation

At this point, it is likely you will have made a connection between the dream and your waking life situation, and will have identified some of the emotional issues involved. Simply identifying what the dream was about may be satisfactory to you. However, if you wish to gain further self-understanding from the dream, continue with this additional step. The following exercise may reveal the deep personal myths or inappropriate beliefs and decisions that compound the waking life situation, and influence your behavior and feelings.

Module 4A - Personal Myth

Do you find yourself repeating reactive or unhealthy behaviors, or do you feel stuck in familiar conflicts unable to progress in one direction or the other? Your dreams can help reveal internal myths, fears and beliefs that are at the source of some of those situations. You can use your dreams, and the results from the exercise above, to discover what myths lie at the core of your behaviors and conflicts, and to begin the process of transforming them.

Conflicting Myths

Sometimes we may see a way out of a situation, but are unable to act on that solution out of fear and uncertainty. Conflicting myths and counter-myths, fears and beliefs, leave us stuck. The "I like/I dislike" and "I desire/I fear" role-play questions were designed to create possible clues to conflicting myths that are compounding your situation.

Originating Decision

Personal myths, that unconsciously affect our behavior, often originate with decisions made at a moment of crisis in our distant past. Our limbic system tries to keep us safe by storing these decisions as emotional triggers, so that we avoid getting hurt by the same situation again. Unfortunately, they often become generalized and inappropriate in the present. You can discover and perhaps re-qualify the originating decision, by using the dream to recall and revisit the original moment of crisis.

Module 4A - Personal Myth

1) **Conflicting Myths**: Reflect on your current situation and the feelings involved. Do the role-play statements (particularly the 'I like/I dislike', 'I fear/I desire' pairs), or the color associations, relate to a conflict in that situation? Describe the conflict in terms such as:

"I need or desire ____ because ____ but if I ____then I fear ____ will happen".

2) **Originating Decision (optional):** Reflect on the situation and describe the feelings involved. Go back to one specific situation earlier in life, which brings to mind similar feelings. What happened, who was involved and how did you feel? What decision did you make about yourself, life or the others involved at the time? Does this decision feed the myth and affect your present behavior?

3) **Reflect:** Are these beliefs logical, healthy and appropriate, allowing you to progress, or are they exaggerations and misconceptions that are holding you back?

Module 4B - Impasses

Has the work to this point revealed conflicting fears or myths that often leave you stuck, inhibiting your progress? In such a situation you may feel you are at an impasse, unable to move in one direction or another, because you fear that all options available to you won't work. Some impasses are simply points of indecision, while others are more serious, driven by long-standing myths and fears. For example, a common impasse is that of wanting more out of life, but being reluctant to assert yourself for fear that, if you do, you will fail or be rejected. This is an impasse between a desire and a fear. The fear may be fed by a deeper myth that goes back to childhood, such as experiencing rejection or punishment each time you tried to assert yourself. Resolving an impasse requires that something happen to overcome or transform the myth that leaves you stuck. Either an opposing counter-myth must gain enough strength, or new information must enter in to create a new option or new myth. Such impasses can show up as an impeding action in the dream story. An impasse may be seen as a barrier to progress, something that is keeping the dreamer imprisoned, trapped, lost or stuck, keeping the dreamer from achieving their goal or objective. On the other hand, the impasse may reveal itself in the role-play of a dream element, the contrasting "I like/I dislike" and "I desire/I fear" statements.

The Impasse Within A Dream Image

The role-play exercise in Module 3A will often reveal such impasses when expressing the "I like/I dislike" and "I fear/I desire" statement pairs. An impasse between the opposing forces of fear and desire can be seen in the "clever dog" dream example from chapter 4. *"Two unknown men were trying to convince us to let them kill a dog they considered aggressive and threatening. The dog suddenly decided to roll over and play dead, in order to spare its life. At that point the dog turned into a cute puppy, and the men stopped, convinced that the dog was no longer a threat. At that point a street lamp illuminated the dog."* Role-play of the dog revealed the following statements: *"I like being a dog because people are afraid of me and don't mess with me; what I dislike about being a dog is that people are always trying to hurt me. What I fear the most is being hurt, and what I desire the most is for people to accept me."* The dreamer was caught in an impasse between the myth: "I have to act aggressively or people will hurt me" and the opposing desire "I want people to accept me."

The Impasse Within The Dream Story

Impasse imagery in the dream story can be seen as: literal barriers in our path (walls, bridges to cross, mountains, gates and doors); forces that stop us from moving in the direction we desire (inability to run in a dream, getting lost); people and things we encounter that impede our progress (person on the path we must deal with, policeman, parent, controlling person, something we fear, darkness, monster); being immobile, trapped or stuck (cages, rooms, basements, etc.), things that prevent you from achieving your goal (telephone that won't work, car that breaks down), etc. Impasses may also appear as non-imagery: fears preventing you from moving forward, situations such as being lost, or the inability to see your way. Ask where you are trying to get to or what you are trying to achieve in the dream, if anything. Is this analogous to something you are trying to achieve in waking life? For example, a statement such as: *"In my dream I am searching for a way home,"* might be a metaphor for a waking life search *"to return to things the way they were."* Then ask yourself "What is impeding my progress?" For example, this dreamer was reluctant to consider a wonderful new job opportunity her friends had found for her, because the salary wasn't what she wanted: *"I was following some friends. They crossed a narrow bridge. I was afraid to cross, since it looked like it would not support me."* Fear is the greatest barrier in both waking life and in dreams. The fear of failure can manifest in a dream as: *"I cannot continue because I am afraid of falling."* Overcoming a barrier in the dream can be a metaphor for an action you can take in waking life to overcome something that is holding you back.

Module 4B – Impasses within the Dream Story

1) **Review the storyline** of the dream and ask yourself, "where am I trying to go or what am I trying to achieve in the dream?"

2) **Impasse imagery:** Pick the image in the dream that prevents you from progressing or obtaining your goal in the dream.

3) **As the impasse image, speak to the dreamer (role-play the image):**
   a) "I am _____(name and describe yourself as the image)_____"
   b) "My function or purpose is to _____"
   c) "I am holding you back because _____"

4) **Switch, and as the Dreamer, speak to the Impasse Image:** Put yourself back into the dream, face the image and tell it what you want it to do to let you progress, for example: "You are preventing me from _____, I want you to _____"

5) **Switch again, and as the Impasse Image, answer the Dreamer**
   a) "My answer to you (the dreamer) is _____"
   b) or "My advice to you (the dreamer) is _____"

6) **Optional Exercises: a) Continue the dialogue** by alternating roles (maybe physically switching places). **b) Do the role-play:** Complete the "6 magic questions" on the impasse image to reveal further content within that image.

7) **Compare to Life:** Does the dialogue or argument sound familiar? What waking life situation does this bring to mind? Is the dialogue leading to a point of resolution? If so, does that resolution feel like progress or does it just put you back where you were?

8) **Define the Impasse:**
   a) Based on the above, re-state the impasse in your own words in a way that captures the conflict, with a BUT statement that identifies the impasse point, like this:
   "I need _____ because _____ **BUT** if I _____then I fear _____ will happen".
   b) Is this statement and the associated desires and fears: logical, realistic and healthy, or unrealistic and inappropriate?

STAGE #3
Transformation

At this point, you likely have a deeper understanding of how the dream story relates to your life story. You may also have become aware of some uncomfortable or painful emotions and fears, as well as conflicting personal myths and impasses that are contributing to the situation. You may have found that your behavior in this situation is influenced by a deep personal myth based on decisions made earlier in your life. In order to progress and transform an inappropriate myth or impasse, an alternative or new myth is often required, along with a successful experiencing of that alternative.

Sometimes dreams attempt to transform an inappropriate myth through compensation, as illustrated in the "clever dog" dream above. In this case, the dream provided an alternative (playing dead) to compensate for the impasse in which the dreamer was stuck. It then went one step further and rehearsed the alternative and rewarded the results by showing the threatening males backing down and the successful action of the dog being illuminated by a streetlight. You can help your dreams with this process by recognizing the compensating activity, bringing the new myth into your waking life and acting on it.

If, as is often the case, the dream does not provide an obvious compensating message, or positive ending, you can still use the dream to help alter or transform inappropriate myths. The procedure below will show you how to continue the dream and take it to a new conclusion in order to provide a compensating metaphor. **A word of caution, however. At this point, if issues have surfaced that seem severe or highly emotionally charged, and appear beyond the scope of a simple self-help technique, then it is best not to proceed. The following procedure should not to be considered a substitute for therapy or professional help.**

Depending on your particular situation, working with the dream alone may not be adequate to begin a healing process. Many well established self-help and therapeutic techniques are available to deal with emotional issues which have surfaced in dreamwork. There are also some new approaches evolving for dealing with embedded emotional reactions, phobias and trauma brought up by your dreams. One such approach is the developing field of "energy psychology." I mention it here because it can also be used to help instill the "new behaviors and next steps" in Stage #3 of the dreamwork process. Emerging from globalization, energy psychology protocols combine western therapeutic techniques, such as imagery, self-statements and subjective distress ratings, with methods from eastern healing traditions such as acupressure and yoga. They can be used for self-help or in a therapeutic setting (for trauma and serious issues), and are based on the assumption that psychological problems have a counterpart in your energy system, and can be shifted at that level.

The methods are quick, easy to learn and non-invasive. One energy psychology technique involves mentally focusing on an emotional situation (such as one revealed by your dream), while manually stimulating a series of acupressure points on your upper body (through tapping or holding), and saying a brief statement related to the emotions that you wish to desensitize. The technique appears to produce neurological shifts that can rapidly impact problems or goals in a desired direction. In general, energy psychology protocols are reported to be effective in rapidly reducing fears, phobias and inappropriate emotional reactions. See the Resources appendix at the end of the book for more information.

Module 5A – Working with the Compensating Element

In chapter 4 we learned that Jung saw dreams as bringing about balance by compensating for misconceptions and neglected parts of the personality.[23] Perls saw this process as a natural tendency toward completion, a "gestalt."[15] Compensation is a necessary first step toward correcting internal misconceptions, structuring a new healthier model of self, and overcoming myths that no longer work, leaving you at an impasse. Dreams compensate by: 1) creating events that bring about reversals or new alternatives; and 2) rehearsing successful scenarios which result in positive dream endings.

Compensation is found in many forms as discussed in chapter 7. It can be seen as a voice that offers guidance, a new or alternative path, a new solution, or a parable in the dream story. It may be something unexpected or revealing, or unexpected portrayals and odd combinations of imagery. It can also show up as guiding characters, characters that speak with authority or power, a voice, or written words. Humor can be the compensation, as seen in a silly image or something that makes you laugh in the dream. The color of a dream image can also compensate for the content within the image it combines with.

Not all dreams have an obvious compensating element, and if yours does not, then look at how the dream ends. The compensation is often found in the successful ending of the dream story itself, as illustrated in the "clever dog" dream. A successful ending rehearses and illuminates new paths or behaviors that were previously unavailable to you, often symbolically "illuminating" the accepted result, as it did in that dream example.

Module 5A – Dream Compensation

1) **Look for the compensating imagery:** a character in the dream that guides you, an audible or written message, a dream event that provides an unexpected reversal, a strange mix of images, a new path or approach, or the action at the end of the dream that is rewarded with a positive dream ending.

2) **Review the Compensating Action:** Reflect on the dream story before and after that event: a) State your actions, thoughts and direction before the compensating event. b) What was the specific act of compensation? c) How did this change your actions/thoughts/direction in the dream? d) Did the dream reward the results?

3) **Relate (as a metaphor) to your waking life situation**:
   a) Before: How does the dream story before compensation relate to your life story?
   b) After: How does the dream story, after the compensating event, relate to a possible alternative in your waking life situation?
   c) The Message: What is the compensating message? Can you relate it as a metaphor to your waking life situation?
   d) Restate as a Solution to your Waking Life Situation: Restate the compensating metaphor as a practical solution or action you might take in waking life. (Do this with caution, since the dream ending is a metaphor and rarely a literal message).

4) **Check It Out:** Is it a healthy solution, allowing you to progress beyond the conflict or impasse, or does it leave you stuck again? If it leaves you stuck, do not pursue it. Or look again at how you restated the solution.

Module 5B – Completing the Dream

If the dream ended positively, consider the positive ending, and compensating event that brought it about, as a potential metaphor for a solution to your waking life situation. If the dream did NOT end in a satisfactory resolution, then you can use the dream to help establish that new metaphor. By spontaneously creating a new dream ending, one that resolves the dream situation, you may be able to establish a new metaphor or analogy that resolves your waking life situation. An inappropriate personal myth can be transformed by trying out new decisions or alternatives that move past the fear or misconceptions.

Note that the counter-myth provided by your new dream ending may not always be practical, and may be an overcompensation or a shadow of the old myth that leaves you stuck in the same place. Therefore, it is necessary to test that new ending regarding appropriateness and healthiness. If it is impractical or an overcompensation, find a practical balance between myth and counter-myth before taking action. If it is an unhealthy solution, then re-examine the metaphor or perhaps try a more appropriate ending.

When you create an appropriate new dream ending, it is important to describe all the actions you take in bringing about that new ending. It is those actions that may be analogous to actions you could take in waking life to bring about a transformation.

Module 5B – Completing the Dream

1) **Review how the dream ends:** Go back into the dream near the end, to perhaps the most emotional point. What are you trying to achieve in the dream and what is inhibiting progress? How does the dream end? How might that relate to the lack of resolution in your waking life situation?

2) **New Ending:** Without thinking about it, using the first thing that comes to mind, make up a new ending that resolves the dream in a satisfying manner. Once you have the new ending, fill in any missing detail by further imagining what specific actions or events must have occurred to bring it about.

3) **Waking life analogy:** How might the new ending, and specifically the actions you took to get there, be analogous to something you can do in your waking life to resolve the situation or conflict the dream is dealing with?

4) **Re-state** the new ending as a possible solution to your waking life situation. Remember that the dream ending is a metaphor, so you have to draw analogies that fit your waking life situation.

5) **Check It Out:** Do an appropriateness check. Is it a healthy, practical resolution that allows you to progress in a positive direction - or - does it go too far to be achievable or perhaps leave you stuck again? If it is not healthy or appropriate, do not pursue it.

Module 5C – Act to Transform the Myth

The most important part of any transformation is experiencing the alternative action in a real life situation. Cognitive recognition, of both an inappropriate myth and the means to correct it, does little to actually make the change. In order to change behavior, we must experience a reversal of these decisions in a way that brings a successful, non-threatening outcome.

Another fun and effective exercise, that helps to maintain the compensating solution in waking life, is to remember an image from the dream that will remind you of the solution each time you encounter similar situations. This might be thought of as a dream "totem." Some examples include a guiding character, a surprise event, a strange image combination, spoken or written words, etc. It may be an image that changed form within the dream, or when you applied the new dream ending (as was the image of the "clever dog" laying on his back in the example above). Once you understand the compensating message and the associated image, then take this image as the dream "totem" and bring it to mind whenever you need to remind yourself of the solution.

Module 5C – Act to Transform the Myth

If the solution from module 5 A or B appears healthy and appropriate, then:

1) Next Steps: Describe the specific **next steps** you can take in waking life to carry it out.

2) Next Opportunity:Describe specifically **when** you might be able to take the next step.

Imagine yourself going through the actions, and then discipline yourself to follow those steps at the next opportunity. Transformation requires that you experience the change.

3) Dream Totem: If there is a defining image associated with the compensating solution or new dream ending, use this image in waking life as a reminder of your "solution," each time you find yourself in a similar situation.

CHAPTER 11
EVERYDAY DREAMWORK

Dreams are no longer the exclusive province of the shaman, the priest, or the psycho-analyst. Dreamtime and its products properly belong to the dreamer – S. Krippner[19]

A common motivation for personal dreamwork is a desire to understand the meaning of your dreams and perhaps to use them for self-help. Dreamwork is also commonly included in therapeutic approaches. For most purposes, all that is required is a fairly simple approach. Therefore, in this chapter I provide the basic steps (the selected modules from chapter 10) that I recommend for everyday dreamwork. If your motivation is to simply understand the dream, then the first stage (exploring the dream) is adequate. If you want to use the dream to help transform your life, then continue with stages #2 and #3.

STAGE #1
Exploring the Dream

Module 1 - Record the Dream: The first step is to record the dream. It is also wise to record any emotionally significant situation going on in your life at the time. If the dream has multiple segments, separated by abrupt scene and storyline changes, it is often best to treat each segment as a separate but interrelated dream. Sketching the dream scene, as if viewed from above, and sketching any curious or important imagery, is also advised.

Module 2 - Dream Orientation:

1) **Metaphors:** Orient yourself to the dream by first underlining statements in the dream story that might figuratively describe a situation also going on in your life at the time. Describe the connection between these metaphors and your waking life situation.

2) **Key Elements:** Next, circle or underline what you consider to be the most important dream elements (characters, objects, actions), as well as any unique colors (unique in that it is not the natural color of that dream element).

3) **Collective Clues:** Finally, review the dream while referring to module 2C for collective clues (right/left placement and direction of motion; dark/light illumination; like/opposing image pairs; geometric shapes, numbers and patterns of motion; compensating events providing a reversal in thinking such as a guidance, humor, surprise, a voice or words; unknown masculine and feminine characters).

Module 3A – Imagery Work: Go back into the dream and "become" the dream image. Speak as the image, in the first person present tense, and record your statements. If you have difficulty imagining yourself "becoming" a dream image, then put yourself back in the dream and bring that dream image into view. Ask the image each of the 6 questions and answer those questions as you think that dream image might respond.

1a) Who or **what are you** (Describe yourself and how you feel): "I am _____ "

1b) *Alternatively* - If the dream character is someone you know, then as that person:
    a) Describe your personality. b) In what ways are you like the dreamer?
    c) In what ways you are different from the dreamer?

2) What is your **purpose or function**? "My purpose is to _____ "

3) What do you **like** about being the dream image? "I like _____ "

4) What do you **dislike** about being the dream image? "I dislike _____ "

5) What do you **fear** most as the dream image? "I fear _____ "

6) What do you **desire** most as the dream image? "What I desire most is _____ "

Relate to Waking Life: Do one or more of the statements sound like a way you feel, or a situation in your waking life? Focus on a specific situation when you felt this way. Focus on the point of greatest emotion. Who was involved and what you were feeling at the time. Do the "I am" and "My purpose" statements sound like a role you are playing in waking life? Do the "I like" versus "I dislike" statements sound like a conflict going on inside you? Do the "I fear" and "I desire" statements sound like waking life fears and desires, perhaps feeding the conflict? Is the desire a reasonable outcome to pursue, or unrealistic in this situation? If the dream character is a person you know, does some aspect of this character's personality relate to a manner in which you are approaching the waking life situation, or alternatively, does this dream character have a personality trait that you admire or wish you had more of, in order to better handle this waking life situation?

Module 3B – Color Work: Once you complete the imagery work, look at the color of the image you worked on, or select one or more key colors you recall from the dream.

1) **Emotional Themes:** Depending on whether they are individual colors, mixed colors or color pairs, use tables 9-2 or 9-3. Pick the closest color match in the table. In lieu of the tables, you can ask yourself what feelings surface when you imagine yourself illuminated with the color, but the tables may provide deeper associations.

2) **Emotional Triggers:** Read the statements for that color and select the statement(s) that trigger an "aha" response or connection with a situation in your waking life.

3) **Review** the waking life situation and your feelings at the time. Relate that connection to the imagery work and to the dream.

STAGE #2
Exploring the Life Situation

Module 4 - Exploring the Underlying Myth: The role-play statements will generally reveal the situation and feelings in your waking life with which the dream is dealing. Reflect on a specific situation and the "I like" and "I dislike" and/or the "I fear" and "I desire" statement pairs. Do they relate in some way to conflicting feelings and thoughts related to that situation. If so, then try to rephrase the statements in your own words, in a way that captures the conflicting beliefs or decisions, such as:

"I need or desire __ because __ BUT if I __ then I fear ___ would happen".

Originating Decision (optional): Reflect on the current situation and the feelings involved. Now go back to one specific event earlier in life, which brings similar feelings to mind. What happened, who was involved and how did you feel? What decision did you make about yourself, or the others involved at the time? Does this decision feed the myth and affect your present behavior?

Check it Out: Are these beliefs logical, healthy and appropriate, allowing you to progress, or are they exaggerations and misconceptions that are holding you back?

STAGE #3
Compensation and Transformation

Go back into the dream and review what you (or some character you identify as you) are trying to achieve and how the dream ends. How does that relate to something you are trying to achieve in waking life?

Module 5A - Dream Compensation: Did a dream event provide guidance, a message, an unexpected reversal or a new approach, OR did the dream end with a positive resolution?
1) How might this compensating event or dream resolution be a metaphor for solving your waking life conflict or situation?
2) Restate the actions, which were taken by the dream to resolve the dream situation, as a solution to your a waking life situation.
3) Check it out: Is this a healthy, appropriate resolution that allows you to progress?

Module 5B - New Dream Ending: If the dream remains unresolved or ends badly, then use this exercise to try to create a compensating metaphor:
1) Go back into the dream to the most emotional part and review the dream to the end. Using the first thoughts that come to mind, make up a new ending that resolves the dream in a satisfying manner.
2) Fill in the missing details, as to how that ending might have been brought about.
3) How might the new ending, and your actions to bring it about, be seen as an analogy for a new way to deal with your waking life situation?
4) Check it out: Is this a practical, healthy, appropriate resolution that allows you to progress, or does it overcompensate or leave you stuck again?

Module 5C - Next Steps: If the resolution is healthy, practical and appropriate, then:
1) What specific next step(s) can you take in your waking life to bring it about, and
2) When is the next opportunity for you to start?
3) Dream Totem: If there is a defining image associated with the compensating solution or new dream ending, use this image in waking life as a reminder of your "solution" each time you find yourself in a similar situation.

Dreamwork Example

Dream Title: *Flip-flopping change purse*

Module 1 - Dream Record

In my dream, I was having a long dialogue with an associate about an upcoming battle. When I awoke, I realized that I had been talking to a leather change purse! My associate in the dream was a slightly rounded but rectangular-shaped zippered change purse, red on the top side and a green/brown color on the under-side. I kept flip-flopping it over trying to decide which side and color I liked best.

Sketch

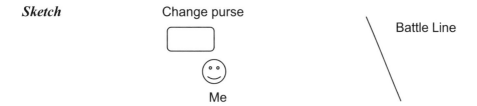

Life Record: *The day before the dream, some of my colleagues and I were preparing ourselves for a possible upcoming battle to try to get approval for something we were working on. I was concerned about what stance I should take in the meeting regarding some of the issues I felt strongly about.*

Module 2 – Dream Orientation

a) ***Key Imagery:*** *Change purse;* ***Color****: Purse = red on the top, green-brown on the underside*

b) ***Possible Metaphors:*** *"Upcoming battle" and "battle line" = relate to the upcoming battle in waking life: "Change" = change in me; change of values?; "flip-flop"= my indecision*

c) ***Collective Clues:*** *red above and green-brown underneath = red as conscious motivation or myth, green-brown as counter-myth; Battle line to the right = conscious focus;*

Module 3A - Imagery Work = *the Change Purse*

I am : *I am a change purse. I am floppy, soft but leathery. I can hold whatever you want.*

My purpose is to: *hold valuable things and keep them together in one place so they won't get damaged or parts of them lost.*

I like: *that I serve a valuable function and am flexible enough to hold anything.*

I dislike: *that I don't fit any particular need. I'm just there in case someone wants to use me.*

I fear: *that no one will see a specific need for me and just leave me in the drawer.*

I desire: *to be always used to contain the most valuable things.*

Relate to Waking Life

a) Do the **"I am" or "purpose"** statements above sound like a role you are playing? *Yes, I am engaged in an activity where I feel I am "holding valuable knowledge and keeping things together in one place so that parts don't get damaged or lost," being a person that has been around the longest.*

b) Do the **"I like vs. I dislike"** statements sound like an inner conflict? Describe: *I do like that "I serve a valuable function in this activity and feel I can remain flexible." But I also realize that I don't have a well-defined role that "fits a particular need" and that I, or my opinions, can be considered optional. That is uncomfortable.*

c) Do the **"I desire" and "I fear"** statement sound like waking life desires or fears? *I want my contributions to be regarded as valuable, but seem to be driven by a deeper fear that "no one will see a specific need for me" and will leave me out of things.*

Module 3B - Color Work   *Color Pair = Red, and Green-Brown*

a) ***Color Questionnaire:*** Which statements best fit your waking life situation?
   Red (table 9-2) = *I want to be assertive and forceful! To succeed and achieve!*
   Green-Brown (table 9-3) = *I need security, recognition and fewer problems. I want to overcome difficulties and establish myself, even though I'm tired and feel I'm being asked to do too much.*

b) ***Describe the waking life connection:*** *This appears to be a conflict within me. Although I want to be forceful and take on more responsibility, in order to be considered of value, I am really taking on too much now.*

c) Reflect: How does this relate to the dream and to the imagery work above?

The conflict revealed in the two colors seems to be two ways of approaching the situation that I am "flip-flopping" over. In the imagery work, the sense of holding valuable knowledge, and wanting to make sure things are done correctly, seems to be connected to the desire to be assertive associated with the red side. The fear of being seen as having no value, and being discarded, is connected to the green-brown desire for recognition and to remain secure with the group. There is also an underlying fear that if I am too forceful, I will be discarded.

Module 4 - Underlying Myths

a) Conflicting Beliefs: *"Too much is being asked of me now, and if I assert myself so that things go correctly, I will end up taking on more – versus - if I don't assert myself, I may be seen as having no value and be discarded* (myth)."

b) Originating Decisions: *The first time I recall the feeling of being suddenly unneeded, of having no value, comes from being laid off once very early in my career. I felt I was no longer of value. My decision was to make sure that I did so much work, that I would be invaluable and there was no way anyone could get rid of me* (the origin of the myth).

Module 5 - Transformation

a) New Ending: *The change purse suddenly changes to a single color, a beautiful bright orange, and I decide not to join the battle but to play a guidance role and convince the group that a battle was unnecessary.*

b) Life Analogy: Relate this new ending as an alternative solution for your waking life situation. *Looking at table 9-2 at orange, the following statements stand out: I want a wider sphere of influence; contact with others; I feel driven but need to overcome my doubts or fear of failure. These statements refer to the same desire for influence, but from a more friendly standpoint, with a focus on overcoming my self-doubts (the real issue). It is a more focused solution, as opposed to the flip-flopping between being overly assertive in order to win and achieve* (myth), *and totally letting things go by being quiet in order to remain safe* (counter-myth). *These objectives are something I can achieve if I don't treat the situation as a "battle," that is if I go in with the attitude of guidance* (the new myth) *rather than to win and succeed by taking on all the responsibility.*

c) Check it Out: Is the alternative solution healthy and appropriate?

Yes. By approaching the situation as a collaboration with others, and sharing my expertise, rather than approaching it as a battle that I have to win and fix all by myself, I will gain a wider sphere of influence and companionship and thus overcome doubts and fears. By sharing the load, I will not spread myself too thin.

d) Next Steps: If the solution seems healthy and appropriate, what are your next steps?

What: *I will regard myself as a guide and collaborator, and let things happen within the group.*

When: *I will try this at the upcoming meeting.*

e) Dream Totem: The defining image for the solution was the element that changed in the new dream ending. The color orange is one element that changed, but the more memorable image might be the image of the dreamer as a collaborator.

CHAPTER 12
WORKING WITH THE WHOLE DREAM
DREAM MAPPING

The only correct interpretation of a dream…is one that gives the dreamer a joyful "aha" experience of insight and moves them to change their life… - Ann Faraday

Working with the whole dream is usually more involved than is necessary to gain self-understanding from a dream. I offer this example, however, to give you an idea of how to use all of the modules. It also reveals how much amazing content there is in a dream, when each element is explored. It is interesting to see how the dream introduces and deals with so many associated myths, conflicts and personality fragments; how it rehearses or tests a particular strategy, and compensates for the misconceptions of the ego in order to bring about closure. The example also illustrates the results you might expect to achieve from the various dreamworking approaches described in chapter 10.

Dream Mapping

I also introduce a technique here that I call Dream Mapping, for working on the interrelationships in the dream, by mapping them into one large picture. In almost every case, I recommend sketching the dream as if seen from above, in order to orient yourself to the dream and view the interactions and collective clues. In order to "map" your dream, I suggest extending the dream sketch to a full page, so that you can place your dreamwork associations with each image next to that image on the map. The final result is a map of the interrelationships between the content within each dream image. See the example below.

When you draw the dream, pay attention to the orientation of dream elements and direction of movement as it appeared from your vantage point in the dream. Also, note numbers, colors, geometric shapes and patterns such as circles, squares, spirals, crosses, circular movement and groupings of 3 or 4 objects or colors. Note images that are a barrier to progress, including physical barriers such as walls, bridges, and people or things in your path. If the dream scene is a busy one, leave room to place notes in the margins so that you can point to the imagery. If there is some strange dream image that stands out, you might want to draw that separately at the bottom.

Using the Modules with the Whole Dream

Pick the modules from chapter 10 that you are most comfortable with, or that are most applicable to the dream you are working on.

Module #1 – Record the Dream

Use module 1 as described in chapter 10, recording the dream and your life situation at the time, and try using the Dream Map approach to draw the dream using a full page.

Module #2 - Dream Orientation

When working with the whole dream using the Dream Map, there is opportunity to orient yourself to all of the elements of the dream. Begin by noting associations and collective clues on the map. Note how I placed possible collective clues in [brackets] in the example. Relative placement and direction of movement in the dream becomes more apparent with the visual Map. Identify the key elements of the dream by placing them on the drawing and labeling them with their modifiers such as color.

Module #3 – Imagery Work

You could begin by using module 3C to define or form associations with the dream imagery and note them on the Dream Map. I recommend, however, that you begin with module 3A and 3B (role-play and color). Doing the role-play and color work first will not only provide more meaningful work, but will also provide additional associations that can be later used in module 3C if you care to use it.

Modules 3A and B – Role-Play and Color

Pick what appears to be central image of the dream and a few additional key images or elements, and role-play those elements. As you will note from the example, immediately after the role-play I use the results to define the conflict or myth within that dream image as best I can. The conflict or myth is then placed next to the image on the Dream Map. If you compare the deeper associations from role-play (3A), to the more cognitive associations from (3C), you will see that the role-play statements provide much more meaningful information for mapping. Next use module 3B for the color and place the statement that you most "connect" with on the Dream Map.

Module 3C - Association (optional)

As you can see from the example, although the associations are less informative than information from 3A and 3B, once they are placed into the dream narrative to create a new narrative, an excellent relationship between the dream story and waking life events is established. This level of association does not go to the deeper issues, but it does nicely relate dream events to waking events.

Module #4 - Personal Myth and Impasse

At this point, you should fully understand what the dream is about, and be able to see a relationship between the dream story and your life story. If you want to continue the dreamwork to further explore your inner story, then continue with module 4.

Module 4A - Personal Myth

If you have completed module 3A (role-play) on one or more dream images, then you should have a sense for some of the conflicting myths, fears and decisions with which the dream is dealing. If you have not already restated the role-play work in terms of a personal myth, then do so as directed in module 4A (see the example). Restate any conflicts you see in the role-play work in terms such as:

"I need or desire _____ because _____ but if I _____ then I fear _____ will happen"

Module 4A also provides an optional procedure for discovering the original decision behind the personal myth by going back in time, perhaps to a traumatic situation in childhood, or a crisis a few years ago, when you can recall feeling the same way. It is interesting to explore how decisions made at times of crisis in the past can stay with us and become generalized, thus feeding the myth and influencing present day behavior.

Module 4B – Impasse

In the dream, if there is something that is obviously holding you back, preventing progress or, as in this example, creating a state of immobility and tension, then note it as a possible impasse image. If there is not, then continue on to module 5. If there is an impasse image, use module 4B to define that impasse and note it on the Dream Map. Note that working with the impasse imagery may reveal additional conflicting myths.

Module #5 – Compensation and Transformation

At this point, after working on a number of dream images, you will likely see that the dream has attracted a number of emotional issues into a complex pattern it is trying integrate and resolve. If you wish to help the process out a bit, then you can use the dream to suggest a course of action. Again a word of caution. If the issues that have surfaced seem severe or highly emotionally charged, and not something you feel comfortable dealing with using a self-help procedure, then it is be best not proceed with this step. This procedure is not to be considered a substitute for therapy or professional help.

You can use the dream for guidance through: a) recognition of the dream's own compensating message (if there is one), or b) creation of a new metaphor for compensation. This is relatively simple when working on one dream element, conflict or myth, as in chapter 11. But when you have worked on the whole dream, there is much to choose from. Testing the dream with both modules 5A and 5B can help sort this out.

Module 5A – Compensation

First determine if there was a compensating message in the dream. Note the message in the dream example that follows. It was a voice that stated "No, you are OK." Look through the various conflicts, myths and decisions that this compensating message appears to be directly addressing, and work on that one using module 5A.

Module 5B – New Ending

If there is not a clear compensating message in the dream, then it is best to simply choose one issue to work on. Look through the various statements relating to conflicts, myths, early decisions and impasses above, and pick the one that has the greatest emotional impact to you. Then follow module 5b and create a new dream ending. This new ending can act as a compensating metaphor.

Module 5C – Next Steps

In either case, check out the apparent message and determine if it is healthy and appropriate, allowing you to progress. If it is appropriate, then determine the next action steps to bring it about.

STAGE #1
Exploring the Dream

Module 1 - Record the Dream

1A - Record the Dream

Dream Title   "I am OK"

I am living in a small village. <u>*Some foreigners have invaded and taken over the*</u> <u>*government*</u> *(feeling is of helpless Vietnam villagers). I am with my fellow villagers inside of a meeting place, like a dining lodge, at a camp. The invaders are gathering us up and the leader, in order to identify and separate the group, states: "everyone that lives beyond four, tense up." A large group is tensing up and the remaining people are moving away to the right near some brown wooden tables. <u>I am confused, not knowing</u> <u>what the command means or what I should do,</u> since I don't know if I live within or beyond four. I tense my fists. Someone behind me says, "No, you're OK." I relax and know that I can now move to the right, feeling I am one of the lucky ones allowed to stay in the village. I ask the leader what will happen to the others, and he states that they will be led out (to the left) and dealt with in some (undetermined) fashion. I look out the window to the right at the beautiful blue lake, with a feeling of growing contentment that I might simply be <u>left alone with my friends and my boat</u>.*

1B – Record Life

There has been a management take-over and I have a new boss who does not know me or value my knowledge or leadership capability. He is here to determine who in the organization will stay and who will be eliminated, based on some unknown set of criteria. For the first time in my career, I feel out of control of my situation and unappreciated. I thought about just giving up on my career and enjoying my friends and other interests.

C – Draw the Dream

Draw the dream setting as if looking at a map from above. Sketch any unusual imagery.

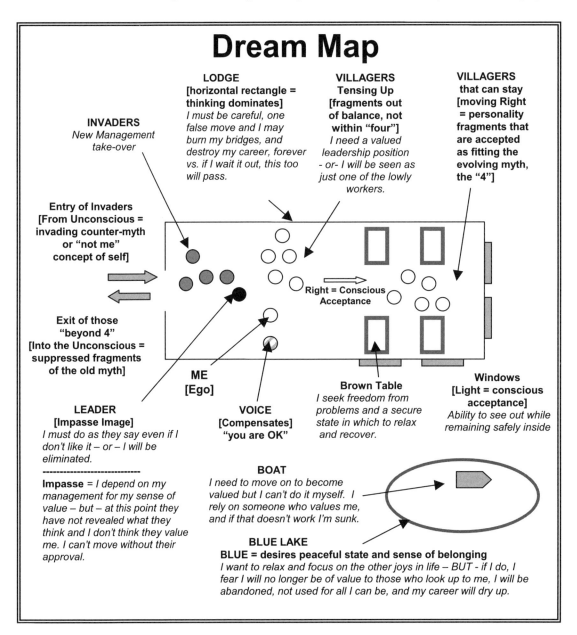

Dream Map

INVADERS
New Management take-over

LODGE
[horizontal rectangle = thinking dominates]
I must be careful, one false move and I may burn my bridges, and destroy my career, forever vs. if I wait it out, this too will pass.

VILLAGERS
Tensing Up
[fragments out of balance, not within "four"]
I need a valued leadership position - or- I will be seen as just one of the lowly workers.

VILLAGERS
that can stay
[moving Right = personality fragments that are accepted as fitting the evolving myth, the "4"]

Entry of Invaders
[From Unconscious = invading counter-myth or "not me" concept of self]

Right = Conscious Acceptance

Exit of those "beyond 4"
[Into the Unconscious = suppressed fragments of the old myth]

ME
[Ego]

VOICE
[Compensates]
"you are OK"

Brown Table
I seek freedom from problems and a secure state in which to relax and recover.

Windows
[Light = conscious acceptance]
Ability to see out while remaining safely inside

LEADER
[Impasse Image]
I must do as they say even if I don't like it – or – I will be eliminated.

Impasse = *I depend on my management for my sense of value – but – at this point they have not revealed what they think and I don't think they value me. I can't move without their approval.*

BOAT
I need to move on to become valued but I can't do it myself. I rely on someone who values me, and if that doesn't work I'm sunk.

BLUE LAKE
BLUE = desires peaceful state and sense of belonging
I want to relax and focus on the other joys in life – BUT - if I do, I fear I will no longer be of value to those who look up to me, I will be abandoned, not used for all I can be, and my career will dry up.

Module 2 – Dream Orientation

Module 2A – Metaphors in the Dream Story

a) Look for Figurative Phrases (underlined): 1. *"Some foreigners have invaded and taken over the government."* 2. *"I am confused, not knowing what the command means or what I should do, since I don't know if I live within or beyond four."* 3. *"Left alone with my friends and my boat."*

b) Compare with Waking Life: 1. *We just had a management take-over (taken over the government) and I now have a new boss who is foreign to our organization. 2. Prior to this "foreign invasion," I was highly valued by management and had control over my group and career. Now I am confused, not knowing what the new boss wants or what I should do, since I don't know where I stand. 3. There are times I feel it would be best to abandon my career goals, and to begin to enjoy the other things in life, to go off "with my friends and my boat."*

Module 2B – Note the Dream Elements

a) Characters: *Foreign invaders; the leader; other villagers; person (voice) behind me*
b) Objects: *lodge, tables, window, boat, four*
c) Words and voices: *"everyone that lives beyond four, tense up"; "no you're OK"*
d) Nature Imagery: *lake*
e) Activity: *invaded; gathering us up; tensing up; moving away to the right; I tense my fists; I relax; move to the right; led out (to the left);*
f) Setting: *small village near a lake; in a meeting place like a dining lodge at a camp*
g) Sensations: *tension in my hands*
h) Emotions: *feeling like helpless Vietnam villagers; confused, tense; feeling I am one of the lucky ones, feeling of growing contentment*
i) Descriptors: *<u>small</u> village; <u>helpless</u> Vietnam villagers; <u>brown wooden</u> tables; <u>lucky</u> ones; <u>beautiful</u> <u>blue</u> lake*

Module 2c - Recognizing Collective Imagery

a) **Conscious** elements (light, right): *Those "within the four" that could stay; boat*
b) **Acceptance or Awareness** (movement to the right, illumination): *Those that were accepted and allowed to remain moved towards the right where the windows were.*

c) **Unconscious** (dark, left, behind, unknown frightening): *Invaders and leader that entered from the left. Voice behind me (symbol of the Self?)*

d) **Suppression** (movement to the left or into the darkness): *The villagers outside of "the four" will be taken out (to the left) and dealt with in some unknown fashion (fragments of the personality belonging to the old myth will be suppressed into the unconscious where their future is not known)*

e) **Conflict** (pairs of equals): *2 males at the point of conflict (dreamer vs. leader)*

f) **Impasse** (something impeding progress): *The controlling leader of the invaders (note: this impasse creates the "tensing up" and not knowing where to go)*

g) **Compensating Forces** (guidance, reversals, voice or words): *The person from behind (inner Self?) stating "No, you're OK".*

h) **Forces of Unification** (four): *"Everyone that lives beyond four, tense up" (fragments of the personality that don't fit within this desired balanced state will cause tension)*

i) **Transformation** (Death/Rebirth Cycle): *Uncertain future of villagers moving to the left, hopeful future for those on the right*

Module 3 - Imagery Work

Module 3A – Role-Play (6 "Magic" Questions)

1) **Pick Key Dream Images:** *invaders, the leader, villagers, lodge, tables, window, boat, lake.* Key images for role-play might include a villager (the suppressed), the leader (the suppressor or impasse image), the lodge (the environment), the lake or boat (the alternative hope).

2) **Role-Play (6 magic questions):**

Villager:
1) **I am** *a villager. I was once a proud and valuable individual, but now I am helpless and of no known value in the eyes of the new government.*
2) **My purpose is to** *be an important part of the village structure.*
3) **What I like is** *to be a valued member of the village.*
4) **What I dislike is** *that even with all my capability, I am seen as worthless.*
5) **What I fear is** *to be devalued and considered just one of the lowly villagers.*
6) **What I desire most is** *to rid myself of the influence of these invaders and be free and proud once again.*

Life Situation: *This is the way I feel on the job. The management take-over left me with a new boss who does not acknowledge my value. I feel helpless, no longer valued, and fear I will lose the respect of my peers and staff.* **Restate as a conflict:** *I need to find a solution to this situation that will keep me in a valued leadership position – or - I will be seen as just one of the lowly workers.*

Invading Leader:

1) **I am** *the leader assigned by the new government to manage this village.*

2) **My purpose is to** *separate those who will stay from those who must go.*

3) **What I like is** *I am in control and have a future with the new government.*

4) **What I dislike is** *I must do what the new government wants, even if I don't like it.*

5) **What I fear is** *that if I fail, I too will be eliminated.*

6) **What I desire most is** *to have this sad situation go quickly and smoothly.*

Life Situation *The new boss did come in to separate those who will stay in the new organization from those that will be eliminated.* **Restate as a myth**: *I must do as they say even if I don't like it – or – I will be eliminated.*

Lodge:

1) **I am** *a grand old lodge that has been here for years. I've seen many of these crises, and "this too will pass."*

2) **My purpose is to** *be a protective environment where people come together for food and relaxation.*

3) **What I like is** *the villagers are like my family. I like it when I am the center and they come to me for important events.*

4) **What I dislike is** *that I am just here and have no control over the events.*

5) **What I fear is** *that all it takes is one fool, and I can be burned down forever.*

6) **What I desire most is** *to have things back the way they were before the invasion.*

Life Situation *"This too will pass" is a perspective I enter when I need to relax and protect myself.* **Restate as a conflict:** *I must be careful, because one false move and I may burn my bridges, and destroy my career forever – vs. – if I wait it out, this too will pass.*

Blue Lake:

1) **I am** *beautiful and calm. I will take you away from it all.*

2) **My purpose is to** *be a place where people can relax and enjoy life.*

3) **What I like is** *everyone likes me.*

4) **What I dislike is** *I feel I am wasted at times, since no one uses me for all I can be.*

5) **What I fear is** *that I will be abandoned and dry up.*

6) **What I desire is** *to be attractive to all who look at me.*

Life Situation: *This sounds like an attractive alternative to trying to continually succeed with a career in management, but it has a fearful downside.* **Restate as a conflict:** *I want to relax and focus on the other joys in life – BUT - if I do, I fear I will no longer be of value to those who look up to me. I will be abandoned, not used for all I can be, and my career will dry up.*

Boat:
1) **I am** *a boat. I can take you wherever you want to go, under your own control.*
2) **I Like** *being able to move around wherever I want on my own.*
3) **I Dislike** *being confined to this small pond. I rely totally on someone else to move me to a bigger pond.*
4) **I Fear** *I will sink if I am not properly taken care of.*
5) **I Desire** *to be moved to a larger pond where I'm able to move where I want to go.*
Life Situation: *I desperately want to find an alternative means for meeting my need to feel in control of my destiny again. But I fear that I may be a big frog in a small pond, and I am totally dependent on someone else or my management to promote me or move me into a place where I can be all I know I can be.* **Restate:** *I need to move on to become valued, but I can't do it myself. I rely on someone who values me, and if that does not work, I am sunk.*

At this point, note the number and depth of the various conflicts and personal myths that are revealed by this approach. It is surprising to note just how many different myths can be present, and interact within a situation the dream is dealing with. By itself, each role-play exercise provides more than enough material to be worked on in one session. Taken together, they reveal the overwhelming number of issues and conflicts that the dreamer must sometimes sort through, in dealing with a complex situation. As you continue from this point, it is advisable to sort through all of this and pick or formulate just one core myth or conflict to work on.

Module 3B – Color Work

Brown (Table):
   Statement from the color table: *I seek freedom from problems and a secure state in which to relax and recover.*
   Related life situation and feelings: *This reflects my frustrations.*
   Compare the color and image work to the life story: *This seems to relate to the counter-myth of just relaxing and enjoying my friends and giving up on the old myth of having to be the leader.*

Blue (lake):

    Statement from the color table: *I desire a tranquil, peaceful state of harmony offering contentment and a sense of belonging.*

    Related life situation and feelings: *This fits the counter-myth of letting go of career aspirations and being left in peace with my friends and my boat.*

    Compare color and image work to the life story: *This fits the role-play of the lake - "I am beautiful and calm, I will take you away from it all."*

Note that the brown table, on the right side of the room, represented what "those who were allowed to stay" were moving toward – the counter-myth represented by the blue lake and the boat. All related to a counter-myth of focusing on friends and relaxation, and abandoning the myth of having to be the leader, whom everyone approved of and looked up to, in order to feel valued.

Module 3C – Associative Dreamwork (optional)

1) Memory Associations: *Vietnam village = A situation in which the people were regarded as having no value, or as the enemy, regardless of their true nature.*

2) Define the Dream Element and its Function:

    Invader = takes over by strength, not by popular acclaim
    Leader = manages those under him, the one they look up to for direction
    Command = what I am supposed to do
    Villagers = people who live as a community
    Lodge = a structure that protects those who meet within it
    Tables = a structure that holds easily accessible sustenance for those sitting at it
    Window = to permit one to see outside, while remaining safely inside
    Lake = a source of unseen life (fish) and a place for recreation
    Boat = a thing of joy and recreation on water

3) Rewrite the Dream Story - insert the element definitions into the dream story: (Note that by doing the role-play and color work first, as well as element definition, you have a wider choice of associations to insert in place of the dream elements in the narrative):

I am in place <u>where people live as a community</u>. Some foreigners have invaded and taken over the government. <u>This is a situation where people are regarded as having no value, or as the enemy, regardless of their true nature.</u> I am with my companions inside of a structure that normally protects those within it. Those who have taken *over by strength and not by popular demand are gathering us up. The new manager, in order to identify and separate us, states: "everyone that lives beyond the desired state, tense up." A large group is tensing up and the remaining people are moving toward a state of freedom from problems and a secure state in which to relax and recover. I am confused, not knowing what I am supposed to do, since I don't know if I live within or beyond the desired state. I tense my fists. Someone behind me says, "No, you're OK." I relax and know that I can now move to the right, feeling I am one of the lucky ones allowed to stay in our community. I ask the new manager, what will happen to the others, and he states that they will be eliminated and dealt with in some (undetermined) fashion. I look out the window to the right at a tranquil, peaceful state of harmony offering quiet contentment and a sense of belonging, a source of unseen life and a place for recreation, with a feeling of growing contentment that I might simply be left alone with my friends, joy and recreation .*

4) Relate or Rewrite as the Waking Life Story:

We have been taken over by new management. They have reduced everyone to being considered of little value, or even bad, for the future of the company, regardless of their true nature. Our organization was supposed to have been one that was protected, but it is not. They are gathering us up and separating us into those who are the desired type (those who can stay) and those that are not (those who must go). Those who feel they are "outside" the desired type become tense. Those who have been given some indication that they are desired (at least for a time) feel secure and can relax a bit. I am confused, not knowing what I am supposed to do or what I should do, since I don't know if I am one of the desired ones or not. I am tense.

I finally gain a sense, based on some recent events, that I will be OK. I begin to relax and start thinking that I may be one of the lucky ones allowed to stay in the organization – but I am not sure. When I ask my management what will happen to those that won't fit into our new organization, he states that they will be laid off. At this point I am less concerned about my leadership status and more about survival, and begin to think about abandoning my career aspirations and focusing on finding a peaceful state of harmony, that offers a sense of belonging with my friends, and recreation. As I consider this, there is a growing feeling of contentment.

STAGE #2
Exploring the Life Situation

Module 4 – Myths and Impasses

Module 4A - Personal Myth

1) **Conflicting Myths**: Do the role-play statements (particularly the 'I like/I dislike', 'I fear/I desire' pairs), or the color associations, relate to a conflict in your waking life? Re-state in terms of conflicting desires or fears (note that there are a number of conflicting myths associated with each role-play exercise above, so pick one to work on): *I want to relax, abandon my leadership focus, and focus on the other joys in life – BUT - if I do I fear I will not be valued by all who look up to me. I may become abandoned, not used for all I can be, and my career will dry up.*

2) **Originating Decision (optional):** Reflect on the situation and then describe the feelings involved. Go back to one specific situation earlier in life, which brings to mind similar feelings. Note what happened, who was involved and how you felt. What decision did you make about yourself, life or the others involved at the time? *In this situation, I felt a sense of shock that I was suddenly no longer valued and perhaps should abandon my career goals. This recalls an event in my childhood in which, even though I considered myself quite capable, I was not chosen for the team. I felt humiliated and lowly and wanted to quit sports. Myth = To be considered of value I must play with the big guys, and if I can't, I will quit.* Does this decision feed the myth and affect your present behavior? *Once again, I am in a situation where "the big guys" don't recognize my value. My first thought is to abandon my career goals and quit.*

3) **Reflect:** Are these beliefs logical, healthy and appropriate, allowing you to progress, or are they exaggerations and misconceptions that are holding you back? *The myth that I need to play with the big guys (be in management) in order to be valued is flawed – I have many other valuable characteristics. The counter-myth that I need to abandon my career, in order to enjoy the other things in life, is equally flawed.*

Module 4B – Impasses within the Dream Story

1) **Review the storyline** of the dream and ask yourself, "where am I trying to go or what am I trying to achieve in the dream?" *I am trying to stay with the villagers as a valued member of the group.*

2) **Impasse imagery:** Pick the image in the dream that prevents you from progressing or obtaining your goal in the dream. *The leader of the invaders.*

3) **As the impasse image, speak to the dreamer (role-play the image):**
   a) I am *the leader of this invading group. Don't try to persuade me one way or another. I simply have a job to do and must do as I am told.*
   b) My function or purpose is *to select those who are within the four who can stay, from those outside who must go.*
   c) I am holding you back *because you can't decide where you stand.*

4) **Switch, and as the Dreamer, Speak to the Impasse Image:**
   I want you to tell me where I stand. Am I ok to stay or not?

5) **Switch again and as the Impasse Image answer the Dreamer**
   My advice to you is that you must decide where you stand. You can't depend on me for that.

6) **Compare to Life:** *I can't depend on my management to tell me where I stand or what to do. It is up to me to determine my true value as it relates to dealing with this situation.*

7) **Define the Impasse:**
   a) Re-state the impasse: *I depend on my management for my sense of value – but – at this point they have not revealed what they think and I don't think they value me.* Note: This is a true impasse as the dreamer has nowhere to turn, since his total support system lies with his management's perception.
   b) Is this logical and healthy, or unrealistic and inappropriate? *It is unhealthy to place my perceived value in the hands of others.*

STAGE #3
Transformation

Module 5 – Compensation & Transformation

Module 5A – Dream Compensation

1) **Look for the compensating imagery:** *the voice behind me*

2) **Review the Compensating Action:**
   a) State your actions before the compensating event. *I was frozen in tension because I did not know whether I could stay or not (within or beyond the four).*
   b) What was the specific act of compensation? *The voice stated "No, you are OK."*
   c) How did this change your actions/thoughts/direction in the dream? *I relaxed and began thinking about other values and enjoying being with my friends.*
   d) Did the dream reward the results? *Yes- by relaxing the tension and presenting a future possibility of staying and just enjoying the lake and the boat.*

3) **Relate as a metaphor with your waking life situation:**
   a) **Before Compensation:** *I was frozen in tension over not knowing whether the new management was going to value me and let me stay, or eliminate me.*
   b) **After Compensation:** *The alternative is shown as relaxing and taking on a thankful survival mode, giving up career goals and enjoying other things in life.*
   c) **The Message**: *"No, you are OK" seemed to reveal an inherent value within me that did not depend on any confirmation from management.*
   d) **Restate as a Solution to your Waking Life Situation:** *Relax, you have inherent value that does not depend on management recognition, and even if you lose your leadership position, there is a wonderful alternative to enjoying the other things in life.*

4) **Check It Out:** *This provides a new myth, a healthy view of the situation that resolves the tension and opens up opportunities to be satisfied with other values in life.*

Module 5B – Completing the Dream

1) **How does the dream end?** *It ends with me feeling OK about myself, being thankful to simply be a survivor, and enjoying the other things in life such as friends and recreation – BUT – I have not moved in that direction yet in the dream.*

2) **New ending**: *I move to the right with my other villagers and then out the door to the lake and my boat, and just forget about the leader.*

3) **Re-state** the new ending as a possible solution to your waking life situation: *I abandon the myth of my value being tied up in a management position (both depending on the approval of management and having to be the leader in order to feel valued). I finally relax and focus on other things in life.*

4) **Check It Out:** *This is a healthy, balanced position that permits me to accept and enjoy the possible outcomes without being dependent on them.*

Module 5C – Act to Transform the Myth

Transformation requires that you experience the change. Therefore, if the solution from modules 5A or 5B appears healthy and appropriate, then:

1) **Next Steps:** *Do just what I am required to do at work. Relax on my free time at night and weekends. Open up to and prepare myself for other opportunities elsewhere. I can stop trying to second-guess what I must do to become acceptable to this new management. If worse comes to worse, I know I have inherent value and can use it to move on, even if it does not result in a high level management career.*

2) **Next Opportunity:** *Begin right away at work tomorrow.*

3) **Dream Totem:** In the end, the image that the dreamer perceived as representative of the new myth was *"the image of the lake and boat with my friends on board."*

APPENDIX A
RESOURCES

www.DreamLanguage.org

Visit the author's website at the above URL for:
- periodic updates on the topics included in this book
- ordering additional copies of this book, in hard copy or CD, and future updates
- learning about the latest facts and findings on dreams and dreamwork
- upcoming events, courses and workshops
- links to other dream related resources

Innersource

Information and programs for developing optimal health, personal growth, spiritual development and well-being through Energy Medicine, Energy Psychology and Conscious Living programs for professionals, lay persons and students.

www.Innersource.net

The International Association For The Study Of Dreams (IASD)

The IASD is a nonprofit, international, multidisciplinary organization dedicated to the pure and applied investigation of dreams and dreaming. Its purpose is to promote an awareness and appreciation of dreams in both professional and public arenas; to encourage research into the nature, function, and significance of dreaming; to advance the application of the study of dreams; and to provide a forum for the eclectic and interdisciplinary exchange of ideas and information. IASD is open to anyone who studies, explores, or works with dreams. Membership represents about 30 countries and people from all disciplines including: psychology, psychiatry, social work, education at all levels, religious studies, anthropology, medicine, the expressive and performing arts, literature, philosophy, humanities and business. Membership benefits include the professional journal *Dreaming* and the magazine *Dream Time,* discounts to conferences plus many on-line benefits. For information on the organization, or to become a member, please go to the web site: **www.asdreams.org**

Energy Psychology

Visit www.EnergyPsychEd.com for information on:
- self-help home-study programs to learn new methods for bringing about changes in emotions, thought and behavior (*Energy Psychology Interactive Self-Help Guide*, or *Introduction to Energy Psychology* - 2DVD set)
- professional home-study training programs for therapists who wish to incorporate energy psychology methods into their practice (*Energy Psychology Interactive: Rapid Interventions for Lasting Change*, book & CD-ROM)
- research summaries and articles on energy psychology
- the best introduction to the field, *The Promise of Energy Psychology: Revolutionary Tools for Dramatic Personal Change* (D. Feinstein, D. Eden, G. Craig)

Visit www.energypsych.org for information on:
- the Association for Comprehensive Energy Psychology (ACEP)
- energy psychology conferences, resources, workshops, articles and research

The Haden Institute

The Haden Institute Dream Leader Training is for therapists, clergy and individuals who wish to lead dream groups or enhance their therapeutic skills. The purpose of the training is four-fold: 1) To train and certify people to lead church and community dream groups; 2) To help professionals and others to integrate dream work into their chosen profession; 3) To enhance and encourage responsible dreamwork across the nation; 4) To help recover the ancient Biblical tradition of listening for God's word to us in our nightly dreams.

The founder/director of The Haden Institute is Bob Haden, M Div, S.T.M, Priest, Jungian Psychotherapist, Spiritual Director and Diplomate of The American Psychoanalytical Association. The Institute also sponsors a two-year Spiritual Direction Training for all vocations in the US and Canada, as well as an annual Summer Dream Conference in the Blue Ridge Mountains of North Carolina. For more information see www.hadeninstitute.com, contact **bob@hadeninstitute.com** or call 828-693-9292.

BIBLIOGRAPHY

1. E. Hartmann, *The Functions of Sleep*, 1973, Yale University Press

2. D. W. Stewart, and D. Koulack, "The Function of Dreams and Adaptation to Stress Over Time," *Dreaming: Journal of the Association for the Study of Dreams*, December 1993, Volume 3, No. 4, p. 259

3. S. R. Palombo, *Dreaming and Memory*, 1978 Basic Books Inc., p.13

4. C. G. Jung, *Man and His Symbols*, Dell Publishing Co. NY, NY, 1973

5. P. Garfield, *The Healing Power of Dreams*, 1991, Simon and Schuster

6. M. Ullman, S. Krippner, A. Vaughan, *Dream Telepathy*, 1973, Macmillan Publishing, NY. NY.

7. R. A. Moody, *Life After Life*, 1975, Mockingbird Books

8. R. Monroe, *Journeys Out of the Body*, 1973, Anchor Press/Doubleday

9. S. LaBerge, *Lucid Dreaming*, 1985, Ballantine Books

10. S. Springer, G. Deutsch, *Left Brain Right Brain*, 3rd Edition, 1980, W.H. Freeman & Co., NY, NY

11. M. S. Gazaniga, "Right hemisphere language following brain bisection: a 20 year perspective," *American Psychologist 38* (1983) pp. 342-346, cited in [1]

12. M. Humphrey, O. Zangwill, "Cessation of dreaming after brain injury", *Journal of Neurology, Neurosurgery and Psychiatry* 14 (1951), pp. 322-325, cited in [1].

13. K. Hoppe, "Split brains and psychoanalysis," *The Psychoanalytic Quarterly,* 46 (1977), pp. 220-224, cited in [1]

14. N. D. Cook, "Callosal Inhibition: the key to the brain code", *Behavioral Science,* 29 (1984), pp. 98-110, cited in [1].

15. F. S. Perls, *Gestalt Therapy Verbatim*, Bantam Books, Real People Press, 1974, pp. 27-76

16. C. G. Jung, "The Stages of Life", Part 1 of *The Portable Jung*, Edited by Joseph Campbell, The Viking Press, N.Y. 1971

17. C. G. Jung, "Relations Between the Ego and the Unconscious", Part 5 of *The Portable Jung*, Edited by Joseph Campbell, The Viking Press, N.Y. 1971

18. C. G. Jung, "Dream Symbolism in Relation to Alchemy", Part 11 of the *Portable Jung,* Edited by Joseph Campbell, The Viking Press, N.Y. 1971

19. D. Feinstein, "The Dream as a Window to Your Evolving Mythology," in S. Krippner, *Dreamtime & Dreamwork*, Jeremy P. Tarcher Inc. Los Angeles, CA., pp. 21-33

20. J. Campbell, *Historical Atlas of World Mythology*, vol. 1, Harper & Row, San Francisco, CA, 1983, referenced in [5]

21. C. G. Jung, "The Transcendent Function", Part 9 of *The Portable Jung*, Edited by Joseph Campbell, The Viking Press, N.Y. 1971

22. J. Henderson, "Ancient Myths and Modern Man" in C.G. Jung, *Man and His Symbols,* Part 2, Dell Publishing, N.Y. 1973

23. C. Hall & V. Nordby, *A Primer of Jungian Psychology*, A Mentor Book, Canada 1973, Ch 6

24. A. Faraday, *The Dream Game*, 1974, Harper & Row

25. M. Luscher, *The Luscher Color Test*, edited by Ian A. Scott, Pocket Books, New York, 1971

26. F. Birren, The *Symbolism of Color*, 1988, A Citadel Press Book

27. F. Birren, *Color Psychology and Color Therapy*, University Books, Inc. New Hyde Park, N.Y., 1961

28. C. G. Jung, *Mandala Symbolism*, Princeton University Press, 1972

29. J. Campbell, *The Portable Jung*, Part 11, Viking Press, N.Y., 1971, pp. 323-455

30. C. A. Riley II, *Color Codes*, University Press of New England, 1995

31. F. Birren, *Color and Human Response*, John Wiley & Sons Inc, New York, 1978

32. C. E. Ferree and Gertrude Rand, "Lighting and the Hygiene of the Eye", *Archives of Ophthalmology*, July 1929

33. B. Brown, *New Mind New Body*, Harper & Row, New York, 1974

34. H. Ertel, *Time Magazine*, 17 Sept 1973

35. K. Goldstein, "Some Experimental Observations on the Influence of Color on the Function of the Organism", *Occupational Therapy and Rehabilitation*, June 1942

36. B. Edwards, *Drawing on the Right Side of the Brain*, J. P. Tarcher, Los Angeles, Ca., 1989

37. R. L. Van De Castle, *Our Dreaming Mind*, Ballantine Books, New York 1994

38. J. J. Ratey, A *User's Guide to the Brain*, Vintage Books, a Division of Random House, New York, 2001

39. Hobson et al., "Dreaming and the Brain," *Sleep and Dreaming*, Cambridge University Press, New York, 2003, pp 1 - 50.

40. G. William Domhoff, *The Scientific Study of Dreams*, American Psychological Association, Washington DC, 2003 pp 9 - 38

41. W. H. Calvin and G. A. Ojemann, *Inside the Brain*, New American Library, 1980

42. G. Alain, Hôpital Sacré-Cœur of Montreal, University of Montreal, "Replication of the Day-residue and Dream-lag Effect", presented at the *Twentieth International Conference of the Association for the Study of Dreams*, Berkeley California 2003

43. J. Panksepp, "The dream of reason creates monsters," *Sleep and Dreaming*, Cambridge University Press, New York, 2003, p. 200

44. E. F. Pace-Schott , "Recent findings on the neurobiology of sleep and dreaming", *Sleep and Dreaming*, Cambridge University Press, New York, 2003, p. 342

45. L. M. Hoss, "The Relationship of Dream Recall Frequency to Performance Measures of Right Brain-Mediated Information," unpublished Masters Thesis submitted to *Radford University*, Radford Virginia 1981

46. P. Bakan, "Dreaming, REM sleep and the right hemisphere: A theoretical integration," *Journal of Altered States of Consciousness*, pp. 285-307 in [45]

47. L. Goldstein, N. W. Stoltzfus, and J. F. Gardocki, "Changes in inter-hemispheric amplitude relationships in the EEG during sleep," *Physiology and Behavior*, 1972, pp. 811-815. reported in [45]

48. M. Hiscock and D. B. Cohen, "Visual imagery and dream recall," *Journal of Research in Personality*, 1973, 7, 1; 9-188. reported in [45]

49. Shapiro, Hong, Buchsbaum, Goldschalk, Thompson, Hillyard (1995), "Exploring the relationship between having control and losing control to functional neuroanatomy during the sleeping state," *Psychologia 38*, pp 133-145

50. M. T. Blagrove, L. Burron, C. Bradshaw (2003), "Dream Recall Frequency is associated with openness to experience but not sleep length," *SLEEP* 26, pA91

51. Webb and Agnew, (1970), *Science* 168; pp 146-147, reported in [50]

52. Backeland, E. Hartmann (1971), *Comprehensive Psychiatry* 12; pp 141-147, in [50]

53. M. Schredl (2003), "Effects of State and Trait Factor on Nightmare Frequency," *SLEEP* 26

54. Janowsky & Carper (1996) and Mark Solms as reported in [40] page 25.

55. Content contributed by Gayle Delaney, PhD, author of *Breakthrough Dreaming*, Bantam Books 1991

56. Patricia Garfield, *Your Childs Dreams*, Balantine, NY 1984

57. C. Hall, and R. Van de Castle, *The Content Analysis of Dreams*, Appleton-Century-Croft, New York, 1966.

58. A. Siegel and K. Bulkeley, *Dreamcatching*, Three Rivers Press, New York 1998

59. A. Siegel, *Dream Wisdom*, Celestial Arts, Berkeley 2003

60. E. Hartmann, *The Nightmare*, Basic Books, NY 1984

61. Fosse, Hobson, and Stickgold, 2003, "Dreaming and Episodic memory: a functional dissociation," *Journal of Cognitive Neuroscience*, 15: 1-9,

62. D. Kahn, *Consciousness in Dreaming: Awareness of Feelings*, presentation at the conference, Towards a Science of Consciousness, 2004

63. W.B. Gibson and L.R. Gibson, *Psychic Sciences,* Pocket Books, N.Y., 1968

64. B. Brennan, *Hands of Light,* Bantam New Age Books, 1987

65. R. Hoss, "The Appearance of Color in Dreams", *Dream Time, a Publication of the Association for the Study of Dreams*, volume 16, Number 4, 1999, page 10

66. R. Hoss, C. Hoffman, *Significance of Color Recall in Dreams,* Presented at the 21st Annual Conference of the International Association for the Study of Dreams, in Copenhagen, June 2004

67. B. Andreas, *Still Mostly True,* 1994 by Brian Andreas, West Coast Print Center, Berkeley, Ca.

68. P. Berne and L. Savary, "The 3 Logics of the Brain," *Psychotherapy Networker*, Sept/Oct 2004

69. Fosse, Fosse, Hobson and Stickgold, "Dreaming and Episodic Memory: A functional dissociation", in *Journal of Cognitive Neuroscience* vol 15, pp. 1-9, 2003. And Fosse, Fosse and Stickgold "Response to Schwartz: Dreaming and episodic memory." *Trends in Cognitive Sciences* vol 7, August 2003.

70. C. Gorman, "Why We Sleep," *Time Magazine,* 20 December 2004

71. D. Feinstein and S. Krippner, *Personal Mythology,* Jeremy P. Tarcher, Inc., Los Angeles, CA, 1988

72. M. Ullman, and N. Zimmerman, *Working With Dreams*, Jeremy P. Tarcher, Inc., Los Angeles, CA, 1985

73. dreambank.net, a database of over 18,000 dream reports with access provided to the author for the purposes of content analysis, courtesy of G. William Domhoff, PhD

74. S. Krippner, and M. R. Walsman, *Dreamscaping,* Lowell House, Los Angeles, CA, 1999

75. V. Kautner, information provided from a dissertation in progress in 2005 at Saybrook on the experience of 9 people, ages 62 to 79 participating in an Ullman dream group, using the Amedeo Giorgi phenomenological approach.

76. M. Emery, *The Intuitive Healer,* St. Martin's Press, New York, 1999

77. D. Feinstein and S. Krippner, *The Mythic Path*, Tarcher/Penguin Putnam, 1997

78. D. Eden with D. Feinstein, *Energy Medicine,* Tarcher/Penguin Putnam, 1998

79. S. Krippner, D. Feinstein, a technique presented as part of a 5 day intensive *Mythology for your Future* at Esalen Institute, Big Sur, CA, in 2005, attended by the author.

80. S. Krippner, F. Bogzaran, A. Percia De Carvalho, *Extraordinary Dreams and How to Work with Them*, SUNY Press, New York, 2002

81. C. Green, *Out of Body Experiences,* Hamish Hamilton, London 1968

82. A.T. Funkhouser, H-P Hirsbrunner, C. Cornu, M. Barhro (1999), "Dreams and dreaming among the elderly: an overview," *Aging & Mental Health* 3(1): 10-20.

83. L. M. Giambra, R.E. Jung, A. Grodsky (1996), "Age changes in dream recall in adulthood," *Dreaming* 6:17-31.

84. M.L. von Franz, (1998), "On Dreams & Death," *Chicago: Open Court*

85. E. Hartmann, *Dreams and Nightmares,* Perseus Publishing, Cambridge Mass. 1998

86. D.L. Barrett, "Just how lucid are lucid dreams?", *Dreaming: Journal of the Association for the Study of Dreams*, Vol 2(4) 221-228, Dec 1992.

87. D.L. Barrett, "Flying dreams and lucidity: An empirical study of their relationship", *Dreaming: Journal of the Association for the Study of Dreams*, Vol *1*(2) 129-134, Jun 1991.

88. D. L. Barrett (Ed.) *Trauma and Dreams,* Cambridge, MA: Harvard University Press, 1996/hardback, 2001 paper.

89. D. L. Barrett and J. Behbehani, "Post-traumatic Nightmares in Kuwait Following the Iraqi Invasion," in *The Psychological Impact of War Trauma on Civilians: An International Perspective*, Stanley Krippner & Teresa M. McIntyre (Eds.), 2004.

90. D. L. Barrett, *The Committee of Sleep: How Artists, Scientists, and Athletes Use their Dreams for Creative Problem Solving—and How You Can Too,* NY: Crown Books/Random House, 2001/hardback.

91. D. L. Barrett, "Royal Road" in Rosner, Rachel I.; Lyddon, William J.; Freeman, Arthur (Eds.), *Cognitive Therapy and Dreams,* Springer Publishing Company, 2003.

92. Cited in R. Adelson, 'Hues and Views", in the *APA Monitor on Psychology*, Feb 2005, pp. 26-29

93. E. Hartmann, personal contribution to this book. Some of the cited work was presented at the 22nd Annual Conference of the International Association for the Study of Dreams, June 2005, Berkeley, CA

94. C. Hoffman, *The Seven Story Tower: A Mythic Journey through Space and Time.* Insight Books, Plenum Press, New York and London, 1999.

95. R. Haden, material provided for inclusion in this book by the Bob Haden, founder of the Haden Institute, Asheville, North Carolina

96. J. Taylor, *Dream Work - Techniques for Discovering the Creative Power in Dreams*, Paulist Press, Mahwah New Jersey, 1983

97. J. Taylor, *Where People Fly & Water Runs Up Hill - Using Dreams to tap the Wisdom of the Unconscious*, Warner Books, New York, 1992

98. J. Taylor, *The Living Labyrinth - Universal Themes in Myths, Dreams, & the Symbolism of Waking Life*, Paulist Press, Mahwah New Jersey, 1998

99. T. Sutton, B. M. Whelan, *The Complete Color Harmony,* Rockport Publishers Inc.: Gloucester, Massachusetts. 2004

100. R. Hoss, *Working with Color In Dreams*, IASD Conference, Leiden, Netherlands, 1994. Note that the author thanks the dreamer for permission to publish this report.

101. Content provided for this book by J. Lasley, author of *Honoring the Dream: A Handbook for Dream Group Leaders,* Mount Pleasant: DreamsWork Publications, 2004

102. A. Arrien, *Signs of Life: The Five Universal Shapes and How to Use Them,* Tarcher/Putnam: New York. 1998

103. E. Hartmann, *What Influences Dream Recall?*Presented at the 22nd Annual Conference of the International Association for the Study of Dreams, June 2005, Berkeley, CA

104. G.W. Domhoff, *The Past Present and future of Dream Content Research*, presented at the 22nd Annual Conference of the International Association for the Study of Dreams, June 2005, Berkeley, CA

105. N. Hamilton, *The Role of Dreams in the Study of Human Transformation*, presented at the 22nd Annual Conference of the International Association for the Study of Dreams, June 2005, Berkeley, CA. Also refer to N. Hamilton and D. Hiles, *Retreats, Dreams: New Transpersonal Research*, 2000 B.A.C. Research Conference

106. H.R. Schiffman, *Sensation and Perception: an Integrated Approach,* John Wiley & Sons, New York 1976, pp. 216-220

107. T. Burckhardt, *Alchemy*, a Penguin Book, Baltimore Maryland 1972, pp. 182

108. R. Hoss, "The Significance of Color in Dreams", *DreamTime*, a publication of the International Association for the Study of Dreams, Vol. 22, Number 1, Spring 2005

109. C. Hampden-Turner, *Maps of the Mind*, Macmillan Publishing Co.: New York 1981

ABOUT THE AUTHOR
ROBERT J. HOSS, MS

Bob Hoss is the Executive Officer and former President of the International Association for the Study of Dreams (IASD), an organization that sponsors education and investigation in the field of dreams and dreamwork. He is a frequent guest on radio and TV, and has been an internationally acclaimed lecturer and instructor on dreams and dreamwork for over 30 years. He has served as Chairman of IASD, President of the Texas Parapsychological Association, and as a member of the research board of the Texas Society for Psychical Research. He is also on the faculty of the Haden Institute and serves, or has served, on the adjunct faculty of Scottsdale and Paradise Valley Community Colleges in Arizona and at Richland College in Texas. As a scientist, his approach to dreamwork is influenced by research and the neurobiology of dreaming. His research into the significance of color resulted in the development of a unique tool for working with color in dreams, which is included in this book. His dreamworking technique is derived principally from training in Gestalt therapy, the work of Carl Jung, plus other eclectic and humanistic dreamworking approaches, including group and individual approaches. He has been an invited teacher and lecturer at the Haden Institute, the Association for Humanistic Psychology, the Human Potential Institute, IASD conferences worldwide, the Toronto Dream Festival, the American Holistic Nurses Association, HARA, Association for Research and Enlightenment (ARE), University of Texas, and many others. Visit the web site at **www.dreamlanguage.org.**

INDEX

INDEX OF TABLES

How To Order

❖ **On-Line Order with Charge Card:** www.dreamlanguage.org;
   www.ASDreams.org (go to on-line bookstore); www.Amazon.com
❖ **Email Order or Inquiry**: Order@DreamLanguage.org
❖ **Fax Orders To**: 480-907-1870
❖ **Mail Orders**: Innersource -Dreams, PO Box 213, Ashland, OR 97520

Quick Order form for Email, FAX and Mail Orders

Please send me the following version/quantity of:

Dream Language: Self-UnderstandingThrough Imagery and Color

	Cost (US)	Quantity	Amount
1 Hard copy book (254 pages)	$20.00	_____	_____
E-Book download or CD-ROM	$12.00	_____	_____
***Discount for Instructors or Dream Groups:**			
Set of 4 books	$60.00/set	_____sets	_____
Shipping (see below):			_____
		TOTAL	_____

Please send me FREE information on:

☐ **Speaking Engagements** ☐ **Workshops/Seminars** ☐ **Other Innersource products**
☐ **Add me to your mailing list __For Dreams ___For Innersource**

Shipping: **U.S.** $2 per book or CD (subject to change without notice)
   Outside US or Bulk Orders: Contact us for shipping costs.

Payment: ☐ **Check or Money Order enclosed (for mail-in only, fax and e-mail orders will be invoiced) - Make all checks payable to: Robert Hoss**

Name: _____

Mailing Address: _____

Phone: _____ **Email** _____

***Institution/Organization (for group discounts)** _____